THE WORLD CONQUERORS

BY THE SAME AUTHOR

The Case of Tiszaeszlar
Red Storm
The Work of Gyula Gombos
besides numerous Plays and Poems.

THE WORLD CONQUERORS
THE REAL WAR CRIMINALS

Translated from the Hungarian
of
Louis Marschalko
by
A. Suranyi

LONDON
Joseph Sueli Publications
1964

CONTENTS

PUBLISHER'S NOTE

In a great many cases, the Translator has been able to check
the quotations from books and newspapers with the originals.
Where this has not been possible, the Publisher asks the
reader's indulgence for differences due to translation.

INTRODUCTION

FOR more than a century, under various pretexts, a battle has been waged for power over the nations. The exercise of power has become the supreme aim of many people. Bankers, politicians, clergymen, trade union leaders and Communist Party secretaries are all in the hunt for power. The storm troops of the dictatorships are no longer shouting the old Socialist slogans. They declare openly and trumpet brutally " Power is what we want ". And the so-called Democratic parties, though trying to keep it a secret, have also in their hearts actually adopted the dictatorial battle-cry, " Power is what we want ". Power, like possession of the magician's wand has become their obsession in life and it does not matter how it is achieved, whether through Conservative or Labour parties or through the Christian churches.

The structure of modern society with its overpopulation has as a consequence developed the idolatory of power. The golden calf has been taken off its pedestal and has by now become a secondary emblem only. The gold, the wealth and all parts of the symbolic sacred animal of Capitalism can be apportioned, distributed or sold by any one who has the power to do so, as if it were meat in a butcher's shop. The Church aims to attain power by controlling the human soul, the Marxist through the autocracy and omnipotence of material means, the banker by his gold or by holding in his hand the control of the Press, the Bolshevist by the sheer brutality of the tommy-gun. But all parties, groups, sects, democracies, dictator-ships and churches have one thing in common: they all want power. And this is quite understandable, as power often appears to be absolute, more even than all the gold in Fort Knox. For if that gold were evenly distributed among all the people on earth the share per head would be so small that it would hardly be worth anything.

But power over empires, states, societies and continents is infinite. It can be distributed like the five loaves and two fishes apportioned by Christ. It secures ministerial posts, episcopal positions and benefits, senior ranks in the police force, party secretaryships as well as other major and minor offices. But only for those who are the followers of power or who belong to the organisation of the bosses holding power. Included are those belonging to the herd following the party leader, trade unions, boss, dictator or bankers; those who are members of some democratic union, Christian trade unions or, of course, any of the masonic lodges.

So it is quite understandable that in these days nearly every slogan and school of thought is directed at one thing only — the seizure of power. " Let us pray " say the churches, but behind their words it is not always Christ's kingdom that is built, but the wordly power of some high priests engaged in double-entry book-keeping. " Freedom " shout the Communists to their bamboozled Party members and followers but as a background to this empty slogan loom the torture chamber, gaol, detention camp and the gloomy hovels of Siberian slave-labourers. Here we find side by side the misery of exploitation and the power and wealth of the privileged Communist ruling classes. " Democracy " is the slogan proclaimed throughout the Western world, but it is well known that the voting system here does not represent the power of the people, but merely screens the mysterious influence and hidden rule exercised by secret cliques.

Behind these false façades is hidden the substance of the most satanic dream of the world conquerors — to become the masters of the whole world ! How can this ambitious goal, the dream and aim of Cæsars, dictators, bankers and trade union potentates ever since Ezra and Moses and through Alexander the Great to Stalin, be achieved ? Conventional armies have become obsolete for furthering this purpose. The hydrogen bomb might wipe out both parties. Both parties can be attacked by rockets. Such a conquest is now impracticable, so the plan is to conquer the world by " peaceful " means, such as by the cheque book, by Unesco, by re-education, by a new moral code and by peace-propaganda. From this idea Lenin developed and built up his diabolic strategic system to seize and expand power, and this system under the name of Bolshevism has proved until now to be irresistible everywhere where people were unaware of the details of this power-technique.

The supposedly cultured world failed to realise, however, that Lenin's Bolshevism was a component only, such as were also

7

Marxism, Freemasonry and Capitalism itself. For there existed another more thorough, universal and gigantic scheme which had been working already for over a century and a half, its aim by now very nearly accomplished. On the basis of ancient doctrines this latter scheme was not going to conquer global power for any of the " isms ", parties, sects, churches, professional organisations or social classes, but exclusively—for one nation only.

The plans for Lenin's system were to some degree rough and superficial. Their greatest weakness was akin to that of a general who lets the enemy know in advance the point of attack and the strength of his forces and the tactics he intends to employ. Whereas, the other, the great fundamental plan, proved much more effective because, similarly to historically successful military operations, it has carefully guarded its secrets from outsiders and indeed often from initiated persons also. Its greatest asset was that it appeared much more general than, for example, the schemes of the trade union leaders limited to the class struggle, or the tactics of church leaders restricted to the spiritual level.

It was perfect and absolute Totalitarianism.

This planning, even to-day, does not attempt to capture global power by means of any particular movement or political system but through the simultaneous use of all creeds, churches, material-isms, political doctrines and patterns of power. It wishes to get built into all positions, movements, churches, masonic lodges and trade unions. It wants to take possession of all key positions in the most opposing movements, in the churches, parties and trade unions. It desires to hold in its hand both Bolshevism and Capitalism, materialism and idealism, to capture or hire spiritually all writers, artists, politicians and the mob. It aims at not being visible anywhere but at being present everywhere and at directing and controlling everything. To divide and rule! To march detach-ed but at a given moment to assault united.

Anybody now surveying the world and world affairs may well realise that this plan has already taken shape. The atomic fission of human society has achieved perfect success. Mankind is divided not only by the natural God-created races and nations. Even the nations are split up now. East and West Germany are divided, as are also North and South Korea. China, Indo-China and Trieste are split up or separated while Europe is divided by the Iron Curtain. Populations are split up and divided into white and coloured persons, capitalists and Bolsheviks, employers and employees, moneyed classes and working classes, Catholics and Protestants, suppressors and suppressed, victors and vanquished. But, as we will see later, all this chaos, disorder and division is directed by the same iron will, by the same secret force acting according to the interest of the leaders of a single race of 15 million people. They are to be found behind the well-padded doors of world capitalism as well as behind the thick walls of the Kremlin. It is they who instigate enraged crowds to strike and demonstrate while at the same time giving wage rises and promoting inflation. They attack Christianity while acting simultaneously as trustees of the gold and other assets representing the earthly power of the churches "whose kingdom is not of this world". They are the atom scientists and the anti-atom humanists; they are the masters and the murderers of the Communist secret police, yet at the same time they condemn the murders of the nations in UNO. They are the arch-enemy of patriotic ideals; they preach against the sovereignty of states and against racial discrimination, while all the time representing a racial nationalism of a vehemence so far unknown to have ever reigned over the nations of the earth.

Our globe with all its Continents—either openly or secretly—is already dominated by this Jewish nationalism. By using certain methods this fact can be demonstrated just as the presence of atomic radiation can be demonstrated by the aid of a geiger counter. For instance, should any nation, state, press or politician, parliament or any other person commit any act not forbidden by law or by the moral code against another state, class or person, then in this sublime age of democracy everything is free and permitted without risk. But should anyone commit the same act against Jewry or even against one Jew, the Jews will wipe off from the face of the earth this offending entity, whether it be an individual or a great nation. This will be effected, if necessary, by the atomic bomb or by the victorious Red Army or by the aid of any of the "democratic" constitutions, perhaps by the use of terror prisons of the cheque book or tommy-gun.

Amongst many other things this invisible seizure of power owed

9

its success to misapprehension and oversight on the part of anti-Jewish people during the last century. They regarded the Jew as an internationalist, which is not the real reason for opposing him. On the other hand, one could not justify his behaviour in destroying his fellow-men any the easier because his motives were based on race, creed, or birth, which, in fact, is what does motivate them. So we are convinced that it is our God-granted right and human duty to fight against the reign of terror exercised on a supernational level by a small fanatical nationalist minority which has subjugated the world and driven mankind far along the road to total extinction.

By the flash of the atomic bomb we should see at last that we are living in a false, dishonest, deceitful world-order, in a disorganised society on the eve of a universal catastrophe. This Satanic tribal nationalism holds world power in its grasp. It holds the hydrogen bomb, and in its mad blindness could destroy the whole of the globe and, with it, humanity. Is all this a bad dream or a nightmare ? To answer this question we must learn more about this tribal nationalism and its tactics. Then we shall see that the nightmare will resolve itself into reality and fact.

ONE

THE OLDEST "NAZISM" IN THE WORLD

". . . and ye shall possess greater nations and mightier than your-selves."—Deut. xi. 23.

WITHOUT a detailed study of the Old Testament, i.e. Torah, we can neither find the solution to those Jewish aspirations bent on capturing world power nor understand the events of the present day. Those who are not intimate with the first five books of the Old Testament, i.e. the Pentateuch, might readily conceive doubts that any such Jewish intentions exist at all, and they will usually dismiss any references thereto as " anti-Semitic " delusions. Such people are unable to realise that Jewry is standing on the threshold of total world domination.

Since the end of the second World War and the defeat of German National Socialism they will label anybody a Nazi who dares to refer to these appalling facts; he will be accused of prepar-ing a new dictatorship and, perhaps, planning another massacre. By making the word " Jew " taboo they are suppressing the freedom to express one's opinion and thoughts and at the same time making sure that people all over the world will not be able to see clearly in the moment of danger. The accusation of Nazism is handy, cheap and popular ! The so-called man in the street knows as much about National Socialism as the big Jewish press organs find fit for him to know and, therefore, in his ignorance he considers Jewry a " persecuted race " and to him the mere utterance of the word "Jew" represents "anti-Semitism".

So having his mind poisoned by propaganda, the man in the street, is disinclined to realise that everything which he now curses and condemns in German National Socialism, those principles for which its leaders were hanged in Nuremberg in the name of " world-conscience ", have existed for the last three to four thousand years. During the "Führership" of Moses, everything was the same in the totalitarian regime of JAHVE. The Jewish race-protection laws of those days and Jewish tribal nationalism have survived to outlive the leader of German National Socialism himself. For the conception of racial superiority, together with its religious and political cults are not Hitlerian inventions.

When Hitler, Goebbels and Rosenberg availed themselves of a racial conception they were doing nothing else but using against Jewry the weapons of Jewry. Everything that world-Jewry, under the disguise of the flag of the Allied Powers condemned, was actually of its own make and device. Jewry actually hanged itself at Nuremberg. For the laws relating to and establishing racial segregation were first published in the books of the prophets Ezra and Nehemiah, and not in the Rassenschutz-Gesetz (Race Protection Act) of Nuremberg. The first concentration camps were devised not by Heinrich Himmler but by King Solomon. The motto of total "annihilation" and total "extermination" of the defeated enemy first appeared in the orders of Moses, the Jewish Fuhrer.

Hitler only proclaimed that the Germans are a superior race to the Jews. On this point Moses went to far greater extremes in announcing that Jewry is of direct divine origin and the chosen people of God and, consequently, sacred. Each and every Jew is personally sacred and he who offends a Jew, offends God Himself ! This is tacitly held even to-day in the opinion of Jewry.

What else is this if not the most exaggerated Chauvinistic form of racial Totalitarianism? It is quite clear that this haughty and ancient consciousness of racial excellence and sanctity remain very much alive up to the present day, when we see Jewry protesting against the trial of an indicted Jew before any Gentile court, for when they regard and treat an affront against one Jew as an affront against the whole of Jewry. According to the four-thousand-year-old standards of Jewish nationalism, any insult against a Jew is a direct insult against God and a crime against the sacred seed of Abraham.

The first and most important commandment of Moses, the great state administrator, is designed to safeguard racial purity. The ever-recurring motif of the Old Testament is this order of Moses, who, before the conquest of the promised land, points at the neighbouring peoples and then says to the children of Israel:

". . . Thou shalt make no covenant with them, nor show mercy unto them. Neither shalt thou make marriages with them; thy daughter thou shalt not give unto his son, nor his daughter shalt take unto thy son." (*Deut. vii.* 2-3.)

Four thousand years later, German National Socialism had the same object in view when marriage, friendship and commercial activities with Jews were forbidden by the Nuremberg laws.

The judges put forward by the Jews in the Nuremberg show trials could not emphasise enough in the name of " world conscience " that the German racial laws were barbaric. But at the same time these judges were unaware that by their sentence it was the Jews themselves they were condemning. For when the Jews returned from Babylonian captivity

". . . they separated from Israel all the mixed multitude." (*Nehemiah xiii.* 3.)

And the diary of the "Nazi" prophet continues:

" In those days also saw I Jews that had married wives of Ashdod, of Ammon, and of Moab, and their children spake half in the speech of Ashdod, and could not speak in the Jews' language, but according to the language of each people, and I contended with them, and cursed them, and smote certain of them, and plucked off their hair and made them swear by God, saying, ye shall not give your daughters unto their sons, nor take their daughters unto your sons, or for yourselves. . . ." (*Nehemiah xiii.* 23-25.)

Nehemiah, the prophet of the race protection laws of those ancient times, nevertheless only curses and beats up those corrupting racial purity whilst Ezra acts with much more vigour and energy. He tells us in his book that the Jews have taken wives among the daughters of the Canaanites, Hittites, Jebusites, Ammonites, Moabites, Egyptians and Ammorite according to the abominations of these people, and that therefore the holy seed was mingled with the people of those lands. (*Ezra ix.* 1, 2, 12.) Ezra orders the polluters of Jewish racial purity to come to Jerusalem and he exposes and denounces them in his book and quoting the divine law, demands that they shall dismiss their non-Jewish wives — and there were

13

among them wives who had borne sons already — relates the Old Testament. It does not matter! All have to perish who desecrated the holy seed, mothers as well as half-caste children. In the theocratic state, the racial God-Fuhrership will not tolerate mothers of foreign origin or cross-bred children. The prophets cannot foresee that two thousand years later in Mr. Sulzberger's *New York Times* this same " lack of toleration " will be stamped and condemned as deadly sin against God when the laws of Ezra and Nehemiah are applied against the Jews themselves. The " Christian " churches teaching and preaching the Old Testament brand the Hitlerian laws of Nuremberg as " ungodly " and yet show full and pious understanding towards the ruling of the new Israeli parliament when, in 1953, it banned marriage betwen Jew and Gentile.

Such racial discrimination might appear to be a dark superstition, a heresy. Nevertheless, the Jewish laws regard racial purity as a commandment of the utmost importance.

" An Ammonite or Moabite shall not enter into the congregation of the Lord; even to their tenth generation shall they not enter into the congregation of the Lord forever." (*Deut xxiii.* 3.)

The later descendants of the Jews took this commandment of Moses so seriously that, according to Houston Stewart Chamberlain, Jewish girls who had evidently become pregnant by Gentile men were sent away to other communities, where the expectant mothers, together with their children were killed. American Jewish rabbis as recently as 1949, issued decrees banning intermarriage between Jews and Gentiles.

The magic of the sanctity of the " holy seed ", the consciousness of being the master-race, burns in the Old Testament with the fierce glow of the most fanatical nationalism of all times. The Jews killed and destroyed the non-Jewish peoples of ancient times in obedience to the religious and national laws of the God-Fuhrership and when we think of the Nuremberg trials of the modern " war criminals " it makes us realise how much more the Jewish kings and prophets of old deserved condemnation on the very same score. But the so-called Christian churches condemn nothing, yet continue teaching Gentile children that most pornographic and bloodthirsty book — the Old Testament. The so-called Jewish holy books on the other hand clearly boast of revenge, relating most macabre accounts of

14

the slaying and extermination of entire nations. They proclaim the slaughter of the innocents, including even babies if they are non-Jewish, as the fulfilment of the highest national duty and as a deed most pleasing to God.

" . . . thou shalt smite them, and utterly destroy them; thou shalt make no Covenant with them, nor show mercy unto them." (*Deut. vii.* 2.)

The Judean master-race is at liberty to commit crime, According to Torah and the prophets the slaying and destruction of other races and peoples is not only a religious duty but an absolute right of the Jewish nation and this right includes the prerogative of ruling over others.

The prophet Isaiah already depicts this coming world-power in resplendent and brilliant colours, as follows :

"Thus saith the Lord God : Behold, I will lift up mine hand to the Gentiles, and set up my standard to the people: and they shall bring thy sons in their arms, and thy daughters shall be carried upon their shoulders. And kings shall be thy nursing fathers, and their queens thy nursing mothers; they shall bow down to thee with their face toward the earth, and lick up the dust of thy feet. . . ." (*Isaiah xlix.* 22, 23.)

"And the sons of strangers shall build up thy walls, and their kings shall minister unto thee . . . Therefore thy gates shall be open continually; they shall not be shut day nor night; that men may bring unto thee the forces of the Gentiles, and that their kings may be brought. For the nation and kingdom that will not serve thee shall perish; yea, those nations shall be utterly wasted. . . ." Thou shalt also suck the milk of the Gentiles, and shalt suck the breasts of kings. . . ." (*Isaiah lx.* 10-12, 16.)

Not only on the ground of racial prejudice, but on the basis of direct divine commandment, the Jews feel themselves entitled to subjugate strangers and to treat as slaves all those who fall into their power.

"And Solomon numbered all the strangers that were in the land of Israel . . . and he set three score and ten thousand of them to be bearers of burdens and four score thousand to be hewers in the mountain . . . " (*II Chronicles ii.* 17-18.)

After Moses' race-protection "Nuremberg Laws", after the

15

racial segregation and world-power mania of Ezra and Nehemiah, we now see the first concentration camp and slave labour establishment in which foreigners work for the master-race. They are related as an accomplished fact without ever being condemned by a humanitarian court. The schemes of the Soviet terror chambers and the forced labour camps of the Kaganovitch Empire were conceived in the land of Israel.

It is the Old Testament and not *Mein Kampf* that must be studied in order to see that the gas-chamber made world famous by the Sulzberger Press was actually the invention of the chosen people. The prophet Samuel tells us how the "humanitarian" race in the ecstatic rapture of victory dealt with its defeated enemies:

"And he brought forth the people that were therein (in the Ammonite city of Rabbah—translator) and put them under saws and under harrows of iron and under axes of iron, and made them pass through the brick-kiln; and thus did he unto all the cities of the children of Ammon. So David and all the people returned unto Jerusalem." (*II Samuel xii,* 31.)

The first concentration camp, the first gas-chamber (a brick-kiln) in the world were in the land of Israel. And the first ghetto was established in Jerusalem and not in Europe.

"The Jew shaped his own fate!" wrote Houston Stewart Chamberlain referring to these things.

This Jewish tribal nationalism which created the race-protecting laws, the ghettos, the concentration camps and the gas-chambers of ancient times, never died out. It continued slaying and killing neighbouring peoples and races. Whenever it was defeated it arose again! It chanted the melancholic sounds of its irredentism by the waters of Babylon during the Captivity and after the liberation it began to build the New Jerusalem with the vehemence of a revived nationalism. It had suffered but was awaiting the new Messiah, the Jewish nationalist deliverer and political leader, the new Fuhrer, who would place world power over all the nations in the hands of Jewry.

Jewry has never abandoned this grandiose national dream. During the Zionist Congress of 1897 at Basle, Dr. Mandelstein, Professor of the University of Kiev, in the course of his speech opening the conference on August 29th, emphatically stated that "The Jews will use all their influence and power to prevent the rise and prosperity of all other nations and are resolved to adhere to their historic hopes, i.e. to the conquest of world power ". (*Le Temps*, September 3rd, 1897.) By such fanatical nationalism the first ghetto was established in Jerusalem and the complete separation from non-Jews accomplished. (*Joel, Chapter iii.* 17.)   It was promised that Jehovah, the celestial Fuhrer would dwell in Jerusalem for ever and that all non-Jewish people would be excluded from God's presence.   It is taught by the Jewish Rabbis that all non-Jewish people must be excluded from sharing the new world or taking any part in it; they can only be tolerated as a despised herd. (*Traktat, Gittin, Fol. 57, Babylonian Talmud.*)

Jewish tribal nationalism faced the most perilous times in its history following the birth of Christ. This was, or could have been, a fatal moment in the history of Jewry. It was also a bitter disappointment. The Jews were shocked to learn that He was not the Messiah they were awaiting. He was no nationalist liberator, to rid them of the Roman soldiers. He was anti-nationalist, or, as He would be called to-day, an international rebel—One who, in the temple, dared to kick over the merchants' wares, to overthrow the desks of the money-changers and to evict the representatives and agents of the local money authorities. It was just as if a determined McCarthyist were to raid the New York Stock Exchange with a whip in his hand. This new prophet did not believe in the racial superiority of Jewry, but in the brotherhood of all mankind. According to the standards of Jewry His racial origin is highly doubtful and open to suspicion, because He came from Galilee, and in Jerusalem everybody could recognise His disciples by their Galilean dialect. In the streets of Jerusalem this Master and His disciples preached against the doctrines expounded by the most powerful authorities on the Jewish Chauvinistic way of life and on Jewish nationalism, i.e. they preached against the Sanhedrin and against the Pharisees, Scribes and Sadducees. This Master and His disciples did not believe in a separate tribal alliance between God and the Jews. In contradiction to the tenets of the Chief Rabbis, Peter, the fisherman from Galilee, tells Cornelius the captain and centurion of the Roman Empire that " all nations " are pleasing to God which fear Him and act righteously. These disciples teach in the name of the Lord Jesus that Romans, Jews and Greeks are all human beings and that there is no exclusive deliverance reserved for any single nation that there is no special Messiah for Jews only, that there is no racial superiority for the followers of Jehovah as all are human beings, children of the one and only God.

He told them that He was the deliverer not only of the Jews but of all mankind and that He was not prepared to accept the supremacy and rule of any master-race. Therefore, He had to be crucified.

" Crucify Him!" they shouted to the Roman governor, who — an opportunist state official similar to the eternally shameful figure of the public prosecutor of Nuremberg—faced the mob's concentrated hatred in confusion of spirit. " Crucify Him " — after all, this Messiah might well prove not to be the descendant of the Holy Seed of Abraham.

Houston Stewart Chamberlain in his book entitled *Die Grundlagen des neunzehnten Jahrhunderts* (The Foundations of the Nineteenth Century) deduces clearly the fatal consequences attending Jewry's entry into world history and is the earliest author to discover that Christ, insofar as racial descent is concerned, was not a Jew. Chamberlain was the first author who came to the conclusion that the name of Galilee itself is actually " Gelil haggoyim ", meaning " heathen or Gentile Land " where non-Jewish settlers lived. They were easily distinguished by their dialect. " The possibility that Christ was not a Jew and that there was not a drop of Jewish blood in His veins is so great that it nearly equals to certainty ", he writes in the book quoted above — Volume 1, page 256.

The question " Was Christ a Jew ? " is posed by Ferenc Zajthy, the Hungarian historian, in his monumental book *Hungarian Millennia* in which he proves that the Jews themselves doubted Christ's Jewish descent. Zajthy points out that in the seventh century B.C. Shalmaneser drove the whole population of Galilee into captivity in chains and that not a single Jew was left there. The Scythian pastoral tribes who subsequently settled into the home of the displaced population adopted the Jewish creed with its religious teachings, but, as the Jews themselves termed it, they were

" under Jewish laws " only. The Jews never accepted them as true descendants of Abraham's Holy Seed.

" . . . Search and look : for out of Galilee ariseth no prophet " (*John vii.* 52) the Jews told the apostles. Prophets can arise from Jewish racial communities only.

The ancient Jewish laws protected Jewish individuals to the utmost, and the death sentence could only be pronounced on a " estih " i.e. on a person who tried to persuade Jews to abandon their creed or who attempted to cause a rift in their racial unity. Ferenc Zajthy describes how, according to the ancient Jewish laws and customs, the way of escape was all the time kept open for even such a person when under the death sentence. On the way leading to the place of execution observers were posted at every hundred steps. The observers' duty was to report if any new witnesses gave a sign by raising their arm that they were willing to come forward and testify in order to save the life of the condemned. In the case of any new witnesses coming forward the laws ordered new trials to be held or an amnesty to be granted.

It is peculiar, though under the circumstances quite natural, that in the procession following Jesus to the Cross, no witness volunteered to testify and save Him. Among those who received Him on Maundy Thursday with jubilant festivities not one raised his hand. Nor did any of those who heard His teachings and saw His miracles. No witness volunteered to save Him. And here we have the decisive proof that He was not a Jew in that nobody was permitted to come forward. Because, according to the laws of the Jewish state, re-trial was permissible for the descendants of Abraham's holy seed only. From this right the Goyim, the Gentiles, the strangers, the descendants of those of all non-Jewish blood were excluded, as well as those who came under the jurisdiction of the Jewish laws but were not Jews racially. So excluded were the hated Galileans, the Cushians and the Huvilains that, according to the Jewish laws, they were to be pressed under the water and drowned by any wayfarer, happening to pass who should see them struggling in the water.

We Christians accept the theory of the Immaculate Conception, i.e. the tenet that Christ was, in fact, the son of God and thus he has no raciality. But in this case it is even more certain that Christ's divine origin, whole personality and teachings represented

19

a power revolution against the tribal Chauvinism of the Jews.

The Christian Middle Ages (labelled the Dark Ages by the propaganda of Jewish intellectuals) were very much aware of the importance of Christ's resistance against Jewish tribal nationalism. We will have the opportunity later to show how this Christian clear-sightedness became more confused after the French Revolution and the Jewish emancipation. From that time until the present day the artificial befogging and obscuration of all Christian ideals has been in progress, and by now the darkness is so impenetrable that many movements and lines of thought confuse Christianity and Judaism. Even worse than this, some Christian priests in their ceremonial are adopting that fanatical hatred which is a characteristic feature of Jewish Rabbis (e.g. the prayer of the American Protestant padres read out before the dropping of the atom bombs on Hiroshima and Nagasaki).

The nationalism convicted at Nuremberg lived only twenty years. But Moses' *Mein Kampf* with its dogma of racial nationalism was preserved and diligently studied by Jewry throughout many thousands of years. The intensity of this ancient nationalism has never abated, not even during the times of "Galuth", i.e. homelessness.

After the Babylonian captivity, Jews and members of Diaspora from the Roman Empire settled around Alexandria. They were all free Roman citizens and "liberal-minded" people and still continued sending considerable annual gifts to the temple of Jerusalem. After the Dispersion (Diaspora) the flame of this nationalism became more intense and vehement. Seven hundred years ago, Moseban Majemon, one of the most brilliant writers of Jewish script, gives us yet another description in Mischneh Torah, in resplendent colours, of the possibilities of the Messiah's arrival and of the attainment of world power by his nation.

"The world became familiar with those things pertaining to the Messiah and to Torah," he wrote, continuing: "These things became known in far-away lands and amongst many uncircumcised peoples. The Christians were conversant with many things though formerly the Messiah was known by Israel alone."

Maimonides also admits that Christianity made the world familiar with the Old Testament, i.e. with Torah, but adds that its interpretation was erroneous and that the errors will be evident at the

20

arrival of Jewry's political Messiah who, as leader of Jewry's armed power, will subjugate the non-Jewish nations of the world and will exterminate, together with their women and children, all those who refuse to accept the laws of Noah. (*Jewry and Christianity*, by Canon Lipot Huber, p. 141.)

During Galuth, Jewish nationalism became transformed into a religious irredentism, with Torah and Talmud acting as its *Mein Kampf*. The Mosaic *Mein Kampf* is preserved everywhere and kept in the Torah shrine of even the smallest village. This national Creed was copied again and again by scribes on papyri, their eyes tired and inflamed by the work, through the letters of which the language of the lost land was learned by children and practised by adults. The Temple was destroyed but the national way of life never ceased to exist. That religious nationalism which, together with Torah in days of old pervaded the land, spread to every place on earth where Jews were living. And this nationalist teaching prescribed not only the rules of life, the form of prayers, the quality of clothing, methods of general hygiene, and dietary regulations, but also shaped and developed the nationalist ideology. Torah remained the same in Belz, Frankfurt or New York as anywhere else. Jewry, dispersed, took refuge from the world in their own reserved ghetto, fortifying their spirit by the study of Torah and Talmud.

One of the greatest mistakes of the " anti-Semites " was to regard the Jew as an internationalist. The Jew was never an internationalist, but the conscious representative of a tribal nationalism that sought domination over all the other nations on earth. He lived in various lands, occupied positions of different social levels but fundamentally remained a Jew.

During the preparatory sittings of the Sanhedrin summoned by Napoleon in 1806, Rabbi Solomon Lippman Cerfberr said: " We have forgotten whose descendants we are. We are neither ' German ' nor ' Portuguese ' Jews. However dispersed all over the globe we may be, we still remain the same nation."

Doctor Leopold Kahn summed up these sentiments when speaking about Zionism in a Jewish school at Pozsony (Bratislava) in 1901—" Jews will never be assimilated and will never adopt the customs or morals of strangers. The Jew will remain a Jew under all circumstances."

This venerable Rabbi was right. Jews lived in different countries, occupying different social levels, but remained everywhere Jews. If a Jew took off his kaftan and enjoyed forbidden foods, dressed in tails or a dinner jacket, he yet remained a representative of the same creed, the same blood relationship and the same nationalism. Perhaps he might not be living literally up to the words of his religious rites, but his racial consciousness and awareness of racial obligations remained unchanged, whether on the Papal Throne, in the Soviet Politbureau or in the State Department at Washington. The Jewish author David Moccata writes in his book *The Jews in Spain and in Portugal* that for generations Jews lived in Spain disguised, intermingling with all the social classes but occupying all the key positions of the state, especially those in the Church.

Jews can always argue that there is such a thing as assimilation. They point at Jews who assumed the language and customs of their adopted countries, married Christian women and became statesmen of Christian empires. But they cannot refute the fact that the Jew who apparently becomes a true Englishman or true German or a most excellent Polish patriot still remains consciously a Jew (and the state of the world to-day bears evidence of this fact), consequently his allegiance lasts only so long as it does not clash with his Jewish origin.

Another extremely efficient weapon of the Jew is his ability, like the chameleon, to assume the colours of his habitat. In France he merges into the background of the local environment, as he does in Hungary, in England and everywhere else. But although he tries to appear an Englishman in England and a Yankee in America, this is a disguise only and calculated for defence as well as for conquest. In New York and Brooklyn, where outside of Russia itself the largest crowds of Russian Jews and Polish Jews live, one rarely sees a Jew wearing a kaftan or a beard. Relatives waste no time giving a good shave to the new immigrant; they know only too well that beards and earlocks provoke " anti-semitism ". They sense that any open appearance of Jewish nationalism would arouse opposition among their hosts. The Protocols of the Elders of Zion warn them of this. " Secrecy is the foundation of our power . . . " Therefore in Soviet Russia, the Jew is either a bolshevik revolutionary in strict adherence to the party line, or an officer of the secret police with a sub-machine gun, in America a Yankee-like banker, and in France a radical patriot. Of course, he must also be a party member in Soviet Russia and probably a Democratic elector in New York.

But, whatever political convictions they profess, whatever nationality they may have assumed, they always remain Jews at heart, following the craving of their Jewish nationalism. Sometimes, appropriately enough, it happens that the Jewish aims coincide with the aspirations of their adopted countries. But, in fact, they never accept the authority of any " stranger ", obeying the Mosaic law, ". . . thou mayest not set a stranger over thee, which is not thy brother " (*Deut. xvii.* 15), i.e. who is not a member of the Jewish race.

With the development of civilisation, this adaptation to environment became more complete. This was best seen in the professions, such as the stage, the films and journalism. The film industry in Hollywood was once regarded as the national industry of America. Those who directed this industry occasionally made good American films. But under cover of the " stars and stripes " they attempted to inculcate a Jewish mentality and a spirit of false values into the American masses, and as we will see later, it was from this Hollywood camouflage that the hundred anti-American Bolshevik film-stars emerged. The Bolshevik Jew in his attempt to conquer world power threw away his mask.

It was consistent with the nature of a four-thousand-year-old Nationalism that Jews should endure persecution, mockery and contempt. But the more they suffered, the stronger their belief grew that the time would come when they would be the masters of all peoples. Thus, Jewry tolerated even anti-Judaism. Often they themselves failed to understand why they were persecuted, derided and sometimes even murdered. For the Jew felt that he was God's creature the same as any other human being, even though " anti-Semites " might doubt it. So he was often insulted and humiliated and labelled a swindler and ridiculed and cartooned. Most people, apparently, remained unaware that his objectionable activities served a higher nationalism—that typical Old Testament sort of nationalism which is irreconcilable towards all other peoples and which aims at the subjugation of all nations. The relationship between the nationalism of the Old Testament and German

National Socialism may be compared to that of earth and sky.

German National Socialism was ready and willing to co-operate with other peoples. It was hostile to one race only — Jewry. Whereas the Jewish type of "Nazism" is hostile to all races and to all non-Jewish social and ruling castes.

Generations in the ghetto taught the Jews that those racial laws which kept them together as a nation could also enable them to become the masters of all nations. To this, apart from modern developments, there was added another favourable racial feature—their indisputable talents and high intelligence. Jewish writers, artists, business men and bankers — regardless of the methods adopted—were reaping the highest awards of Western civilisation. For the small Jews, left behind in this race, all the successes were Jewish successes, all the achievements were Jewish achievements. Not only the Press but the most simple Jew revered Disraeli, the great "English" statesman, together with Heine, the great "German" poet and Marx, the most capricious international revolutionary. What is this if not the conscious splendour of an unrivalled nationalism or extreme "Nazism"? A nationalism that brooks successful apostasy and is unwilling to execute even a criminal if it knows that he also is a descendant of the seed of Abraham, a nationalism that encourages the successful apostate to return to the fold which he had rejected.

And so we nearly always find Jews making headway all over the world, either as poets, bankers, English Conservatives or Portuguese revolutionaries, all believing they are predestined to reign over the peoples of the earth. So far they have succeeded in everything. It is clear, therefore, that the tenets laid down in Torah, the Talmudical principles and the Jewish secret institutions created during the Middle Ages are still effective instruments serving towards the achievement of world power.

"It is our vocation to rule the world," proclaims this aggressive minority. "Either as American banker or as Soviet Commissar we form but one nation."

It is the chief purpose of this book to show that Capitalism and Bolshevism, the two great ruling systems of our modern age, are not two opposing movements but that they rather present two different forms of expression of the same Jewish ambition to obtain world power. One of them, possibly, is more cautious than the other, nevertheless, both are the same. The attempt to bring about a conflict between Capitalism and Bolshevism is therefore a most terrible deception. The enmity directed towards Christians and Arabs proceeds from both these systems. The "man in the street" as the symbol of the uneducated and uninformed masses, may think that the capitalist world will be able "to fix" Bolshevism all right but the true fact is that the latter is nothing else but an extension of the former. Bolshevism is the offspring of Capitalism or, perhaps, it is the result of the blunders of Capitalism. Bolshevism is the adopted child of the Jewish Liberal capitalist system. Those who try to find some difference or contradiction between the two systems must never forget that in Hitlerian National Socialism, the big German capitalist entertained the most friendly relations with German socialist workers. Why therefore could not the Jewish Bernard Baruch have been on the best possible terms with Lazar Kaganovitch or even with the small Communist leader of Brooklyn?

"We are one nation", stated Theodore Herzl, the founder of Zionism. "We are neither American Jews nor Soviet Jews, but only Jews!"

By the turn of the last century, having regard to the results achieved, it appeared as if the unity of the holy seed and its calling to win world power had begun to crystallise into reality. This was visualised in the imagination of the Jewish authors, poets, bankers, socialist revolutionaries and Communist apostles. A world-conquering nationalism had arrived. The "anti-Semites" themselves failed to notice and evaluate this development, and the events of 1945 had to transpire before a realisation came concerning the indisputable mental and racial unity of "capitalist democracy", on the one hand and of Soviet "peoples' democracy" on the other. It is hardly necessary to remark that this realisation was attained by an exceedingly small minority. The anti-Semites saw and understood the Jewish "racial solidarity", the "dishonest business methods" and the "Judaisation" of their own countries only. Meanwhile, what was considered by some to be a "Jewish crime" was a virtue in the estimation of Jewish nationalism. The racial consciousness of the master race, i.e. Mosaic nationalism, attained its present form by the end of the 19th century. Its slogan forged for Bolsheviks and bankers alike was: "Let us march independently and be victorious together!"

So the world conquerors began their march and set out to subjugate the globe and to become rulers of all nations.

TWO

THE MEANING OF CHRIST'S RESISTANCE

In the Middle Ages men still recognised the cleavage between the spirit of the New Testament and the Jewish " nazism " of the Old Testament against which Christ rebelled. In Christ's person the ideal of human brotherhood was fully accomplished. The Old Testament contained the materialistic covenant of a single race with its Jehovah. Christ brought deliverance to the whole of mankind. He made the covenant in the New Testament for all of us. The idea of universal love and the whole inner meaning of the New Testament was the antithesis of materialistic Judaism with its obsession of pre-determined power. The greatest lie of history is the statement alleging that Christianity was born out of the Jewish religion. On the contrary, Christianity came into being as the very negation of Jewish nationalism and racial predestination. The apostles themselves taught this:

" Ye know", Peter said, " How that it is an unlawful thing for a man that is a Jew to keep company, or come unto one of another nation; but God hath shewed me that I should not call any man common or unclean." (*Acts x.* 28.)

The Jews were amazed to be told that the Goyim also may enjoy and share the divine grace of the Holy Ghost. They complained that the apostles sat down at the same table with uncircumcised people. They staged a demonstration in Athens against Paul the Apostle because he brought Greeks into the synagogue and defiled the Holy Place.

Peter's statement, already quoted, uttered during his visit to Cornelius the centurion, together with the quotation below, sound like a defiance of the prevailing Jewish tribal arrogance:

". . . of a truth I perceive that God is no respecter of persons: but in every nation he that feareth Him and worketh righteousness, is accepted with Him." (*Acts x.* 34-35.)

But the teaching of Paul and Barnabas in Antioch sounds even more defiant:

"Then Paul and Barnabas waxed bold, and said it was necessary that the word of God should first have been spoken to you: but seeing ye put it from you and judge yourselves unworthy of everlasting life, lo we turn to the Gentiles." (*Acts xiii.* 46.)

By Gentiles they meant the Goyim, i.e. the non-Jewish peoples. "And (God) hath made of one blood all nations of men. . . ." (*Acts xvii.* 26) says Paul in Athens. And he says this because from the God-created blood-brotherhood, one nation, one race—the Jews—excluded themselves by their own fierce tribal nationalism.

"And art confident" Paul writes concerning the Jews, "that thou thyself art a guide of the blind, a light of them which are in darkness, an instructor of the foolish, a teacher of the babes, which hast the form of knowledge and of the truth in the law . . . thou that makest thy boast of the law through breaking the law dishonourest thou God? For the name of God is blasphemed among the Gentiles through you, as it is written." (*Paul to the Romans ii.* 19-20, 23-24.)

The Apostles everywhere teach and preach Christ's revolutionary ideas which are the very negation of Judaism, of that tribal reservedness and of that Jewish " nazism ".

"For the heart of this people is waxed gross, and their ears are dull of hearing, and their eyes have they closed; lest they should see with their eyes and hear with their ears and understand with their heart and should be converted, and I should heal them." "Be it known therefore unto you that the salvation of God is sent unto the Gentiles and that they will hear it." (*Acts xxviii.* 27-28.)

But the Jews crucified the apostle of this faith and have not to the present day abandoned their belief that they are the chosen people and therefore the lords and masters of all peoples on earth. The dispersion of Jewry began with diaspora, after the Babylonian captivity and was completed by the demolition of Jerusalem. As a result of this the long pent-up demoniacal force was spread abroad; the ambitious aim to rule over all nations accompanied by an exclusive racialism penetrated the ethnic and religious confusion of those ancient times. It is not necessary to discuss here in detail how it was—though Jewry was not pure-bred as a race being composed of cross-breeds of various peoples and remnants of different races—that nevertheless this racial conglomerate was shaped and moulded by Ezra and Nehemiah into the only homogeneous pure race in the world. Even at the end of the nineteenth century various American anthropological investigations came to the conclusion that " the Jewish race retained its ethnical purity throughout ". (*Political-Anthropological Revue,* March, 1904, page 1003.)

Houston Stewart Chamberlain writes that from Theodosius until the year 1800 there were only 300 persons of non-Jewish stock actually adopted by Jewry in the racial sense. From this extreme racialism proceeded a mentality which hated and despised all other peoples, whilst being at the same time ambitious to conquer. In Europe appeared the materialistic and uncompromising spirit of the Old Testament, which never abandoned its Messianic dream of that time to come when the destruction of all peoples and the mastery over greater and mightier nations would be accomplished.

It is therefore easy to understand that the ancient world, as well as the Middle Ages, drew the obvious inference from this, and separated themselves from the Jews not only ideologically but physically also. Over the people of those days the biblical account of the descent of the Holy Ghost and of Peter's sermon on that first Whitsun morning still exerted a considerable influence:

". . . save yourselves from this untoward generation." (*Acts ii.* 40.)

The Middle Ages created the ghetto but at the same time by this act preserved the Jewish race. Generally speaking Jewry was able to sustain its policy of racial purity because this was recognised by the Christian world in the form of the ghetto. But, unfortunately, this did not prevent the Jews from infiltrating into the life and economic systems of the Christian states.

We can learn the history of this Jewish influence from the ancient world. Nearly a million Jews were settled in Alexandria and its suburbs after the Babylonian captivity, where they played the same rôle and exercised much the same power as Jewry does in New York to-day. In the Roman Empire, especially in Rome, the power and influence of this nationalist tribal minority reached quite formidable dimensions. Cicero, the great Roman statesman, during the proceedings of a court action made his address to the court in such a subdued voice that he could only be heard by the judges.

29

He explained the wisdom of acting in such a fashion by stating that Jewish solidarity constituted a force formidable enough to ruin anybody giving evidence against them. Throughout diaspora and from early times the Jews possessed organisations akin to those we now know as masonic. They initiated certain influential Gentiles who were prepared to declare themselves to be half-Jewish and through whom they were able to establish their influence in the highest places in public life. It can be established that behind Nero's persecution of the Christians were members of diaspora. Poppea Sabina, the wife of the Emperor, was a Jewess and a member of diaspora and she succeeded in persuading the Emperor through the help of his favourite courtier, a Jewish actor named Alityrus, to exterminate the Christians. Throughout historical times the Alityruses and Poppeas of this world have been behind its Neroes and Roosevelts !

Jewish influence played as much part in determining the downfall of the Roman Empire as in causing the ruin of the Spanish Empire. In the Spanish Empire Jews had, as Heman writes, the control of all spiritual and material powers from the tenure of land to the highest ecclesiastical positions, and through their usury they exercised much influence over court circles and the entire nobility. In the end they were able to extort for themselves such fantastic privileges that in a court of law the oath of one Jew was accepted as of greater value than the oaths of two Gentiles. They repeated the same form of power-grab later in Germany and in the Hapsburg Empire. In the sixteenth century a Jew called Imre Fortunatus and his associates played a tremendous part in the preparation for the downfall of the Hungarian Empire by fostering corruption in public affairs to such a degree that the Empire became unable to resist the attacks of the expanding Turkish power at the Battle of Mohacs in 1526.

The spiritual leaders and statesmen of the ancient world and Middle Ages were very much aware of this Jewish influence. From Tiberius, the Roman Emperor, to Goethe, all men of vision looked upon Jewry as a national danger. " A ministry from which the Jew obtains all his requirements, a household, the wardrobe and finances of which are under the control of a Jew or a commissariat which is under the management of a Jew must indeed be endowed with the undrainable qualities of the Pontine marshes", writes Goethe.

Possibly the great Napoleon was the most clear-sighted of all when he exclaimed : " These Jews are like locusts and caterpillars and they will devour my France ! "

It was clearly seen even as late as the eighteenth century that Jewish influence had nothing of the much-vaunted humanitarianism about it, since it was a minority movement which became a " state within a state ". Though some states did not recognise the danger, nevertheless the Jewish conquest was usually stopped at the last moment. Ferdinand and Isabella, the Catholic, expelled them from Spain and elsewhere restrictive measures were taken to check them but the most important thing was that the influence of Jewish " nazism " was nowhere permitted to gain a foothold in public affairs. The ghetto at least served as a good institution in keeping up ideological and intellectual barriers against the Jews so that the Christian religions and cultures were not so exposed to mortal danger and to that of being visibly engulfed as they are to-day. It is important to note that up to the French Revolution the Jews had no direct influence on the masses. At the most they were only able to increase their influence over some court circles by the help of their money-bags, but they never had an opportunity of establishing any direct control over the people or of exploiting them by further-ing the interests of their own nationalism.

One point only of the so-called Jewish problem passed unnoticed in the Middle Ages. Namely, that the growing influence of Jewish nationalism and its encroachment was not an instinctive activity originating from greed, selfishness or any other " Jewish character-istic " as the " anti-Semites " termed it. The demoniacal urge was already consciously at work, and the nationalism of the Old Testa-ment, of Torah and of Talmud were impelling the Jew to undertake a quest not for money, nor for riotous living and wealth but for world power. Money merely served as the means towards this aspira-tion, while the attainment of mastery over the whole world remained the supreme aim. For this, not even a Jewish central government was required though such existed from time to time. Talmud and Torah were quite sufficient. These books which gave much better instruction than any government as to the conduct of Jewry, were to be found in all synagogues and in all Jewish houses.

The various countries and empires were more or less able to keep this world-conquering dream under control while its execution in different lands was unco-ordinated. The danger grew very considerably with the expansion of the limits of the known world and when, through the medium of the press, radio and other organs of propaganda, the different countries and peoples drew nearer to each other. Then the aspiration of this Jewish minority nationalism to dominate was to operate effectively not only against single countries but against all lands and peoples simultaneously and with full force. At the same time, with the rise of Protestantism, a certain Jewish mentality began to obtain a foothold within Christianity itself.

Luther saw clearly that the difference between universal humanity and Jewish tribal " nazism " was irreconcilable. His great treatise written on the Jewish question is the proof of his clearsightedness. But, apart from the rise of Protestantism, the Old Testament obtained a greater influence through the teaching of the Bible in church sermons and through religious education in the schools. The Protestant preachers, Hungarians, Swiss, Englishmen, Dutchmen and Germans alike turned more and more to the prophets of the Old Testament for parables and quotations. During the religious wars all the most withering curses of the Old Testament were invoked on the heads of opponents. The mentality of the Old Testament thus penetrated the Christian faith through the empty phraseology of rhetoric. Christianity began to regard itself as an extension or subsidiary of the Jewish religion instead of stressing its truly opposing character. As a result of this error, a Jewish mentality of intolerance, accompanied by a spirit of hatred, became established in the civilised Christian world and generation after generation grew up imbued with the materialistic and unimaginative teachings of the Old Testament.

English Protestantism became especially subjected to the influence of the Old Testament. The mentality of the English merchant-princes and the spiritual attitude of the Puritans likewise became identified with the principles of the Jewish Old Testament and found in it the justification of a certain business conduct. In the nineteenth century some deluded English scholars even tried to prove that the inhabitants of Britain were actually descendants of the lost tenth tribe of Israel. Werner Sombart, the famous authority on capitalism, showed conclusively that the roots of capitalism are as much Jewish as Protestant.

One thing, however, can be stated as certain. With the advent of Protestantism the former unity of the Christian world was broken up. Christ's Church separated into Catholicism and Protestantism. Through this breach Mosaic nationalism boldly penetrated the Christian world and Christian spiritual life. Under the pretext of enlightenment and progress the inhabitants of the ghettos began to shout loudly for emancipation, the very thing which, even Voltaire, the greatest champion of progress, had regarded as a mortal peril. Under the guise of philanthropy and enlightenment Christianity itself strove for Jewish emancipation. It appeared unable to see that this might mean one day the death of Christianity — of Catholicism, of Protestantism, or orthodoxy and of unorthodoxy alike.

The despised Middle Ages were well aware that this possibility was always present because of the fanatical force of Jewish religious " nazism " directed against Christianity, the source of most of which is to be found in Talmud. In 1888 the Minerva Press published a striking account which was never refuted about the findings of an investigating commitee called together in 1240 by St. Louis the King of France. The King wanted to know why the Jews were so hated in France. He convened a Royal Court over which he presided. Talmud was presented an expounded to the court by a christianised Jew who spoke Hebrew well. To test the authenticity of the Talmudic text the court invited Jechiel the Rabbi of Paris, together with Rabbis Juda Samuel and Jacob, the latter being an eminent orator well known in both France and Spain. The fair-minded king did his utmost to ensure that the rabbis should have every chance to defend Talmud as well as to confirm the genuineness of the Talmudic text. Despite all this, the court was forced to conclude that the Talmudic laws are contrary and even repugnant to the social order, not only of all Christian but even of all non-Jewish communities. As a result of enquiries, the court discovered that Talmud not only repeatedly insults the Virgin Mary but casts doubts that Christ was born from a Virgin, and even states that He was the child of a soldier named Pandara and a woman of the streets. The Christians were appalled when these translations of Talmud were pronounced to be authentic

33

by the invited rabbis. As a result of the final conclusions of this court of enquiry, St. Louis ordered that Talmud be committed to the flames. (*The Hidden Empire*, 1945, p. 27.)

In later times the Christian world paid little attention to the Jews' holy book though, for them, it had become nearly as important as Torah. It was from Talmud that hatred emanated towards Christians and from it also spread a double-morality. It is worth while to note that even as late as the twentieth century there is no authentic translation of Talmud available. It is true that it has been translated by Graetz, a university professor of German-Jewish descent, but all the incriminating parts have been excluded. The Hungarian author Alfonz Luzsenszky has also translated certain parts of the Tulmud. One of the principal concerns of the present Bolshevik dictatorship was to throw Alfonz Luzsenszky into jail where he has most probably perished in a Jewish Communist torture-chamber.

But Talmud continued to foster that Jewish nationalism which lived ever more vividly in the dreams of Maimonides and of the Jewish prophets of the Middle Ages as well as in the heart of Jewry. Well before the outbreak of the French Revolution the Jewish people were active and on the move towards the realisation of the Mosaic covenant. The breach effected in Christian unity, together with so-called enlightenment and social progress, were all favourable to this purpose—the capture of world-power. And now the plan was roughly sketched out we will examine it more closely later under the denomination of " biological class-warfare " or the physical destruction and extermination of the non-Jewish nations, i.e. the event known as " revolution ".

After the First World War the cultured Western world was shocked by a series of articles in the London *Morning Post* entitled " Underground Conspirators ". H. A. Gwynn, the editor of this paper, in his book, *The Cause of World Unrest*, quoting authoritative contemporary reference books until then ignored by liberal historians, points out that the French Revolution was far from having been entirely caused by a revolutionary disposition of the lower classes. At this time both Jewish and masonic powers were already operating, and by buying up all grain stocks, they created an artificial famine and through this famine the revolution of July 14th. As early as 1776, the Spartacus movement, created by Adam Weishaupt, had been

34

established in Bavaria and this movement suddenly re-appeared again in many different guises inciting dangerous outbursts during the various revolutions after the First World War. Gwynn's treatise proves that all the revolutionary movements of the nineteenth century were infiltrated and to a great extent controlled by Jewry. Gwynn established Jewry's rôle in freemasonry with the help of data contained in the book of the converted Jew, Abbott Lemann (*L'Entrée des Izraelites dans la Société Française*) as well as with the evidence collected by the American author and freemason Albert Pike. He proved that Jewry had inculcated a hatred of Christianity into the secret societies, so that under the cover of liberalism they were actually able to remain undisturbed while they worked to undermine the Christian social order. Thus the Jewish "nazism" of the Old Testament, besides its money-power, acquired a new and terrible weapon for the destruction of Christian people. The name of this new weapon was Revolution.

The international socialist organisation began in 1864 with the foundation of the first Internationale, and both its leaders Marx and Lassale were Jews. Both of them were prophets of hatred, seeking revenge for the humiliation of their race. Disraeli in his book *Coningsby* predicts a German workers' movement under Jewish direction and leadership. With all this a new factor appeared in the history of European culture: organised hatred and envy as a systematically engineered force to create classes and societies as well as to destroy them. The intolerance prevalent in Europe was rooted in the spirit of the Old Testament, but even more reeking of the Old Testament and more Talmudic was this engineered hatred, the prophets of which preached exactly the same slogans and promises as the Old Testament when it promised the chosen people that Jehovah would pour out before them all the riches and wealth of the world and that they would only need to work two or three hours a day for their living. The "nazism" of the Old Testament found a formidable ally in the European working classes and later in the American proletariat which had every right to become embittered and hostile to the exploiting capitalistic system. But the proletariat was slow to realise that the originators, operators and beneficiaries of this capitalism were at the same time the representatives of both Jewish nationalism and of the Internationale.

There is no doubt that the seeds of the diabolical Jewish plans were well embodied in Marx's teaching. They aimed to destroy the intellectual *élite,* the aristocracy, the middle classes, the clergy and white-collar workers of all non-Jewish nations by the use of the false doctrine of equality and by arousing the envy of the proletarian masses. They plotted to deprive the nations of their leaders and to degrade humanity to a leaderless and cattle-like herd. This was no longer socialist planning. This was Jewry's own global strategy. Each leaderless man in the herd becomes the blind tool and slave of that Jewish tribal " nazism " bent on conquering the world.

Though Marx had, in fact, championed internationalism, Jewry was never international. It wanted to internationalise the proletariat only. To the proletariat was assigned the rôle to destroy their respective countries together with their religions, so that the international world state could be established possessing one *élite,* one ruling-class—the Jews exclusively!

Jews were to be found in every nation. They spoke the language of their adopted country yet remained Jews, proud and conscious representatives of an exclusive racial conception, of a supernational " nazism ". The shattered forces of Christ's rebellion took shelter from the noisy slogans of " Enlightenment " in the cool naves of the churches. The Christian Faith had been gradually stripped of its innate spiritual inspiration and influence and now became transformed into Jewish Christianity. It clung and adhered in a materialistic way to its worldly influence and to its worldly wealth, instead of following its calling and realising that the time was ripe to preach Christ's teaching with unflagging vigour. At the same time Jewry, having preserved its religious and racial unity, was now able to penetrate the enfeebled Christian communities with great effect. While the flame of Jewish nationalism was burning ever brighter the Christian " rebellion " was losing its faith and becoming timid, sceptical and impotent. The religious nationalism of the Old Testament was able to imbue the inhabitants of the Russian ghettos with faith and racial consciousness. But the Christianity of the New Testament became so faint-hearted that it began to be ashamed of the New Testament as well as of its own creed which it sometimes suspected might be " out of date " or " unscientific " when compared with the slogans of what was known as " enlightenment ".

When faced with the great social problems of the age Christianity proved to be inert and impotent. But at the same time Jewry was able to furnish its own race with faith. Not faith in God, since many Jews were apparently relinquishing their creed, but faith in a fanatical political nationalism. On the other hand, the Christian " revolution " failed to complete its mission on earth, i.e. to support the humble against their persecutors and so achieve social justice through love and not through hatred.

By the nineteenth century Christianity had already become more a formality than a living creed. It could not hope to match the modern conception of Christ's revolution against the idea of the Marxist revolution. The Papal Encyclicals *Rerum Novarum* and *Quadragesimo Anno* were only theoretical interpretations of the attitude adopted by Socialism and by the liberal state-system. Christ's Church militant did not fight as ardently as it should have done. It conveniently resigned to falling back on Christ's well-known maxim, " My kingdom is not of this world ", whereas Marxism stressed the conception of a physical salvation on this earth. This latter idea, of course, was entirely of Jewish origin. Jehovah himself, as well as Ezra and Nehemiah, those extollers of racial purity, had surely promised this very thing, i.e. redemption on this earth, the wealth of the world through the gates of Jerusalem, the eighteen hours' working week and welfare state. The Marxist promise was also redemption on earth, but behind the screen of promises stood Jewish nationalism, because the Marxist leaders knew that the achievement of what they called redemption meant also the establishment of the Jewish world-kingdom.

Christianity was unable to unite and so to follow up the social conception of Christ's revolution On the other hand, Jewry remained undivided in the racial and spiritual unity of its four-thousand-year-old " nazism ".

After the French Revolution, the secret societies, as well as certain governments themselves dominated by Jewish influence, gradually expelled Christianity from public life until its rôle became merely to encourage attendance at the churches. With Christianity so weak and divided what power could have successfully opposed these pressures? The Greek Orthodox Church with its empty formalism, or Roman Catholicism with its bishops sitting complacently in the

37

possession of several hundred-thousand acres of church lands (latifundia) and preaching poverty and justice to the masses, or Protestantism which became more and more saturated with the spirit of the Old Testament? In the circumstances, could any power exist capable of influencing the masses and of bringing them over to the side of the Christian revolution? Christianity began to retain a life apart, refraining from criticising public events, from influencing public opinion or from putting into practice socialist concepts. These rôles were taken over by the Press which was in the hands of Jewish nationalism, by members of the masonic lodges or by the Marxist agitator. Faced with this Marxist " heaven on earth ", Christianity was unable to vindicate the social meaning of Christ"s teaching. Furthermore, it abandoned its leadership and did not stand up for the masses. With the withdrawal of Christianity from public life, there arose in its place a fanatical determination to destroy all the institutions of the Gentiles, both human and divine. Its aim was to deprive them of their leaders and thus establish the final rule of Jewry's world government.

As early as the turn of the nineteenth century, that great thinker Houston Stewart Chamberlain warned the Christian world as follows:

" The problem of the Jews living amongst us is belonging to the most difficult and most fateful questions of the present time." (H. S. Chamberlain, 1, p. 163.)

At the beginning of the twentieth century all doubts concerning the success of the great plan could be put to rest. The leaders of world Jewry had only one thing more to decide, i.e. the actual means to be employed in securing world power. Was this to be achieved through gold or through the tommy-gun? Through plutocracy or through Communist terror directed by the Jewish bosses of the secret police? Should the new synagogue be the seat of the money-changers and scribes or of the terrorist Sadducees?

Or should it perhaps be open to both factions working side by side?

To this great dilemma a certain document, pronounced by the Jews to be a forgery, gives a clear answer.

THREE

WORLD DOMINATION IN THREE STAGES

JEWRY did its utmost to disprove the authenticity of the *Protocols of the Learned Elders of Zion*. To-day, any person who dares to make even the slightest reference to the *Protocols* is labelled an uncivilised barbarian by the Jews.

On June 26th, 1933, the Federation of Jewish Communities of Switzerland and the Berne Jewish Community brought an action against five members of the Swiss National Front, seeking a judgment that the *Protocols* were a forgery and a prohibition of their publication. The procedure of the Court was astounding, the provisions of the Swiss Civil Code being deliberately set aside. Sixteen witnesses called by the plaintiffs were heard, but only one of the forty witnesses called by the defendants was allowed a hearing. The judge allowed the plaintiffs to appoint two private stenographers to keep the register of proceedings during the hearing of their witnesses, instead of entrusting the task to a Court official.

In view of these and similar irregularities, it was not surprising that, after the case had lasted just on two years, the Court pronounced the *Protocols* to be a forgery and demoralising literature. The decision was given on May 14th, 1935, but it was announced in the Jewish Press before it was delivered by the Court!

On November 1st, 1937, the Swiss Court of Criminal Appeal quashed this judgment in its entirety. Jewish propagandists, however, still declare that the *Protocols* have been " proved " to be a forgery.

It is clear, however, that the original text of the *Protocols of Zion* was in the hands of the Jews of Odessa as early as 1890. The *Protocols* were published in 1905 by the Russian Nilus. According to certain versions, their author was the Oriental Asher Ginsberg under the pen-name of Achad Haam, meaning " from the same people ", and his purpose was to try to arouse the Jewish national consciousness. A copy of this book published by Nilus was acquired by the British Museum in 1906, where it can be found catalogued to-day.

While world-wide controversy regarding the authenticity of the *Protocols* continued, their genuineness was established by a higher authority than any court; world history itself. The Jewish programme outlined in 1906 has since been literally and realistically carried out. We may, therefore, consider the *Protocols* from various angles; either as the world plan drawn up by the Elders of Zion of the 33rd degree of freemasonry, as the secret records of the Zionist Congress of Basle, or simply as a pamphlet written by an extreme Jewish nationalist—all this is irrelevant. The only relevant and undisputable fact is that the programme has nearly been accomplished in its entirety. Even more has been accomplished than was foreseen by the Elders of Zion. The world-conquerors have subdued the world. Instead of pursuing in detail the purposeless controversies disputing the authenticity of the *Protocols*, we want to prove one thing only, i.e. that the Elders of Zion have materialised their programme. There now remains but a single step for Jewry to take before announcing openly that world-power is in their grasp. For the time being Jewry appears to be a bit obscured behind the political, economic and spiritual powers ruling mankind, but it is ready to spring into action at any moment. It is preparing to complete that single step, after which the sixth point will be added to the five-pointed star as well as to the white American pentacle, which will thus become the open symbol of the accomplished world-kingdom, i.e. the six-pointed David-star.

There remains another question in connection with the *Protocols* and that is: Did there ever exist any open or secret Jewish organisation to lay down plans for a world-programme? Did a secret Jewish " Government " exist to direct world-Jewry according to the teaching of Torah and of Talmud or, perhaps, of the *Protocols*?

There is no doubt that inside the Jewish community, as early as before the birth of Christ, an organisation known as the Kahal or Cahilla was existent and acting as the political executive body of the theocratic Jewish state. We can therefore presume that the Jewish nation in its exile preserved something from this organisation.

We pointed out earlier that even before the dispersion both the Alexandrian and Roman diaspora had acquired real governmental and political powers. After the dispersal, each Jewish community possessed its own miniature Cahilla, the purpose of which was to arbitrate in legal disputes between Jews, especially in cases where it was undesirable to submit the matter to the Christian courts and thus expose it to publicity. In countries densely overrun by Jews the existence of these Cahillas was well known by everybody. But doubtless there must have been a higher Jewish administrative body as well, what we might perhaps call nowadays an "Emigrational Committee" which kept the Jews together and co-ordinated their political ambitions. There are documentary proofs that this supreme Jewish Cahal kept constantly appearing under different names throughout history. Once it was to be found in Constantinople under the name of the Sanhedrin, and the "Great Satrap" was the head of Jewry. Later on it was seen in various movements, in French freemasonry as well as among the supreme commands of the great powers in the First World War. Traces can be found everywhere of the activities of this secret world-government. In 1920, returning from the unsuccessful peace-conference of Versailles, President Wilson of the United States announced openly:

"There was a secret force at work in Europe which we were unable to trace."

Disraeli, in 1844, in his book *Coningsby,* frankly states that:

"The world is governed by very different personages from what is imagined by those who are not behind the scenes."

In the *Wiener Freie Presse* on December 24th, 1921 the Jewish Walter Rathenau wrote precisely the same thing when he said:

"Three hundred men, each of whom knows all the others, govern the fate of the European continent, and they elect their successors from their entourage."

The functions of the Cahilla (Kahal) are well known in New York, because the Jews often give Cahilla parties. Very interesting exposures about all this are contained in the book, *The Hidden Empire* (1946) in which, on page 35, we find:

"The Jews of the world divide the earth into two hemispheres, the Eastern and the Western. As the United States lies in the Western Hemisphere, we will confine ourselves to that alone.

"The Cahal is understood to be constructed in the Symbol of Seven. The Sponsor for the Eastern Hemisphere is not for consequenc herein; however, both Sponsors for both hemispheres are alleged to be accountable only to AKA'DHAM the Unknown and Uncrowned King of Jewry throughout the Earth whose identity is kept guarded secret."

It is undisputable, therefore, that some kind of central Jewish organisation or government existed all the time which methodically carried out the world-programme of the Elders of Zion. But whether such a government existed or not, the fact must be emphasised that the programme itself was accomplished and this in itself presents sufficient proof of its organisation. The fact must be stressed that world Jewry has already completed the second stage planned by the Elders of Zion and everything is fully prepared to complete the rest soon, and thus to reach the third and final stage.

Fifty years ago, or during the legal proceedings at Berne, the authenticity of the *Protocols* might have been disputed. But the execution of the programme of the *Protocols* with its ardent Old Testament nationalism was forever in evidence. The existence of the *Protocols* was perhaps disputable but not that of its nationalism.

In the *Protocols,* which are most probably extracts only from the real programme, appear the methods by which Jewry is to accomplish world domination. From the somewhat mysterious text the cursory reader will gather that the *Protocols* sometimes talk about dictatorship, sometimes about liberalism and that they plan to achieve world-power sometimes through capitalism and by the power of the Press and sometimes by the practice of what are unmistakably Bolshevik methods. When the *Protocols of Zion* were in the hands of the Jews of Odessa, the teaching of Lenin was unknown. Nevertheless, in the *Protocols* the complete ideology of Lenin, together with the fighting tactics employed by the ruling minority are found. The reader may be surprised to learn that, after all, Capitalism is the political method preferred by the Jews in order to obtain final domination over the world.

After a critical study of the *Protocols* we realise with surprise that the difference between Bolshevism and Capitalism is illusory. The Elders of Zion were clearly aware that Bolshevism is nothing else but the end-product of liberal-capitalism, i.e. both are two different forms of the same totalitarian rule, and the ideology of both essentially consists of the elements contained in materialism, minority-rule, the lavish use of the cheque-book and the terrorism of the tommy-gun.

A re-appraisal of historical events will provide us with the solution to the obscure parts of the *Protocols*. The Elders of Zion planned three stages in the establishment of the throne of King Solomon.

The first stage was to secure for Jewry control over money and capitalism, to establish Jewry's exclusive control over the press and to increase its influence, while at the same time destroying and compromising the *élite* of non-Jewish society. Simultaneously to use the ideal of liberalism as a battering ram for the destruction of the Gentile nations, to bring about the perversion of Roman law as well as of all other legal systems, to arouse envy and discontent among the working classes and to perpetuate hatred between societies and states.

The first stage also included the spreading of dissension between Christian states, the unleashing of wars and the starting of revolutions, but all these activities were still to be pursued within the framework of liberalism.

" We must be in a position to respond to every act of opposition by war with the neighbours of that country which dares to oppose us : but if these neighbours should also venture to stand collectively together against us, then we must offer resistance by a universal war."

For the first stage fighters, the *Protocols* prescribe intrusion into the Christian family, a ceaseless struggle against religion, the monopolisation of the press, the provoking of the workers to revolution and the slow destruction of Christian societies. In the first place all kingdoms must be suppressed, after which the aristocracy must be destroyed, the landed classes pauperised and the spirit of revolution awakened in the masses.

" On the ruins of the natural and genealogical aristocracy of the Goyim we have set up the aristocracy of our educated class headed by the aristocracy of money. The qualifications for this aristocracy we have established in wealth, which is dependent upon us, and in knowledge, for which our learned elders provide the motive force." (*Protocol* I.)

The last sentence of the *Protocol* makes us think of the rôle now being played by Jews in the Atomic Energy Commission.

The authors of the *Protocols* clearly see that in the age of liberal-capitalism free competition is the surest way towards the second stage.

"We will appear as alleged saviours of the worker from oppression," the *Protocols* continue—"as when we invite him to enter the ranks of our fighting forces—Socialists, Anarchists, Communists—to whom we always give support in accordance with an alleged brotherly rule of our social masonry." (*Protocol* III.)

We must not forget that these *Protocols* first came to light as long ago as 1906, and has not this programme been fully carried out since?

During the first stage both the tactics as well as the weapons employed are different. "Our countersign is — Force and Make-believe," preach these "Pharisees" in the *Protocols,* adding at the same time: "Only force conquers in political affairs, especially if it be concealed in the talents essential to statesmen." (*Protocol* I.)

The authors of the Protocols were inflicted with no ideological inhibitions. They foresaw clearly all that has since been accomplished, namely, that the exploitation of finance-capitalism would prepare the way for Bolshevism.

". . . the people, blindly believing things in print, cherishes—thanks to promptings intended to mislead and to its ignorance—a blind hatred towards all conditions which it considers above itself, for it has no understanding of the meaning of class and condition.

"This hatred will be further magnified by the effects of an economic crisis, which will stop dealings on the exchanges and bring industry to a standstill. We shall create by all the secret subterranean methods open to us and with the aid of gold, which is all in our hands, a universal economic crisis whereby we shall throw upon the streets whole mobs of workers simultaneously in all the countries of Europe. These mobs will rush delightedly to shed the blood of those whom, in the simplicity of their ignorance, they have envied from their cradles, and whose property they will then be able to loot. Ours they will not touch because the moment of attack will be known to us and we shall take measures to protect our own." (*Protocol* III.)

It is enough to recall the last thirty or forty years of European and world history to conclude that this is indeed the beginning of the second stage.

44

For this is Bolshevism itself. The single rebel, the proletarian masses filled with hatred and envy, led by the same commissars and agitators who at present control the banking systems, the parliaments and press of the capitalist states. They are all, of course, offspring of the same tribal alliance. They are all representatives of the same double-faced nationalism.

The real hidden face of Talmud shows up here, the distorted features of the bloodthirsty Sadducee, scheming to destroy all other nations, even by massacre if necessary, he who led the great Christian-pogroms of 1945 with as much zeal as the braves of Bar-cochba in A.D. 131 during the great Jewish revolt in the Mediterranean. *Protocol* III goes on:

" The aristocracy which enjoyed by law the labour of the workers, was interested in seeing that the workers were well fed, healthy and strong. We are interested in just the opposite—in the diminution, the killing out of the Goyim. Our power is in the chronic shortness of food and physical weakness of the worker because by all that this implies he is made the slave of our will and he will not find in his own authorities either strength or energy to set against our will."

What else is this if not a nightmarish vision of Bolshevism? Three decades before its outbreak! What else but the programme of the former Illuminati with its Jewish characteristics: " Hunger and persuasion!" This is nothing less than a vivid description of the Russia of Stalin-Kaganovich itself in which — according to the *Protocols*—is to be found the secret police and an institution called the People's Court enforcing absolute suppression and complete exploitation of the workers.

Already we are in the second stage! In Russia, the kolkhoz-slave has to kneel down before the Commissar. In the Soviet the Jewish foreman or factory-director has authority to withdraw ration cards from those workers who are unable to fulfil the prescribed norm, i.e. the ordered amount of forced labour. The six million persons starved to death in the Ukrainian famine, the sacrificed Hungarian, German, Rumanian and Italian prisoners of war who died of hunger, caused by the withdrawal of their ration cards, prove that this part of the programme is fulfilled wherever " Israel is King ".

But the writers of the *Protocols* saw clearly that this was not enough.

That Bolshevism is only the means of breaking, degenerating and bestialising the masses and so reducing them to a human herd. That Capitalism and Bolshevism together with the class-struggle are implements only. All these are not yet sufficient to attain absolute security and an impregnable position for Jewry.

" Remember the French Revolution, to which it was we who gave the name of ' Great '; the secrets of its preparation are well known to us for it was wholly the work of our hands. Ever since that time we have been leading the peoples from one disenchantment to another, so that in the end they should turn also from us in favour of that King-Despot of the blood of Zion, whom we are preparing for the world." (*Protocol* III.)

This is the third stage. The last and the most important! The authors of the *Protocols* tell us that when this is reached, at the last minute Jewry will annul with a single stroke of the pen every principle it had professed to the Goyims. Liberalism and Socialism will be succeeded by a complete and absolute despotism. By an outwardly patriarchal Jewish world-kingdom but one which is essentially cruel and terroristic, ruled exclusively by Jews.

Protocol III explains that it is absolutely necessary for the people to see the incarnation of power and authority in the person of their ruler. He is the God-chosen monarch whose mission is to crush those destructive forces whose origin is neither in the intellect nor in the human spirit but in the animal-like instincts of mankind. To-day these forces are uppermost and they will assume various forms of violence and robbery perpetrated in the name of law and order. They wil disrupt the present social system in order to establish the throne of the king of Israel. But as soon as his power is achieved the rôle of these forces will be over. "Then it will be necessary to sweep them away from its path, on which must be left no knot, no splinter."

Later we will see how prophecies which in 1890 or 1906 appeared to be far from fulfilment became reality; they were fulfilled with astonishing accuracy.

In the West at the turn of the century " storm-troops " of the world conquerors, consisting of the bourgeois, capitalist and middle-class Jewish social strata stood by ready for action, led by the " assimilated " intellectual Jewish progressive *élite*, i.e. by writers and journalists, etc. For the Western Jew was also a pupil of Talmud. Meanwhile, in the East, more than five million members of Jewry scattered over the area between the Volga and Danube, the masses of both Russian and East Polish Jewry, were still dreaming dreams of the Jewish world-kingdom, bending over their Talmuds and Torahs in the synagogues of Belz, Brest-Litovsk and Maramarossziget.

Lajos Fehér, the Budapest-born Jewish scholar, spoke no more than the truth when he pointed out in his great work entitled *Jewry* that Talmud had, in fact, reduced Jewry to a ritual slavery. The strict and detailed ritual rules prescribe some kind of religious duty at all hours of the day. Rubens in his work, *Der alte und der neue Glaube* (The old and new faith) comes to the conclusion that a Jew has to spend half of each day carrying out ritual. There are some 3,000 religious ceremonies prescribed by Talmud to commemorate the death of Moses alone. All these made it impossible for an orthodox Jew to undertake any productive occupation. In such circumstances he was unable to do the fourteen hours' daily work of a Polish, Russian or Hungarian peasant. But not being connected with the peasantry had its advantages. It was easy for Jewry in a comparatively short time to transform itself into a middle-class and to take its place among the intellectual social stratum. As it was not tied to the land, it was free to engage wholly in intellectual activities such as in the reading of the holy books. If we examine the significance of this during the last 2,000 years we understand better why this race has produced so many intellectuals, writers, poets, journalists, politicians and atom-scientists.

Thus Jewry increased fast in stature. It needed only to learn the language of a country to be able to become part of the middle-class, bourgeoisie or moneyed-aristocracy of that country. It was able to occupy more key-positions than any other nation, which naturally included working classes and peasantry as well. From this it was only a step to develop a more grandiose Messianic conception.

Why should not this race of fifteen million people form the ruling classes of every nation on earth by assuming an external English veneer, a Russian manner, an American boisterousness, or French politeness, all the time remaining imbued with the same uniform consciousness of Jewish nationalism?

Purim is the only day of national rejoicing when Jewry may get drunk to commemorate the killing of the first "anti-Semite", Haman, together with his ten sons and of the slaying of 75,000 Gentiles in the city of Shushan and the provinces. Jan and Jherome Tharaud in their pro-Jewish book *In the Shadow of the Crucifix* are at pains to point out that the Jewish nation never knew the meaning of the word "love". Although the saying "Love thy neighbour as thyself" was a Mosaic commandment, nevertheless, this was restricted to the members of the Jewish tribes, and even further to "the next of kin". Meanwhile, Eastern Jewry evolved into a community forming a kind of reservoir of hatred and animosity which was directed towards all those around them.

The Western Jews, the staunch Marxists, expected at first that the proletarian revolution, as prophesied by Marx, would materialise somewhere in the West

And in the meanwhile, in the West, indeed, more exactly, in Brussels, half a century ago, almost in romantic circumstances, the Russian Bolshevik party was founded Among the founders we see a former member of the "Russian" lesser nobility, an expelled seminarist from Georgia, the daughter of a Russian captain of industry and a progressive journalist. With the exception of one or two, they were all Jews.

One-and-a-half decades later, Holy Russia was ground to the dust by Jewish nationalism, which here started directly from the second stage to carry out the plans of the Elders of Zion for the establishment of the Jewish world-kingdom.

FOUR

MILLIONAIRE BANKERS BACK BOLSHEVIKS

BEFORE the First World War a certain picture postcard was freely sold in the Jewish shops of Russia, Lithuania and Poland. On this postcard a rabbi was shown holding Torah in one hand and in the other Nicholas II, the Czar of Russia, cartooned as a white pullet with the Romanoff crown on its head.

Under the picture the following text appeared in Hebrew: " Sä chaliphati sä temurati, sä kaporati."

This means: " This sacrificial animal shall be my absolution, it will be my substitute and expiatory offering."

The Hebrew text is actually part of the prayer called " Kaporah ". The rituals relating to this sacrifice are contained in *Leviticus* (chap. xvi. 15).:

"Then shall he kill the goat of the sin offering, that is for the people, and bring his blood within the veil, and do with that blood as he did with the blood of the bullock, and sprinkle it upon the mercy seat, and before the mercy seat."

Some rabbis opposed this doctrine. But wherever Cabbalists were living among Eastern Jewry, on the day of atonement a white cockerel and a white pullet were usually sacrificed in lieu of the goat.

This postcard was thus an open invitation by Jewry to murder the Czar. Hatred against Czarism was already latent in consequence of the pogroms, but it was kept at boiling point by the Mosaic commandment: " . . . thou mayest not set a stranger over thee (as king) which is not thy brother."

When Bolshevism broke out the Czar and his family were murdered in Ekaterinburg. The Czar's murderers were Jacob Swerdlow, who became later the President of the Soviet Union, Jacob Jurovszkij, Chajim Golocsikin and Peter Jernakow, all Jews.

But all those who schemed for fifty years to bring about the disintegration and subjugation of Russia were Jews also. Fifty per cent of the members of the first Social Democratic Party of Russia, from which the Bolshevik Party was later formed, were Jews. The Polish Social Democratic Party was at first organised as the Jewish Democratic Party, and the situation was similar in Lithuania. Kerenski himself, who became the Prime Minister of the First Republic, was a Jew by birth.

The greatest Russian novelist, Dostioevsky, whose treatise about the Jews is, even to-day, kept carefully hidden away by the co-called Western " free " publishing houses, saw as early as 1887 that the scourge of Judah was poised over the head of the Russian people and that the red shadow of Bolshevism would descend over Holy Russia.

" Their kingdom and their tyranny is coming," he wrote. " The unlimited despotism of their ideology is now only beginning. Under this tyranny human kindness and neighbourliness as well as the longing for justice will fade away; all Christian and patriotic ideals will perish for ever!"

Bolshevism won. And in the moment of its victory, the Jewish intellectuals, the young revolutionaries as well as those poverty-stricken Jews at the bottom of the capitalistic ladder, turned their faces towards Russia. Whether Bolsheviks or not, they were, nevertheless, as Jews becoming aware that those succeeding the Czarist régime were almost all Jews too.

A member of Hungarian middle-class Jewry, László Lakatos-Kellner, had greeted Lenin in a poem by writing:

THE NEW CHRIST HAS ARRIVED,

LENIN !   LENIN !

The official gazette of Hungarian Jewry *The Egyenlöség* (Equality) read mostly by well-to-do citizens, published the following in an article praising Trotsky-Bronstein:

" Jewish intellect and knowledge, Jewish courage and love of peace saved Russia and perhaps the whole world. Never has world historical mission of Jewry shone so brightly as in Russia. Trotsky's words prove that the Biblical and prophetic Jewish spirit of Isaiah and Micah, the great peace-makers, with that of the Talmudic Elders, is inspiring the leaders of Russia to-day."

The American banker, Jacob Schiff, the Kuhn Loeb banking house and American financiers supported the Bolsheviks from the very beginning with huge loans and innumerable large donations. These bankers knew the leaders of Russia just as well as they knew the prophecy of Amschel Mayer, the founder of the House of Rothschild. Over the Rothschild house in Frankfurt a red flag was displayed on a shield. Jean Drault, the French writer, remembered old Amschel Mayer saying to customers in his shop:

" One day this flag will rule the world!"

Karl Marx, grandson of the rabbi of Trier, must have known this flag very well too. He, as well as anybody, was well aware that Jewish capitalism and Jewish Marxism are but two different forms of the same Judaism, of that same world-conquering nationalism. Rothschild's red flag is just as cheerful and bracing a sight for Morgenthau as it is for Kaganovich.

While it is interesting to learn that Bolshevism adopted its red flag from a Jewish banker, it is also noteworthy that the Bolshevik revolutionary greeting, i.e. the raised clenched fist, is a symbol of Jewish origin too. The paper entitled *The Key to the Mystery*, on page 21 of the number dated August 7th, 1939, describes how, on the feast of Purim, held in commemoration of the slaying of 75,000 Gentiles, the Jews still greet each other with a raised clenched fist.

But the Christian world still asks how could collusion be possible between two " deadly " enemies like Capitalism and Bolshevism?

This question was definitively answered in 1918 by the report of the United Secret Service (2nd Army Bureau) naming the persons who financed the Bolshevik revolution in 1916. Under Jewish pressure this report was destroyed by the State Department, but it was too late then. The Rev. Denis Fahey, Professor of Theology, in his book *The Mystical Body of Christ in the Modern World*, and Mgr. Jouin, in his work *Le Péril Judéo Maconnique*, both quote the complete report. We here briefly refer to it but the full text is available. According to the American counter-intelligence and news service, the following big American bankers gave money to Lenin and his comrades for the Bolshevik revolution: Jacob Schiff, Guggenheim, Max Breitung, the banking house of Kuhn, Loeb and Co., the directors of which were at that time Jacob Schiff, Felix Warburg, Otto Kahn, Mortimer Schiff, and S. H. Hanauer. As the report remarks: " All Jews."

The report quotes articles in the *Daily Forward*, the Bolshevik

Jewish paper of New York, describing in detail how large sums of money in dollars were transferred to the Bolsheviks from the assets of the Westphalian-Rhineland Syndicate, a large Jewish business concern. How the Parisian Jewish banking house of Lazare Brothers, the Gunsbourg Bank of St. Petersburg with affiliations in Tokio and Paris, the London banking house of Speyer & Co., and the Nya Banken of Stockholm all sent money to the Bolsheviks.

The statement of the American military counter-espionage and intelligence service established the fact that Jacob Schiff gave twelve million dollars towards the financing of the Bolshevik revolution. As for the Parisian banking house of Lazare, they not only played a considerable rôle in the unleashing of the Second World War, but their former director Mr. Altschul is to-day on the Board of Executives of Free Europe Inc., and is at present occupied with the reorganisation of Europe.

This peculiar ganging up, this conspiracy of Bolsheviks and bankers can only be plausibly explained by Jewish nationalism. Though the prostration of Russia, the land of pogroms, as well as the extermination of the Czar's family, were all criminal Bolshevik perpetrations, nevertheless in the eyes of Jewish nationalism these appeared to be the acts of Jews, the triumph of Jewry, the glorious liberation struggle of religious irredentism. Absolute political power in Russia had fallen openly into the hands of Jewry.

At first, perhaps, Lenin's teachings were not fully understood by the Jewish masses. Nevertheless they saw that nearly all the leaders and rulers of the new Russian states system were descendants of Abraham. Lenin himself was Ulyanov formally only. His father was a member of the Russian lesser nobility. But his mother was the daughter of a German-Jew doctor called Berg. Lenin inherited his mania for destruction and his desperate lust for power from his mother; both characteristics being equally Judaistic. Victor Marsden, the English journalist who was engaged as a correspondent during the First World War in Russia, describes Lenin as follows:

" Lenin, a Calmyc Jew, married to a Jewess, whose children spoke Yiddish."

Herbert Fitsch, a Scotland Yard detective, who, in the guise of a valet penetrated the entourage of Lenin and reported him to be a " typical Jew "!

The *Morning Post* at the same time published a list of the names, pseudonyms and racial origin of the founders of the Secret Government, together with its fifty most important key-functionaries. They were about ninety-eight per cent Jewish.

The London *Jewish Chronicle* of April 4th, 1919, boldly states: "The conceptions of Bolshevism are in harmony in most points with the ideas of Judaism."

Victor Marsden, the *Morning Post* reporter in Russia, states that among the 545 leading Bolshevik officials there were 477 Jews at the birth of Bolshevism.

But the point of view of Jewish nationalism was appreciably different. The Jews paid scant attention to the exterminated bishops, to the slain priests and to the starved or massacred Russian masses in their hundreds of thousands. They appreciated the *Jewish success* only.

The gruesome events in Russia surpass all imagination. Statistics compiled from the early days of Bolshevism and quoted also in the American Congressional Records confirm that during the first years

28 Bishops and Archbishops	150,000 Police Officers
6,776 Priests	48,000 Gendarmes
6,765 Teachers	355,000 Intellectuals
8,500 Doctors	198,000 Workers
54,000 Army Officers	915,000 Peasants
260,000 Soldiers	

were murdered together with the Emperor and his family.

After considering these gruesome statistics one might expect that Jewry, which has been advertised in the Jewish-dominated press all over the world as a humanitarian people, would expel these Bolshevik Jews from its ranks with loathing and contempt. But world Jewry and its great organisations at the best remain silent. And in the meanwhile there is probably not a single country in the whole world where the Communist Party is not under the exclusive direction of Jews.

In Argentina as early as 1918, Solomon Haselman and his wife Julia Fitz began to organise Communism. The Argentine revolution broke out in January, 1919, and its victims in Buenos Aires alone included 800 dead and 4,000 injured. The leader of the revolt was Pedro Wald, alias Naleskovskij, and its Minister of War was Macaro

Ziazin, both Eastern Jews. After the suppression of the revolt, other movements were organised by Jews. There were many Jews and Communists amongst the teachers and university professors. Siskin Aisenberg initiated Bolshevik education of the Argentine youth. Among Yiddish newspapers, Roiter Stern, Roiter Hilfe, Der Poer and Chivolt were all engaged in spreading dangerous Bolshevik propaganda.

The Chilean Bolshevik uprising of 1931 and the Uruguayan Bolshevik rebellion of 1932 were engineered and led by the descendants of the seed of Abraham almost exclusively.

When the short-lived Brazilian revolution was suppressed in 1935, it came to light that the actual leaders were all Jews with the exception of a nominal leader called Louis Carlos Perestes. The Braccor, an Eastern Jewish association, organised the dock workers, and the leader of this revolt known as Ewert was, in fact, called Harry Bergner. This uprising was directed from the Soviet Embassy of Montevideo by a Jewish leather merchant called Minikin. Amongst the leaders of this Brazilian uprising there were many members of the Organizacao Revolutionaria Israelita Brazor, and amongst others we mention the following names: Baruch Zell, Zatis Janovisai, Rubens Goldberg, Moysés Kava, Waldemar Roterburg, Abrahâo Rosemberg, Nicolâo Martinoff, Yayme Gandelsman, Moisi Lipes, Carlos Garfunkel, Waldemar Gutinik, Henrique Jvilaski, José Weiss, Armando Gusiman, Joseph Friedman, and so on.

Of the South American revolutions the Mexican one is particularly interesting for here again a Jewish millionaire leads the Bolsheviks. The Dictator of the Mexican Bolshevik revolution, Plutarco Elias Calles, is the son of a Syrian Jew and an Indian woman. Calles is a freemason of the 33rd degree and his personal fortune amounts to eighty million pesos. His friend, Aron Saez, who played an important rôle as his lieutenant, and who had a fortune of forty million pesos, is a Jew as well. Their persecution of the Church resulted in 20,000 Catholic martyrs. Amongst these were 300 Roman Catholic priests and 200 devoted Catholic youth.

But the American Bolshevik movement was the most typical and characteristic of all. In the U.S.A. the Communist Party was set up on September 1st, 1919, William Z. Foster being its first general secretary. The *Daily Worker,* the Communist New York daily, began its first publication about the same time. The bulk of the followers of the American Communist Party consisted almost entirely of those Jews who had emigrated to the United States from Russia, Poland and those countries lying to-day behind the Iron Curtain. The U.S.A. gave them everything a great and free democracy can give—security from pogroms, prosperity, often wealth and new homes as well as decent wages. Nevertheless, at the earliest opportunity they began to plot for the overthrow of American freedom and for the total subjugation of Washington's household.

The Communist movement originated from the union formed by the employees of the clothing industry. Even to-day this union is almost entirely in Jewish hands and their first question to a prospective new member is: "Do you speak Yiddish?" It is interesting to note that, as in Russia and Poland where the Marxist parties were organised by Jews, in America too the Jewish organisations became the champions of Communist principles. The Jewish Workers Club, the Jewish Workers Union, the ICOR (a company for settlers), the ARTEV (Arbeiter Theater Verband) and the John Reed Club for Jewish writers, were all Jewish and Communistic organisations. The number of Jewish radical and Communist papers as well as Jewish periodicals edited in the U.S.A. reached 600 by 1936, and as early as 1933 the total membership of the Communist Party was estimated by Earl Browder to be about 1,200,000. In the preparatory work of organising American Bolshevism, the National Textile Workers Union and the Workers International Relief played important rôles. The leaders of both these great associations were Jews, Charles Steinmetz, Upton Sinclair, Helen Keller, Albert Einstein, Bishop William M. Brown. The International Labour Defence was a very powerful organisation led by millionaires or by very wealthy lawyers, despite the fact that it was typically Communist.

All these groups, unions and associations hoped to capture America for Bolshevism during the great economic crisis. When, in 1930, the Communists of New York tried to besiege the City Hall, the Communist papers reported with open enthusiasm:

"The Jewish women were fighting like tigresses." (*Weltbolshevism*, page 265.)

All the above-mentioned associations belonged to the non-secret or exoteric Bolshevistic formations of America. None of these open types of Bolshevistic associations presented any real peril. Surely the American worker—be he either a descendant of an early settler from the *Mayflower* or of an eastern refugee—would never turn into a Communist. Consequently, soon after their party was established the American Bolsheviks tried to persuade American youth to join them and serve as the hard core of the world conquerors' storm-troops. They knew only too well that it would be extremely difficult to repeat in America the tricks employed in Russia. They were well aware that the American worker is neither Bolshevist nor Marxist. Therefore their aim was concentrated on American youth; they strove to gain the support of a deluded second generation. Therefore, well before Roosevelt came to power, they organised the Young Communist League, the National Student League (formed from the universities) and the Young Pioneers for children between eight and nine years of age. The undermining of America, of course, was not only brought about by the Communists.

There also existed more peaceful cover-associations and workers' unions which, under the pretext of Marxism or socialism, really served the supranational aims of Jewish tribal nationalism. But the key positions even in those organisations which were not directly Jewish were captured by Jews. The C.I.O., the largest labour organisation was under the leadership of Sidney Hillman, while the American Federation of Labour was founded by Samuel Gompers, an immigrant Jew from England.

After all these facts the reader will not be surprised that when Eugen Dennis was arrested on May 16th, 1950, the famous Jewish writer Albert Kahan commented as follows in *Jewish Life,* the monthly supplement of the New York Zionist paper *Freiheit*:

" When, on May 15th, Eugen Dennis, the leader of the Communist Party, was sent to prison, a shadow fell on the life of every American Jewish man and woman."

Let us now have a look at Europe (omitting Russia), the old continent where chorales and psalms were composed and written, and where during the Christian Middle Ages, Jewry was confined to the ghetto.

In England, the Communist Party, though of negligible strength, is directed by Jews, as are also those organisations called anti-Fascist Leagues or Anti-War Movements, where we can find such names as:

Lord Marley, Ivor Montagu, Hannen Swaffer, Gerald Barry, Bernhard Baron, Nathan Birch, Morris Isaacs and Harold Laski. The noble Lords, Baronets and Knights of Jewish descent have all suddenly taken sides with Bolshevism, which in Russia, allegedly, intends to destroy capitalism.

In France the control of Marxism is and was almost entirely in Jewish hands. Zay, Leon Blum, Denains, Zyrowszky, Mandel-Bloch and the rest, are leading the same revolutionary nationalism which ruined Holy Russia.

In England the Communist Party was represented in Parliament at one time by a Jew called Piratin.

Those principally concerned in organising the French Communist Party were Henri Barbusse, André Gide, Romain Roland and André Malraux. In France, the Jews enjoy the benefits of the French petty Bourgeoisie, were dazzled by the powerful position of Jewry in Soviet Russia and hurried to join French Communist organisations. These carried on their activities under various cover names such as the " International League against Anti-Semitism " or the " Cultural Association of Jewish Proletarians ", etc. The Jewish-Communist organisation known as *Gezerd* can also be mentioned in this context.

The Writers' International Congress held at Paris in 1935 was entirely Communistic. Here it became clear from the first that the authors who were the greatest exponents of the Jewish " humanitarian " spirit also fervently supported the masters of Russian Bolshevism. The signboard of this Congress displayed the word **" International "**, but it was in reality a great tribal gathering of nationalists dazzled by successes in Russia, the participants of which came from various lands and spoke different languages but belonged to the same race.

In Belgium, a Jew called Charles Balthasar is the organiser of the Bolshevik Party, the mainstay of which is the association called the *Gezerd*.

In Sweden similar forces are working for Bolshevism. The Swedish Communist Party was supported by one of the greatest capitalists— Ivar Krueger, the match-king, reports the paper *Der Weltbolshevism,* from information received from Swedish sources. The various publishing houses and lending libraries in the hands of Jews have also greatly helped to promote Bolshevism.

Neither is the situation much different in Norway where Major Quisling, in the light of experience gained in Soviet Russia, started to organise an anti-Bolshevik national party, for he realised that the same people who destroyed Russia were preparing to annihilate Norway.

In Denmark, at this time, Jewish students as well as the Jewish professors Georg Brandes and Davidsohn of the University of Copenhagen directed Communist activities. Their main organisation is the Jewish cultur-association, the I.K.O.R. Axel Larsen, the Jewish administrative leader, confidently announced at a mass-meeting that: "The Danish Communist Party will not rest until it has succeeded in hanging all priests and gendarmes."

In 1932 the Bolsheviks in Switzerland called themselves left-wing Socialists. Leon Nicole was their leader and his assistant, a Russian Jew called Dicker, instigated the uprising of November 9th, 1932, which resulted in thirteen dead and 100 injured.

In Austria, Austro-Marxism is at work and it would be difficult to distinguish between its democratic and communistic shades of thought, although both are inspired by Jews. Friedrich Adler was, from the outset, the chief organiser. He was the first Secretary of the Second Internationale and also the murderer of Stürgh, the Austrian ex-Premier.

In Rumania, Anna Pauker-Rabinovich and other Jews were the champions of Bolshevism. It was they who forced the workers into a bloody railway strike. Their influence was quite terrifying in a corrupt and liberal government like that of Rumania. The paper *Weltbolshevism* concludes an article as follows:

"It is noteworthy how strong the participation of Jewry is in the Communist movement. The most dangerous activities are observed in those areas where the great masses of Jews live." (Page 435.)

Czechoslovakia, the aircraft-carrier of the Soviet Union, was completely undermined by Communist organisations from the very beginning of her national independence. One of the Communist leaders was Slansky-Salzman. The Communist literature and control of all the organising activities are in the hands of Jews.

In Bulgaria, the Communist movements were headed by Jews also. When two hundred officers and civilians fell victims to the plot against

Sveta Nedelja, it came to light that the plot, organised by Dimitrov, was carried out by the Jews Jack and Prima Friedman.

In Greece, the papers *Avanti* and *El Tsoweno* are the official organs of the Communist Party, the latter being the organ of the Communist-Jewish association in Salonica as well.

And if one looks at the Far East, it is clear that here, too, the same hands are setting ablaze the fires of Bolshevism. The leaders of the Chinese Communist Party, Borodin and Crusenberg, were also of the seed of Abraham.

We have deliberately left Spain to the end, as Jewish organisations can be distinctly recognised in the Spanish Civil War. When the fight broke out, the leaders: Zamorra, Azara, Rosenberg and the notorious La Passionaria, whose real name was Dolores Ibauri, were all Jews too. And those who flooded into Spain from all sides to render more unbearable the bloody plight of the Spanish people, were all emissaries of the same racial nationalism already victorious over Russia. Ilja Ehrenburg, Bela Kun, Gerö Ernö, Zalka Máté, the leaders and members of the notorious Rákosi-Roth brigade, all belonged, almost without exception, to the emissaries of this deranged racial " nazism ".

When the hour strikes the mask falls! Christian churches and centuries-old art treasures go up in flames, drunken terrorists shoot at Christ's cross and the same " experts " again expertly crucify priests as they had done in Russia before. They scuttle prison-ships with anti-revolutionaries locked up in the hold, they shoot tens of thousands of captured Christian hostages in the bull-fight arena. The dead bodies of one and a half million victims and martyrs cover the battlefields of a stricken Spain. Behind all the mass misery and behind the miners of Asturias looms the same mystic power that induced the Russian sailors to revolt at Kronstadt. While the " Pink " intellectuals begin to regard this blood-bath in the light of a Passion Play spectacle, progressive bankers provide it with gold and arms. Old Testamental " nazism " thereby paid back Ferdinand's Catholic Spain for the expulsion of the Jews, and two decades later the American Jewish Congress had the impudence to declare that: "**Up to the present day Jewry has not forgiven the Spanish nation for their expulsion.**"

It was fortunate that at that critical time there were heroic

Spaniards on the spot and also European powers ready to send effective help. With the aid of the German Condor Legion and the Italian Blue Arrow Division, the Spanish people defeated these fanatics, thus proving emphatically that the Soviet revolution could likewise have been brought under control had Russia not been deserted in her hour of need by the European powers.

The massacres in Russia perpetrated by the Communists had a horrifying effect on the Christian world. But these crimes appeared as heroic, attractive feats in the eyes of Jewry. In their eyes one thing mattered only, i.e. that over a vast empire, over practically one-fifth of the globe, power was seized by their nationals.

During the interventional war the English trade unions were brought into action by a " hidden " hand to hinder the campaign against Bolshevism. When Poland was overrun by Bolshevism Grand Orient Freemasonry had, with the help of Czechoslovak Freemasons, prevented ammunition deliveries to the Poles. Eventually Hungary's last ammunition reserves were sent to the Vistula front and with this help Marshal Pilsudski won the Battle of Warsaw.

What interest had Western capitalist Jewry in the survival and spreading of Bolshevism? After all, the Western Jew is a capitalist, and Bolshevism proclaims the abolition of capitalism. The Western Jew consistently propagated all the various humanitarian slogans in the lodges, apparently ignoring that the whole system of Bolshevism was an outrage against humanity. The Western Jew appeared to remain faithful to his own religion while Bolshevism was proclaiming atheism. What, then, had Bolshevism in common with Western capitalism? How was it possible for Zionist organisations in New York to hail Bolshevism, and for Jacob H. Schiff to give it money?

Since then history has supplied us with the answer.

What Bolshevism and Capitalism have in common is the ghastly fact that **both of them are equally Jewish.**

The Western capitalist Jew saw no enemy of Capitalism in the Soviet leaders; he saw only Jews. He was able to excuse the Bolsheviks barbarities for they were committed mostly by Jews. According to the strangest beliefs of Jewish nationalism, the Jew is a superman! Jewry is a supernation. The Jew is at liberty to act as he pleases against other races. This is the teaching of Torah and Talmud. The Jew's standing is " beyond good and evil ". In the beginning some Jews condemned Bolshevism for conventional reasons, but later they realised that the only thing to do was to remain silent about it, since Bolshevism, too, was led by Jews.

High Finance in the West was agreed on the maintenance of Jewish leadership in the Soviet Union, whatever the cost. Henry Ford's book the *International Jew* was published at this time, revealing in shocking disclosures how far the judaisation of American life had progressed. Though the Jewish boycott obliged Henry Ford to apologise for his book, he never denied the truth of its contents. After the First World War the Jewish question in America became more and more acute. Through the monopolisation of commerce and banking, the control of the turnover of public commodities, their despotic rule over the press and the poisoning of public education, the encroaching Jewish power began to threaten the American way of life.

The peril was foreseen earlier by great Americans such as Benjamin Franklin who, on one occasion, said:

" There is a great danger for the United States of America, this great danger is the Jew.

" If they are not excluded from the United States by the Constitution, within less than 100 years they will stream into this country in such numbers they will rule and destroy us and change our form of Government for which we Americans shed our blood and sacrificed life, property and personal freedom. If the Jews are not excluded, within 200 years our children will be working in the fields to feed the Jews while they remain in the counting-house gleefully rubbing their hands."

It would make an interesting best-seller to describe how certain mysterious hands spirited away his diary. It can be stated with certainty that at the time when the Bolshevik revolution broke out in Russia, American Jewry was already standing at the first stage of the great plan. During the operational attack to secure the first stage, the control over finance and the press was achieved and influence over public life firmly established. Jewish nationalism in the Western World clearly realised that, despite its ostensibly hostile ideology, Bolshevism must be kept alive, because the way to the second stage in America led by way of Bolshevism—the great Eastern ally—which would help to conquer America and to establish Jewish world power. It is understandable, therefore, that after the Russian revolution the leaders of the 217 American Zionist organisations decided to give every possible financial help to Bolshevism.

"Bolshevism will be devoured by the vermin!" Trotsky-Bronstein exclaims in distress. But American Jewish Capitalism took every care to sustain, rear and industrialise this world menace. So "anti-capitalistic" Bolshevism was soon supported by loans from Loeb, as well as by other long-term credits, by scientists, by contributions and by deliveries of arms. Those giving the money were no Bolsheviks but they were Jews! They were the representatives of a supranational racial solidarity. They gave substantial help to Bolshevism because they had the foresight to realise that if by any chance Bolshevism should collapse this would discredit the reliability of Jewish planning and leadership. Besides, this mishap would bring to light the massacres perpetrated by Jewry in the name of Bolshevism. So to prevent losing the subjected territories of Russia, regarded by now as an actually established part of the planned future Jewish world empire, Jewry gave Bolshevism every possible help. For the Christian nations Bolshevism represented an ideology. But for Jewry it was a Jewish national problem of superlative importance.

But the firm establishment of Bolshevism in Russia was not in it itself enough. To ensure its survival and development as a power it was necessary to weaken the European Christian peoples so that they would not be able to smother the Bolshevik Hydra later on. For Jewish tribal nationalism, the period of the peace conferences following the First World War meant yet one more triumph for dreams of Jewish world domination.

Wilson himself stated on his return home from the Peace Conference at Versailles:

"There was a secret force at work in Europe which was untraceable."

At the Versailles Peace Conference the German delegation contained two Jews. Its advisors included Max Warburg, Dr. von Strauss, Oscar Oppenheimer, Dr. Jaffe, Deutsch, Brentano, Struck, Wassermann and Mendelsohn Bartholdi.

During this period the Christian world failed to notice that the artificially deepened rifts dividing the nations, together with the injustices promoted by the peace treaties, only served to further

Jewish aspirations to world power. In starving Germany, rebellious Spartacus groups together with Socialist and Bolshevik revolutionaries, were splitting up society. Across the Rhine, new nationalisms emerge to fly at each other's throats. In the place of the Hapsburg Monarchy and the former Austro-Hungarian Empire, many small opposing nationalisms prepare to pay off old scores. While the fires of the Bolshevik revolution still smoulder in Italy, the new flames of the Fascist revolution begin to flare up.

Meanwhile, more to the East, due to the support of Jewish Finance, Bolshevism grows stronger and stronger so that the Jews of the Kremlin as well as those of the Loeb directorate, may well chant the credo of their nationalism over distracted Europe.

" Our men are progressing rapidy in Paris, New York and Moscow. We are advancing towards the second stage of the battle. We have divided Christian Europe and from the soil of the injustice sown by us will spring the seeds of a new war. You will see that the seeds will bear fruit in the next twenty years." As the great Lenin said:

" The First World War gave us Russia, while the Second World War will hand Europe to us!"

Oh, Europe, heart-land of civilisation, do you not yet understand? Can you not perceive where Jewish national unity coupled with your own internal conflicts lead? Can you not see the abyss towards which you are being driven by forces imbued with the cruelty and purposefulness of a supranational people. Alas! There are so few who see it even now.

An unknown friar, Sziliczei-Várady Gyula, once wrote prophecies that were soon forgotten in a book called *From the Ghetto to the Throne,* and herein is Nemesis:

" The Western Jew will equip an army of twenty million men in the East to destroy Christianity and human culture and to establish the Jewish world kingdom!"

FIVE

A MOVEMENT MALIGNED

As a result of the suppression of spiritual freedom all over the world, we live in a kind of thieves' kitchen, concocting a flash hypocritical series of slogans in the place of free speech. There are certain taboo-like problems to which one is not supposed to refer. There are certain persons one should not name. There are also certain matters not to be mentioned in the language of Western civilised man. Speaking the truth means facing either the gallows of Nuremberg or the loss of one's daily bread.

Nevertheless we must say a few words about National Socialism.

Christian Resistance should have followed at the moment when Bolshevism broke out in Russia and when the work of Jewry became visible through the Versailles Treaty. The message Christendom should have been the restoration of unity in disorganised Europe, the instruction of the nations and the elevating of the Christian conception of hierarchy, thus guarding the individual against being reduced to herd-level. Bolshevism as well as soulless liberal capitalism should have been effectively mastered by their only real adversary—by Christian resistance all the time pointing the way upwards toward Heaven. Perhaps Christ Himself might have come with His scourge to drive the money-changers out of the House of God, thus restoring justice, goodwill and social peace and once more He might have addressed His Christian people with Peter's forthright words: ". . . Save yourselves from this untoward generation!"

But Christianity was reluctant to adopt revolutionary methods in order to wrench world power out of the hands of those whom Christ, the founder of Christianity, attacked on Maundy Thursday. The spirit of Christianity should have impressed itself upon public life, upon governments and upon the press and trade unions but it failed miserably to fulfil its mission. Germany became a stage for the rootless " fellow-traveller " of the Weimar-Democracy. The leaders of Hungarian and Polish Catholicism tried to preach Christianity to the poverty-stricken masses from the shelter of their large estates. The Italian and Spanish clergy remained in the enjoyment of their worldly wealth. Protestantism, as seen by Axel Munthe, was unable to give faith, or to follow in Luther's footsteps, who, taking his stand with the people, exclaimed: "Here I stand and I cannot do anything else!"

But history will not tolerate unfulfilled duties and unsolved problems. In the East Bolshevism was established, while in the West reigned the atheistic speculative power of gold. The Socialism of Christ was unable to find its wings. Therefore National Socialism had to come.

Opinions may differ as to whether National Socialism was a " *neopagan* " movement from the beginning or whether certain mistakes crept in later. But it is indisputable that National Socialism, after coming to power undertook to fulfil, under various slogans, those tasks that ought to have been performed by Christianity. No doubt it would have been much better had the Christian Churches in the turbulent hours of the upheaval of 1919 declared war on Bolshevistic atheism, on the immorality infesting European societies and on corruption, defeatism, capitalist exploitations and Marxist class-liberation. But the Christian Churches had developed a glass-house Christianity. Unlike Christ, who, though unarmed and "sitting upon an ass, and a colt the foal of an ass" immediately made his presence felt by both word and deed, when he rode into Jerusalem, an anæmic incapacitated Christianity restricted to empty prayers, proved itself to be only a passive witness of historic events. The fatal mistake of the Churches was in not supporting the social aspirations of the masses but rather in backing on every occasion the actual holder of state power. During the period between the two World Wars prayers were said from both Catholic and Protestant pulpits not so much for the living members of the Church community, i.e. for the masses, as for the welfare of the ruling power. Thus, in England, they prayed for the King, in France for the Republic, in Hungary for the Regent, in Italy for Mussolini, later, in Austria for Hitler, just as "pacifist priests" are ready to say prayers to-day even for Kruschev.

In any case, one accusation has to be deleted from the charges, rightly or wrongly brought against National Socialism. In spite of what occurred later, it was not in its early days a movement of the " masses ". It stirred the masses but not with any intent to gratify the needs of the masses. The *élite* of the German intellectuals who were not necessarily identical with the actual leaders of National Socialism came to recognise that the most dangerous point in the scheme of both Bolsheviks and Jews to obtain power consisted in their intention to reduce free and intelligent men to the herd-level, to transform them into a malleable formless mass, which could easily be kept under control by the tommy-gun. Against this, the early years of National Socialism saw the development of lofty aspirations, as well as the growth of the concept of the *élite*. It campaigned not for the class struggle but for higher national morality, for freedom, for social order and justice and for national culture which would not be offensive to others. National Socialism could never have arisen had it not been for the fact, for instance, that learned Jewish professors in Germany set up experimental brothels for children with boys and girls of twelve to thirteen years of age. Could such a national disgrace ever have been perpetrated had the way not been prepared by a series of financial swindles with public funds and by Communist plots?

Hans Grimm, the greatest champion of the German spirit in Europe, the great German writer who later fell out with Hitler, even after 1945 described the conditions that gave rise to the National Socialist revolution as follows:

" An unyielding predilection for an ethnic community and a striving towards national integrity, coupled with a passionate eagerness for Anglo-German co-operation. There was general anxiety for reform in a changing world; this mass movement recognised new values—both spiritual and physical, as was demonstrated by basing the currency upon production instead of upon gold. Furthermore, the claim that quality must be protected against quantity was also upheld and the whole of this great experiment set out to prove that the spirit of Versailles must be abolished for everybody's benefit."

German National Socialism not only proclaimed certain principles but, in its initial stage, at any rate, endeavoured to put them into practice. The promotion of intellectual *élite*, the suppression of the class-struggle, the establishment of peace between capital and labour, the building of homes, the raising of the working classes' living standards, the cultivation of family ties, the well-planned settlement of the proletarian masses and the securing of a peaceful old age through the creation of social insurance, were all constructive forces of indisputable value. Doubtless they still play a basic rôle in present-day German life and make possible the rebuilding of " democratic " Western Germany, although since the German economic and monetary system is now closely geared to the U.S. Federal Reserve Bank network, and so to the power of gold and usury, these constructive forces are to some extent being warped by an unsuitable framework. For it was a tremendous achievement on the part of National Socialism to have established a currency system covered by the value of the nation's work and by the volume of the national production, which at the same time brought about the overthrow of the omnipotence of money as a commodity and also that of the domination of gold.

Although its leaders were not necessarily frequent churchgoers, the National Socialist state accepted and carried out Christian principles by establishing order and social justice. It is clear that for this to be accomplished destructive social forces had to be eliminated. It was inevitable, therefore, that National Socialism had to stand up against the relic of " 1918 defeatism " as well as against the subversive activities of the Jewish spirit. It had to make a stand against the Jewish Bolshevik and the Jewish Capitalist, being aware that the unrestricted autocracy of the Golden Calf only engenders discontent, envy and class-warfare.

It makes little difference whether or not the Jewish question was " over-emphasised " by National Socialism. It is of no importance either that National Socialism actually adopted the racial theory of the Old Testament as one of its instrumental devices; for even had it forsworn these, it would still inevitably have clashed with world Jewry, which could not tolerate the existence of any other nationalism on earth. The National Socialists might have treated Jewry as humanely as possible, but this would not have altered the fact that the secret power exercised by Jews over the German Reich was being taken out of their hand, which was absolutely intolerable for them. Besides, they could not afford to contemplate such creative energy, such striving towards national unity, such influence wielded

67

by an *élite,* all of which were things bearing irreconcilable hostility towards the power aspirations of world Jewry. They could not bear the fact that by the elimination of the power of gold, not only were state power and the means of influencing public affairs wrenched out of their hands, but the secret power as well. In any case, from the moment world Jewry realised that Germany was being ruled by a conscious *élite,* it would have promptly turned against National Socialism with just as much hatred as it actually did when " anti-Semitism " gave an excuse for it.

In loosing Germany, Jewry lost a territory from which it had exerted power. Therefore it was determined to re-conquer it.

For a century, world Jewry, Marxism and liberal capitalism had been adopting mass-production methods to transform the people into unthinking masses, the free individual into the proletarian. They had realised, of course, that only unthinking herds could accept and endure the yoke of Judah.

In Germany, National Socialism at least arrested this process. In spite of his liberalism, the Spanish author Ortega y Gasset, in his work *The Uprising of the Masses,* long ago drew attention to the danger inherent in people being reduced to herd-like masses. Lothrop Stoddard, professor of Harvard University, also insisted that an uprising of the masses must be prevented. By its accomplishments German National Socialism clashed most violently with Jewry's plans, since the rôle of the mob is clearly laid down in the *Protocols* which speak of: ". . . that same blind slave of ours—the majority of the mob." (*Protocol* X.) And again: " From all this you will see that in securing the opinion of the mob we are only facilitating the working of our machinery. . . ." (*Protocol* XIII.)

To achieve world power auxiliary troops are needed. And these consist first and foremost of the masses themselves. To secure the independence of a nation, men of outstanding quality are required. While destruction is the basis of Jewry's world domination, constructive work is the foundation of real freedom.

Thus, to ask whether or not the Hitlerite régime was really bent on war is beside the question. There is no point in assuming that Hitler and the German leaders were madmen. We might, with more justice, admit that National Socialism had war declared upon it from the very moment of its birth. It was condemned to war because it was

68

a system which inevitably made enemies of Bolshevism and world capitalism, i.e. of those forces forever looming in the background! Without making a single " anti-Semitic " manifestation or the slightest unfriendly pronouncement, National Socialism would still have made enemies of Jewry on account of the successful completion of the " levelling up " process.

In this connection we will once more quote Hans Grimm, who states fairly and concisely in his book *The Answer of a German*:

" Between 1933 and 1939 more was done for public health, for the mother and child, as well as for the promotion of social welfare than before and, perhaps we might admit, than ever before! "

At this time even Winston Churchill had a different opinion of National Socialism from that which he professed later. Churchill wrote of Hitler in *Step by Step*:

" If our country were defeated, I hope we should find a champion as indomitable to restore our courage and lead us back to our place among the nations."

But National Socialism was condemned to war for this very reason. At the moment when Hitler took power with the determination of abolishing the system of Versailles and of raising his own people, then somewhere in the veiled secrecy of the lodges and in the mystic inner shrines of Jewish nationalism a declaration of war was immediately decided upon. One problem only remained, i.e. whose nerves would prove the stronger. Who would be able to take up best an appearance of peaceful intentions, and who would be hanged later as war criminals?

" Can we be sure that America will also come to heel?" was the question the Jews must have been asking themselves at this time. " We can be sure that the Soviet Union will be on our side when the great war comes. We can also rely confidently upon the France of Leon Blum, of Reynaud-Mandel, of Lazarus' Bank of the Grand Orient and the Rothschilds. We can be certain that when the time comes the England of the Sassoons, of Rufus Isaacs, of Hore-Belisha, of the Gallachers, Stracheys, and Laskis will fight to further our ends. But suppose the people of the American democracy draw upon the results of experiences gained in the First World War—what then? What will happen if, at a critical moment isolationism, represented by the Mayflower Yankees, gets the upper hand, saying that the

United States have nothing to do with a war between German and Jewish nationalisms?

"Perhaps the Americans will have no interest in fighting for Danzig. But we Jews will! For Hitler is standing on the balcony of his Chancelry supported by eighty million people singing the *Horst Wessel* song.

"Die Fahne hoch!" (Let's raise high the flag!)

The people are marching through the Brandenburg Arch in dense columns of eight after liberating themselves from our domination. Tht fist of the German worker, previously clenched in hatred and envy now unclenches in the friendly salute of the open palm. One of these two nationalisms must perish!

". . . we shall respond with the guns of America or China or Japan!" is written in *Protocol* VII. "Therefore, we must first conquer America to ensure the conquest of the world. We must bolshevise or socialise America from above without it being noticed."

For America's constitutional form is democracy. This is the best constitutional system when the true will of the people prevails, and the worst where secret hands falsify the national will. In America the people are proud of their freedom and of their democratic education. The American worker is as proud of the industrial revolution as the capitalist himself. In America everybody is equal before the law. Both the descendants of the early pioneers whose fathers came on the *Mayflower* as well as those of the little Jew from Galicia, can declare with equal pride: "Civis Americanus sum!" Democracy is the most ideal way of life, provided there is no individual group, party, race or sect successfully fulfilling in secret aspirations detrimental to the rest of the nation. As soon as such a parasitic force develops inside democracy, democracy itself is reduced to nothing. It is transformed into a minority-ruled herd. The right of the vote becomes a myth, since public opinion is being shaped by the press of this alien nationalism. The parliamentary system is debased to that of a theatrical act, for senators will be influenced by an artificially created and therefore false public opinion. The government will be run no longer on the lines originally contemplated, as laid down by the legislature, because the government itself will be manned by the members of this secret force, enforcing a minority will, dictating by their "power of the purse" and directed by the advice of their brains trust.

"We Jews," as the spokesman of this clannish nationalism might put it, "are well aware that in America, England, France and the Soviet Union, as well as in every other part of the world, the rule is: Judah must come first! As long as the interests of America are identical with the interests of Old Testament 'nazism', we will be good Americans, but as soon as our interests begin to conflict with the interests of America, we shall betray her too. Generally speaking, democracy suits us if and when it is led by as many Jews as possible. The so-called freedom of the press is good for us provided the descendants of the seed of Abraham above all can avail themselves of it. Yes! this freedom is a valuable thing but only where we Jews are at liberty to do anything we like!

"Oh, you faint-hearted ones, who listen terror-stricken to the marching S.A. and S.S. troops; be not afraid! By now we are experts in undermining and capturing democracies. We are familiar with the methods of imposing our particular interests on the masses. America, the richest state of the Goyim is being shaken by a mortal economic crisis. The time is ripe to start our all-out offensive which will also give political power into our hands. And ours will be a take-over of a more permanent character than that of Hitler. We are going to conquer America neither by arms nor by theories. We possess a more reliable prescription to call down Nemesis on America. The fate of America was prescribed by our own Führer—Moses! Torah is our Mein Kampf!"

According to Leviticus, chapter 25 (the *Third Book of Moses*), all estates and properties in Israel were to be re-distributed every fifty years. All mortgaged lands and all slaves were to be redeemed. Every half-century there was to be a great social reform in Israel. Old debts were to be cancelled and the poor were to be given a share out of the assets of the rich, or, as we might say to-day, "prosperity" was to be restored, i.e. money, property and land was to be distributed again in equal shares. Every fifty years this was to be heralded by trumpets.

"This social reform," the spokesman for Jewry might continue, "was called the new distribution! In America it will be called the New Deal! These words translated literally into English mean our

71

great social reform, the new distribution. But this time we will not be distributing the assets of the Israelites but of the Americans and, of course, in such a manner as to ensure that the Americans will be left with as little as possible, and our own people with as much as possible.

" This will be the year for sounding the trumpets in America, where in Washington's time the total number of Jews was a mere four thousand. But now our bankers, our socialists and our journalists will be blowing trumpets, and our brains trust will execute the New Deal at the expense of the American pioneer-population. Thereafter the only remaining question will be: Whom are we going to put in the Presidential Chair at Washington?

" Those of you living in despair in your palatial residences in Wall Street or in 13th Street, as well as in the ghettoes of Brooklyn and Bronx, must not doubt that we shall find our man, the real match of Hitler who will, at the same time, place political power over America into our hands. You need only read our directions in the ' forged ' *Protocols*:

" ' Liberalism produced constitutional status, which took the place of what was the only safeguard of the Goyim, namely despotism (autocracy-editor) . . . then it was that we replaced the ruler by a caricature of a government—by a president, taken from the mob, from the midst of our puppet overture, our slaves. In the near future we shall establish the responsibility of presidents!' (*Protocol* X.)

" ' . . . we shall arrange elections,' " this *Protocol* continues, " ' in favour of such presidents as have in their past some dark undiscovered strain, some " Panama " or other — then they will be trustworthy agents for the accomplishment of our plans out of fear of revelations. . . .'

" Who shall, therefore, be the new President, who will place America in our hands and who will execute our orders?

" His name is Franklin Delano Roosevelt!

" But who is this Franklin D. Roosevelt?

Robert Edward Edmondson, under the heading **Famous Sons of Famous Fathers—The Roosevelts,** answers this question in his book, *I Testify.*

On March 7th, 1934, the Carnegie Institute compiled the family tree of the Roosevelts, from which it is evident that the President of the United States is of Jewish descent. His ancestors came to America about 1682: they were Claes Martenszen *Van Rosenvelt,* and on the distaff side Janette Samuel. They were originally of Spanish sephardim descent Jews who had escaped from Catholic Ferdinand's persecution in 1492 and who had gone to England. From the time of their arrival in America the Roosevelt family tree is studded with Jacobs, Isaacs and Samuels.

The *New York Times* of March 14th, 1935, quotes the President as saying: "In the distant past my ancestors may have been Jews. All I know about the origin of the Roosevelt family is that they are apparently the descendants of Claes Martenszen van Roosevelt, who came from Holland."

But according to the Carnegie Institute, Mr. Claes Martenszen Rosenvelt was a Jew. Furthermore Roosevelt's well-known wife is herself a Jewess.

Europe, or to be more precise, Germany, lies between the two jaws of the pincers. Here, from the Jewish point of view, dreadful events were taking place. The collaboration of German capitalists and workers, as well as the solidarity of the middle-classes and farmers demonstrated that the class-struggle is far from inevitable. Marx's theory of destruction was being disproved, whilst the golden calf had wellnigh lost its prestige when it was seen that production and not gold was to be the true basis of the new world. All that has been taught and eulogised for more than a century as world progress has now been destroyed—oh, of course, not by a German corporal, *but by the spirit of the modern age.* Against the tide of world domination surging from the Eastern Hemisphere the symbolic flag of the swastika was arising. This could not be tolerated by world Jewry.

"Yet, fear not!" declares the spokesman. "Around the puppet, Roosevelt, our advisors are now gathering in conference — Felix Frankfurter from Vienna, Morgenthau from Mannheim, Bernard Baruch from Königsberg, and Albert Einstein from Berlin. Samuel Roseman who writes Roosevelt's presidential speeches is there. So are our labour leaders; amongst them our compatriot Sidney Hillman who controls American labour in the administration of our puppet, F.D.R. There is Mr. David Dubinsky, also a fellow-immigrant from Russia, who will transform the Christian American workers into taxpayers for Zionism. The entourage of *our* President will consist exclusively of trustworthy men, such as La Guardia, Mayor of New York, a Jew from Fiume, and Alger Hiss, the protégé of Frankfurter and of Senator Lehman, etc. Bernard Baruch will control the 351 most important branches of American industry and will equip the American boys who are going to fight against Hitler. On behalf of America, Alger Hiss will conduct the talks with Stalin. Einstein, Oppenheimer and David Lilienthal will produce the atomic bomb. As managers of UNRRA, La Guardia and Herbert H. Lehman will help the future Jewish victims of the coming war. Henry Morgenthau, jr., the Secretary of the Treasury, will prepare a splendid plan for the extermination of the German people. Our Mortiz Gomberg will see to it that eighteen million people from the countries of our enemies will become stateless in Europe. Our men will be distributing cheques of eleven million dollars to provide the Soviet with arms.

"What a magnificent dream. Americans will sail across the ocean to punish *our* enemies. In the lodges of B'nai B'rith the Moscow-New York axis is ready to function.

"'Do not worry! Roosevelt will provide the armaments for Russia!'"

Well, did not a little-heeded prophet write twenty years ago:

"The Western Jew will equip an army of twenty million on the East to destroy Christianity and human culture and to establish Jewish world kingdom!"

SIX

THE REAL WAR CRIMINALS

HITLERISM was not the only thing that world Jewry hated. They dreaded even more those movements paving the way for a new understanding amongst the nations of Europe. Jewry's main aim was to discredit these new trends as well as to make them disliked by the rest of the world. While campaigning on one side for full co-operation, they tried to strangle on the other side all those who were collaborating with their enemies—the Germans.

" They unhesitatingly opposed even the slightest thought of making peace!" writes Maurice Bardeche.

But to-day we have definite proof that the Germans tried most earnestly to establish co-operation and partnership among the European *élite*. They were not looking for " Quislings " but for those who were considered good patriots in their own country, people dedicated to the cause of their own native land. An almost exaggerated idealism pervaded the *élite* of the National Socialist revolution. In their own country they stated what they believed to be the truth. They recognised that the individual has social rights. They demonstrated that this is the only satisfactory solution on a national basis, if Bolshevism is to be avoided.

They believed with revolutionary fervour that if they could succeed in liberating the European masses from capitalist exploitation then peace might be secured for a long time. They had seen how Jewish " nazism " interposed itself to disrupt the unity of the German people by means of its money power and its control of the press in order to secure exclusive domination over the entire nation. Having successfully done away with all this by their National Socialist revolution they had high hopes of securing peace and also the co-operation of neighbouring peoples, once the influence of that supranational Old Testament " nazism " was eliminated in these countries too.

This was " New Europe " in the making. And this was the very thing world Jewry had to prevent at any cost, even if it entailed reducing the Christian culture of Europe to the dust. Because, should this plan succeed, more and more states would be released from the grip of Jewish domination.

Therefore the mere thought of European unity, or of any possible co-operation had to be discredited. And because more than the sixty per cent of the press of the Western world is in Jewish hands and, according to American statistics, eighty-five per cent of the American press and 100 per cent of American films, this campaign was conducted on a larger scale than any other propaganda operation in the history of the world.

By misinterpreting the racial concept the Jews pretended that the Germans were claiming sole supremacy for the German nation over all other nations. Thus they succeeded in estranging the other nations from Germany. They distorted the racial theory by insinuating that Germany wanted to conquer the world and on the basis of this theory was claiming world supremacy. The *Nineteenth Century* magazine in its issue of September, 1943, during the height of the war, admitted on the contrary that:

" The general belief that Germany started this war to achieve world power is, in our view, a mistake. Germany wanted to become a first-rate power, but to be a first-rate power and to achieve world domination are two different things. Great Britain is also a world power but she does not rule the world."

The Jews also falsely interpreted the theory of " Blut and Boden " (blood and soil), i.e. the theory that a man belongs to his native soil; the concept of a unity between a country and its inhabitants was so twisted as to suggest that the Germans claimed all those territories in which any inhabitants of German origin happened to be living. By this means they aroused the jealousy of all independent European nations where German minorities were to be found. Poland, Lithuania, Hungary, Slovakia, Yugoslavia, Bohemia, Rumania, and other neighbouring states began to regard with distrust the German Reich.

They tried to explain away Germany's steadily growing export trade as a preparation for war and attempted to make the world forget that Goering's slogan of " guns or butter " had a precedent in the boycott by American Jewry. They ridiculed the sincerely pro-British parts of *Mein Kampf,* at the same time working on the fears of both

76

East and West by quoting certain passages of this book out of their context.

This poisoning of the mind was thus stimulated on a gigantic scale throughout the world. When the German administration tried to stop this trouble-mongering at home it was promptly accused of dictatorial tyranny. As a background to all these forms of anti-German propaganda there was, of course, the undeniable fact that the abolition of the reign of gold together with the establishment of peaceful co-operation between capital and labour was a real shock for Jewry. World opinion was induced to believe that the German worker's living standard was rising only because of rearmament. But, in fact, they knew very well that large workers' settlements were everywhere under construction, and that the existence of the workers' and satisfied families was a living refutation of those things taught by Jewry for over a century.

"What can have happened?" they asked one another in fear. "Have these hated Nazis really wrecked the splendid theory of the Marxist class-struggle which was serving our ends so well?" As Bettelheim expressed it, can great cities such as Berlin, Vienna and Budapest get along without Jews? Can a nation really live without exploitation, without a Jewish nationalist press, without the films, theatre and Jewish "mercenary spirit"? After all, we have kept the whole world under our influence for centuries by suggesting that without our cultural activities, our business sense and supercilious intellect all nations would perish and all "progress" would cease. And now Germany prospers without us—with a prosperity which is the living negation of our arrogant nationalism Anybody looking at these steadily growing garden-cities, at the satisfied and happy people and at the prospering intellectual and economic activities can see that our great nationalist writer, Bettelheim, was wrong when he predicted that world civilisation would perish without the Jews. So far, these Christians are becoming more and more satisfied, while we Jews are losing more and more ground. If the rest of the world learns about this on an international level, and if the foreign tourists and the world's proletariat see that all this is possible without us, indeed, even against us, they will realise that we have lied to them. Our politicians, journalists, trade union leaders, capitalists and labour leaders will all become liars! Therefore we must destroy the proofs!

Therefore, these nice homes with their gardens, together with the new factories, day nurseries, youth camps and hospitals must be wiped off the face of the earth. For we have at our disposal our secret nationalist weapon—the same one used with such effect at the siege of Jericho. Let us, therefore, sound the trumpets for our world propaganda

World Jewry must be regarded as the **sole war criminal** of the Second World War because, in the first place, it prevented reconciliation between the nations and the possibility of co-operation, destroying even the pre-requisites to these aims. With the help of untruthful propaganda and falsehood, and by use of radio and press, it projected a totally false world picture before the eyes of mankind. It created a general world atmosphere in which the mere utterance of the truth in connection with the German question might entail danger to life or loss of livelihood, or suspicion of high treason. All peace offers made by the German statesmen were labelled sheer lies. It derided all sober and honest plans. It made all social achievements in Germany appear as reactionary red tape, all the progress as an anti-progressive obstacle, every manifestation of the *élite* concept as barbarism and all forms of anti-Bolshevism as anti-democratic. Colonel Charles Lindberg, the national hero of America, became suspected of high treason when he dared to state his honest opinion about National Socialism, based on his own personal experience.

Meanwhile, in 1938, Roosevelt, who can only be regarded as a puppet of the Jewish brains trust, sent the following gaily worded wire to Churchill for the promotion of war preparations:

"You and I can rule the world!"

World Jewry declared war on Europe and on Christianity at the very moment Hitler came to power, or perhaps even before. The anti-German boycott movement flared up in America as early as 1932. Jewish organisations published full-page advertisements in the *New York Times* reading: "Let us boycott anti-Semitic Germany." Seeing that this did not have much result, they began to prepare the New York-Moscow axis.

Forest Davis in his book *What Really Happened in Teheran,* the contents of which were reviewed and published in the *Saturday Evening Post* of May 13th and May 20th, 1944, reveals that as early as 1933 Morgenthau was preparing for the resumption of American-

Soviet diplomatic relations. And the first Soviet Ambassador in Washington's land was nobody else but the bloodthirsty Soviet Commissar, Litvinov Finkelstein.

Before President Roosevelt, the direct descendant of the Rosenvelt family, came to power, all this would have been unthinkable. The common denominator that actually brought together American democracy and Soviet tyranny was—Jewry.

James Whiteside in an article, *Mr. Roosevelt and Communism*, describes with appalling vividness in the columns of the *St. Louis Despatch* how as soon as Litvinov appeared on the American scene, a fearful procession of Communists (i.e. of Jews) began its march towards the White House. Roosevelt gave special permission for the installation of a very powerful Soviet broadcasting station in the Pentagon (the American War Office) thus infecting the high command of the American forces with the most pernicious propaganda.

As early as 1933 the editor of the *New York Morning Freiheit*, a Yiddish paper with a circulation reaching several hundred-thousand copies, called upon American and world Jewry to unite all Jews in the war against Nazism. The American Jewish Congress, led by Rabbi Stephen Wise, joined the movement with avidity.

In 1933, also, Rabbi S. Wise, on Hitler's advent to power, announced a " Holy War" on the part of Jewry as follows:

" I am for war!" This memorable announcement was made on May 8th, 1933 (Edmonson, *I Testify*, p. 195).

It is evident that at this time not even the outlines of the German General Staff's plans for 1940 were drawn up, for which Rabbi Wise and Co. hanged the German military leaders.

A speech had previously been delivered by Morgenthau on February 11th, 1933, declaring war on Hitler:

" The U.S. has entered the phase of a second war!" announced this prominent leader of Jewish nazism. (*Portland Journal*, February 12th, 1933.)

In the meanwhile various Jewish and Communist boycott organisations were springing up like mushrooms in the United States, scheming to ruin Hitler's economy. A Joint Anti-Nazi Boycott Committee was already fully active in 1936, while Hitler, even in his wildest dreams, could not guess the exact time when the clock would strike and he would have to try to free himself from the mortal embrace of the Hydra whose coils entwined the world.

It can now be proved historically that the youthful National Socialism was right in fearing that Jewish nationalism would make a fatal ring round the Third Reich from which it would be impossible to break out, even with the help of arms. But was this fear really justified? Who held power in the United States, Great Britain, France and Soviet Russia?

Concerning the question of war guilt and war-mongering, the same motive remains for our consideration which constituted the principle problem of Roman law as well as of any legal system throughout the ages: *cui prodest*? Who will profit from the war? 'Whose interests are promoted by it? The only interest of German National Socialism was the maintenance of peace.

The last attempt to prevent the outbreak of the Second World War was when Ribbentrop visited Moscow to conclude the non-aggression pact with Stalin. On August 23rd, 1939, Hitler summoned to Godesberg 2,000 officers of the General Staff. This " secret " consultation was a bluff intended for Britain. So was the impressive march of endless columns on the roads, and the endless flights of Air Force formations near the Führer's eyrie. Even the most stupid agent of the Intelligence saw clearly that this was a bluff.

Regarding Britain, it was evident that although war had been decided on, it was still possible to make peace. Hitler in a speech lasting four hours declared:

" Do not think, gentlemen, that I am an idiot and will let myself be forced into war because of the question of the Polish Corridor!"

But at this moment an invisible hand reached out to take an active part in directing the flow of events—the same intriguing hand which consistently embroiled matters in the background. After the Godesberg meeting of the General Staff, Soviet Russia signed the non-aggression pact with Germany. This was closely followed by the Bromberg massacre engineered by another invisible hand.

This real war crime, recorded in detail, together with the relevant proofs, in the German White Paper published in the autumn of 1939, was later hushed up in Nuremberg. Although the artificially constructed horror scenes of the " Todesmuhle " (Mill of Death), for the shooting of which wax figures were used in the various scenes, were shown in the cinemas, the film of these horrors which had really happened, as published in the White Paper, were never shown in any cinema. Women with truncated breasts, mangled male corpses with the sexual organs cut off, bodies of German babies and four- to five-year-old children impaled on butchers' skewers. Thousands and thousands of slaughtered innocent people about whom the " humanitarian " world remains silent. These were German victims in Poland, whose population was saturated with three million Jews, and where the Jewish-dominated press had by then whipped up hatred and the desire for war. By this time the German and Polish divisions were standing face to face on the frontiers. It was no longer a question of the Corridor, but a flaming brand had been thrown right into the gunpowder barrel. Whose hand and money was in this massacre? Was it brought about by the extreme patriotism of the Polish people or was it coldly calculated and satanic planning? Was it a Soviet or an English hand? Such a thing is hard to conceive. Nevertheless this is the decisive question in determining war guilt.

To see hecatombs of massacred victims well before war had even started was a thing National Socialist Germany could not tolerate. This situation was forced upon her in order that Britain and France could begin a preventive war against Germany.

And so on September 1st, the next day, the German divisions were really marching. " Since dawn to-day we are shooting back!" said Hitler in the Reichstag.*

" We will, of course, be told to-morrow morning," writes Maurice Bardeche, a French Professor, " that Hitler has attacked Poland. Certain people have been waiting and longing for this moment. They were expecting this attack, having been hankering and praying for it. These men are called Mandel, Churchill, Hore-Belisha and Paul Reynaud. The great league of Jewish reaction was determined to have its own war. This was its holy war. They knew very well that

* Late at night on Thursday, August 31st, 1939, the Editor was listening-in to Gleiwitz, a radio station on the German-Polish frontier but just inside Germany. Suddenly, after midnight, the musical programme stopped and excited German voices announced that the town of Gleiwitz had been invaded by Polish irregular formations marching towards the emitting station. Then the station "went dead". When received again at about 2 a.m. (Friday) Polish was being spoken. Cologne radio gave out that German police were repelling the attackers of Gleiwitz. At 6 a.m. (Friday, September 1st) the German Army invaded Poland.

A few days after the outbreak of war, the Editor saw a small paragraph in the English press to the effect that the Germans claimed, among other things, that the Poles had started the war by invading Gleiwitz early on Friday morning.

only such an attack could give them a chance to capture public opinion. It will not be very difficult to find the necessary proofs in the German archives that certain gentlemen in cold blood prepared the conditions which made this attack inevitable. Woe betide them should the true history of the war ever be written."

Though the first part of the great world plan succeeded, and on September 3rd, 1939, Great Britain and France declared war on Hitler, nevertheless the two most important partners, America and the Soviet Union, were still missing.

The greatest secret of the Second World War is still due to come to light and shock the world. Perhaps it will be told only after the fall of Bolshevism, when the archives of the Kremlin will be available. What promises were made by the western world conquerors to the to eastern? The Soviet Union showed another face towards the German Empire. This face was cool, sedate and sometimes a little mystically Asiatic or patriotic but had no Jewish features. The most horrible blunder made by the leaders of National Socialism was when they believed this change to be genuine. Ribbentrop during his conversation with Sven Hedin said that Bolshevism had changed for the better and that Stalin was a great man. (Sven Hedin, *Without Commission in Berlin.*)

Stalin, the cunning Georgian, however, did not believe the same of National Socialism. Before signing the pact with Ribbentrop, he suddenly demanded another Baltic port. Hitler agreed to this, sending his approval by telegram. On learning this news Stalin remarked shrewdly to Molotov:

"Germany has just declared war on us! My only reason for asking for this port was to test the Germans. I knew all along that if they let us have this port they intend taking it back from us later." (Plevier, Moscow.)

Despite this, both parties were scrupulously observing the full text of the pact, including the division of Poland and the question of oil deliveries. Hitler, Ribbentrop, Göering and even Göebbels were all taking meticulous care not to hurt the sensitive Russian Bear. Stalin bids farewell to Krebbs, the German military attaché, with a kiss. All the signs seem to show that this alliance of fire and water is genuine.

Then one day Molotov, Soviet Commissar, husband of the beautiful

Bolshevik Jewess, Karpovszkaja, and brother-in-law of Mr. Carp (Karp), one of the greatest war industrialists in America, appears in Berlin. The date shown by the calendar is November 10th, 1940. France is lying prostrate, while over the British Isles the great air battle is raging. The German Army is taking a rest. Then Molotov places on the table the Soviet demands. They contain claims to the Dardanelles, the occupation of Finland and the conquest of the Far East. Everything they contain is unacceptable to Germany. These demands can hardly have originated anywhere else but from the Anglo-American opponents of Germany.

The leaders of Berlin were now confronted with the consequences of their greatest error.

Bolshevism, after all, had not changed; it was only wearing a different mask. The power in the Kremlin remained Jewish, only its real character remained invisible until it succeeded in involving Germany in the Second World War. By this time the Kremlin must have had guarantees in hand that the " arsenal of democracy " would help the Soviet with money and arms against Germany.

As we all know, Felix Frankfurter, one of the most influential men of the U.S., had by now prepared the Lend-Lease Act and it was approved by Congress as well. But will this war prove to have been in the interests of America? No, it will not! The war will not be in the interest of the American people but in the interest of American Jewry exclusively, i.e. in the interest of persons like Manuilsky, Beria, Morgenthau and Bernard Baruch, as well as of the emigrants from Germany and of the refugees from France. As is shown by statistics of the Gallup Poll (also in Jewish hands) **on June 3rd, 1941, 83 per cent of the American population was against entering the war.**

What real interest had America in re-crossing the ocean once more? The German admirals, Raeder and Dönitz, had clearly stated that invasion of America was as impossible as an invasion of the moon. Senator Barkley pointed out on March 31st, 1941, that had Germany wanted to attack America the deliveries of arms to Great Britain would already have provided a good reason for this.

Sober American people could see no reason why they should be involved in the war. Charles Lindberg said: " The entry of America into the war would lead to chaos lasting several generations." Mr. Ickes, the U.S. Secretary of the Interior, himself of Jewish descent, replied to this by accusing Charles Lindberg of being the Quisling of America. Eighty-three per cent of the American people, including Republicans and Isolationists, are Quislings too, just because they did not want to march behind Morgenthau!

Roosevelt himself, impelled as he was by the brain trust towards war, was obliged to admit that the Americans did not want to intervene. America cannot even be suspected of having any commercial interest in the war through the arms traffic, for this was an ideological war. Therefore, world Jewry began shouting the command of the *Protocols* as the Christian armies approached Moscow:

" We will answer you with American and Chinese guns."

If mankind were capable of serious thought it would have asked itself : " What was the point in America's entering the war, and especially on the side of the Soviet?"

The responsible German leaders issued the following statement:

" It is quite certain that the peace which will follow the German victories will not be of the Versailles type but will be a peace for the benefit of all nations. The people of those countries occupied to-day will regain their freedom but in the common interests of all nations they will have to compromise with certain legalities and conditions."

At the same time Roosevelt sent the following message to Congress :

" A peace treaty at this time which would give control over the occupied countries to Hitler, would amount to the recognition of nazism and to the likelihood of a new war. We want to secure freedom, including religious freedom, for all nations and for each individual."

" Religious freedom!" says this neat slogan. But freedom of which religion? By this time the Christian armies invading Russia could see for themselves the closed churches by the ruins of Christianity which had been destroyed by Bolshevik Jews, as well as, perhaps, the statue of Judas erected by Bolshevism in commemoration of Christ's betrayer. But from the cataclysm of war, from the surge of blood and fire, from the smouldering ruins of destroyed cities, from the thunder of bombs dropped on innocent children, Roosevelt, the most fateful figure of the 20th century, now emerges!

" This war will be Roosevelt's war!" the right-wing Republicans were saying. But people like Morgenthau, Baruch, Frankfurter, Einstein and Oppenheimer, knew better:

" This war will be our war! World Jewry's war!"

For Roosevelt, this late descendant of the Spanish Sephardim, was the prototype of the 20th-century politician. In him was to be found the personification of the *Protocols*, although he was world deliverer and puppet at the same time. Standing behind were the real masters of America. Freemasonry and the Elders of Zion, Zionist leaders and bankers and the Galician-born trade union Bolsheviks.

" He is *our* President!" they said, " and his war will be our war!"

We have substituted a caricature for the " real government ", say the *Protocols*, with the President elected by our creatures and slaves —the mob.

It is obvious that by now nearly the whole of the American legislative and executive power was in the hands of Jewry. The "anti-Semites" could only see the little Jews crowded in Galician ghettos or the small grocer of Brooklyn. Jews stood also behind the chair of Roosevelt, beside the successor of Washington!

At this time when Roosevelt was trying to involve the United States in war against the expressed wish of 83 per cent of the American population, Jewish power in the U.S. Government was to be seen by the following appointments:

Bernard M. Baruch, the unofficial President of the U.S.

Judge Samuel Roseman, the founder and head of the brains trust, Roosevelt's unofficial advisor.

Professor Raymond Moley, " Favourite Personal Advisor ".

Professor Felix Frankfurter, " Chief Legal Advisor " (Securities Act Author).

Henry Morgenthau Senior, Unofficial Advisor (Jewish State Lawyer-Author).

Justice Benj. N. Cardozo, Unofficial Advisor.

Gerald Shwope, Unofficial Advisor.

E. A. Filene, Unofficial Advisor.

Charles W. Taussig, Brains Trust Advisor.

Nathan Margold, Interior Dept. Solicitor.

Charles E. Wyzanski Jr., Labour Dept. Solicitor.

Professor Leo Wolman, Labour Strike Board.

Rose Schneiderman, Labour Advisory Board (Radical Labour Unionist).

Isador Lubin Jr., Labour Bureau Statistical Expert.

Sol. A. Rosenblatt, Amusement Administrator.

E. A Goldenweiser, Federal Research Director.

Jerome Frank, General Counsel.

Mordechai Ezekile, Economic Advisor Agricultural Dept. (Co-Author A.A.A. Laws).

Herbert Feis, " The Brains of the State Dept.".

Henry Morgenthau Jr., Secretary of the Treasury.

David E. Lilienthal, TVA Director.

Sidney Hillman, Labour Advisory Board.

L. N. Landau, PWA General Solicitor.

L. A. Steinhard, Minister to Sweden.

Professor Albert E. Taussig, NRA Advisor.

Alexander Sachs, NRA Code Authority.

Maurice Karp, NRA Director of Personnel.

Robert Freshner, CCC Forest Army Head.

Robert Strauss, NRA Assistant Administrator.

Donald Richberg, NRA Advisor.

H. I. Strauss, Ambassador to France.

Ferdinand Pecora, Special Investigator.

Samuel Untermayer, Stock Exchange Bill Advisor.

Professor James M. Landis, Federal Trade Commissioner.

(*The Hidden Empire*, p. 12.)

A hidden power, able to keep under its control a country of 150 million people, governing from key positions through its brains trust and from behind the Presidential chair, is a terrible thing to contemplate. But Roosevelt required the help of this far-reaching and omnipotent power in order to involve America in the Second World War.

From American sources no secret had been made of the fact that, after trying in vain to drag America into the war against the expressed will of public opinion, Roosevelt carried on provoking the Japanese with various schemings and plottings until they were left with no other choice but to attack Pearl Harbour. During the German assault against the eastern half of the world kingdom, Japan, the other potential enemy of Bolshevism had to be neutralised, even if it meant the entry of the U.S. herself into the war.

But under no circumstances did Roosevelt want to enter the war before securing his re-election as President for a third term of office. This is the reason why he said in 1940 at Philadelphia in his pre-election speech:

" I say to you fathers and mothers again . . . again, and again, your sons shall not be sent to die on foreign soil unless attacked."

Rear-Admiral Robert A. Theobald, ex-commandant of the American torpedo flotilla stationed at Pearl Harbour, in his book published under the title *The Real Secret of Pearl Harbour,* exposes how Roosevelt prepared and provoked this attack against the U.S. With a series of irrefutable proofs Rear-Admiral Theobald establishes that Roosevelt himself brought about the catastrophe of Pearl Harbour. On November 26th, 1941, he sent such an insulting note to Japan that she was left with no other choice but to attack.

"With the help of the note of November 26th," states Admiral Theobald, " President Roosevelt purposely and irrevocably unleashed the war for the United States. Japan's attempt to avoid the strangle-hold was without success. She had either to surrender or to fight, and there was no doubt about her choice."

Despite the fact that American Intelligence had acquired the secret code of the Japanese fleet several months earlier, so that the American High Command knew in advance of every movement of this fleet, the Commandant of Pearl Harbour received no message at all, inform-ing him that, due to the outcome of diplomatic negotiations, a Japanese attack was imminent. As much as four weeks earlier the chiefs-of-staff knew very well that the Japanese intended to overrun Pearl Harbour. They even knew the exact hour the Japanese warships and carriers left their home ports to attack Pearl Harbour. They succeeded even in intercepting the secret Japanese telegram containing the text of the declaration of war and commanding at the same time that this declaration was to be handed over to the White House at the exact time the first bombs were falling on Pearl Harbour.

This catastrophe could have been averted easily, but President Roosevelt eagerly awaited the attack. He expressly forbade the American fleet to leave Pearl Harbour. Four thousand, five hundred and seventy-five unprotected American soldiers died, eighteen ships, amongst them four great American warships, were destroyed. But Roosevelt and those standing behind him attained their aim!

" I say to you fathers and mothers again . . . again, and again, your sons shall not be sent to die on foreign soil unless attacked!" booms the promise of "our President" amid the thunder of the bombs falling on Pearl Harbour. And now he stands on the deck of the *Potomac* with the same hypocritical face, surrounded by other Pharisees heartily singing "Onward, Christian Soldiers", the well-known Anglican hymn. All the time he knows very well that he will scrap the recently signed Atlantic Charter in much the same way as he broke his promise to American fathers and mothers. To the Pope, Roosevelt writes that the Russian form of dictatorship is not as dangerous to Christianity as the German type of despotism.

Roosevelt, who was a well-informed politician, knew very well that this was not true. So did the advisors standing behind him. Nevertheless, they declared it to the Pope and to the nations of the world. Those advising him and compelling him to make hypocritical promises were well aware that through exploiting his vanity they could lead this "democratic" dictator into any venture.

"F.D.R. is our President!" Yes—the President of men like Litvinov, Frankfurter, Kaganovich and Baruch. Perhaps he is the Messiah himself, whose shadow hovers over the bombed-out ruins of Christian churches, over the smouldering debris of Budapest, Berlin, Vienna, Sofia and Belgrade. To-day it is an acknowledged fact that, before his death, Roosevelt was envisaging himself as the first proclaimed President of the world republic through the medium of the revived U.N. and there were definite plans relating to this already drawn up.

". . . and ye shall possess greater nations and mightier than yourselves" sounds the eternal promise. The fact that Roosevelt "progressed" from peace to war, from the New Deal to the firm of Dupont Nemours, from the Atlantic Charter to the Yalta Agreement, from the promise given to the Pope of establishing and maintaining a just peace to the principle of unconditional surrender, from freemasonic humanism to the Morgenthau Plan and from democracy to friendship with Bolshevism is the tragedy of mankind. All this is an appalling example of a statesman corrupted by Jewry. He is the "philanthropist" who causes the bombing of women and children, the "champion of peace" who prepares war, the "great democrat" who is a much greater dictator than Hitler himself, and the leading "American" who by his actions turns out to be—a Jew.

The most calamitous figure of the 20th century is neither Hitler nor Stalin—it is Roosevelt.

And in those days when Christian armies were so near to the Soviet capital that they could see the spires and turrets of Moscow, and when the Japanese attacked Pearl Harbour, it was only appropriate that Churchill should go to the telephone and say to Roosevelt: " Now we are all in the same boat!"

Stalin, Roosevelt and Churchill! Behind them the Eastern and Western Jews—Kaganovich and Baruch!

" The emblem of our nation, the symbolic serpent, has closed its ring " say the *Protocols.*

Not long after these events, a photograph appeared in *Life.* Harry Hopkins, one of Roosevelt's closest advisers and administrator of Lend-Lease, stands in the middle of a group. On his right, Litvinov Finkelstein presents a greasy grin to La Guardia, who is handing over in accordance with the Lend-Lease Act the first American cheque to the Soviet Union.

It is a sum of eleven thousand million dollars, contributed by the hard work of American fathers and mothers to aid Soviet barbarism and to help the Bolshevik dictator.

Well, had not a visionary written in his ignored prophecy? :

" The Western Jew will equip an army of twenty million men in the East to destroy Christianity and civilisation and to establish the Jewish world kingdom!"

The prophecy of Cassandra has come true and the evidence to prove the identity of the real war criminals has also been established.

Forrestal, who became American Secretary of War during Truman's Presidency, and who was probably killed by the sinister power that dominates the world, records his conversation with Joseph P. Kennedy in his well-known diary under the date of December 7th, 1945, Kennedy had been Roosevelt's Ambassador in Great Britain at the beginning of the last war. The entry in question reads:

" I played golf with Joe Kennedy to-day. I asked him about his consultations he had in 1938 with Roosevelt and with Neville Chamberlain. He thinks Chamberlain was convinced that Britain had no means to enable her to fight against Hitler. Therefore Chamberlain was not entertaining the idea of going to war against the Hitler régime. Kennedy's own view at that time was that Hitler's

Germany will be fighting against Russia without being later involved in war with Britain. William C. Bullitt (also of Jewish decent), Roosevelt's Ambassador to France in 1939, was pressing Roosevelt persistently to take the firmest possible stand against the Germans in the Polish question. Were it not for the ceaseless encouragements given from Washington, the English and French would never have made a *casus belli* out of the Polish question. Bullit maintained emphatically, said Kennedy, that the Germans will not fight. Contrary to this view Kennedy was of the opinion that the Germans will go to war promptly and that they might even overrun Europe. Chamberlain came to the conclusion—said Kennedy—that America and **world Jewry had driven Britain into the war!"**

Let us admit, therefore, that the real war criminals were never brought to trial at Nuremberg.

SEVEN

WHY HITLER HAD TO GO

COULD not all this be merely a nightmare of "anti-Semites"? Is it possible after all for a five- or six-per-cent racial minority to drive an immense country like the U.S.A. into war? Is it possible for the Soviet to fight side by side with the hated capitalists? Let us review the strength of this racial minority in the two giant countries. Let us begin with the Soviet Union since we know by now that her founders and leaders came mostly from the ranks of the world conquerors.

During the great purges the world conquerors sacrificed a few individuals from their ranks. But the places thus vacated were filled by others even more loyal to Stalin's dictatorship. Stalin's wife, Rosa Kaganovich, is the daughter of Lazarus Kaganovich, ex-Commissar of Soviet heavy industry. At the outbreak of war power in the Soviet Union was in the hands of the six members of the Kaganovich family and in those of the head of the secret police; Beria was also of Jewish descent. According to American reports, general conversation in Stalin's home was conducted in Yiddish, even up to quite recent times.

Many of the commissars have Jewish ideas. Molotov's wife is a Jewess, whilst Litvinov Finkelstein, ex-deputy commissar of foreign affairs, so capitalistic in appearance, was the visible link between the eastern and western halves of this tribal nationalism.

In 1935 Yeats Brown brought out his book *European Jungle,* and on page 181 we read that "in the Central Committee of the Communist Party, consisting of fifty-nine members, ninety-five per cent were Jews, i.e. 56 members while the other three members were married to Jewesses; Stalin, Labov and Ossinsky."

Sometimes Jews risk bragging about the power they exercise, for example, in the American *Jewish Chronicle* of January 6th, 1933 (page 19), we find the following:

"In Soviet Russia every third Jew is employed in an administrative capacity!"

91

This actually means that out of the three-and-a-half million Jews in Soviet Russia more than one million hold administrative offices in various key positions of the Bolshevik dictatorship. They are the most loyal, intelligent and fanatical supporters of the Bolshevik system. They become commissars, party leaders, loyal Soviets, provincial governors and senior officers, as well as commissars of the Army and of the N.V.D.

After the great purge ordered by Stalin at the end of 1936, the top rank officials of the forty Soviet Republics, i.e. the party secretaries who were holders of actual executive power, consisted of four Russians, two Armenians, one Georgian, one Buryat and forty-one Jews. (*World Service*, 1936, I 1.)

When in 1941 the European armies crossed the Soviet frontiers, they were shocked to find Soviet rule more Jewish in character than had been proclaimed even by Streicher's propaganda. Beginning at the Polish frontier, in all the provinces up to Stalingrad, Jews exclusively were the leaders of the towns, the commissars in charge of the collective farms and the chiefs of police. All Soviet commissars, all secret police officers and leading officials captured by the Germans belonged, without exception, to the same world-conquering race.

The High Command of the Soviet Army also contained many Jews, and in this connection we find the following quotation in a book entitled *The Hebrew Impact on Western Civilisation,* published in New York in 1951 by Dagobert Davis Runes:

" In the war fought against Hitler there were 313 Jews amongst the Soviet generals."

J. Zaltzman was in charge of the production of tanks, and Abraham Wikbosky controlled the arsenals and gun foundries of the Soviet Union. Mikoyan directed all war production and war contracts.

It is quite understandable, therefore, why these co-racialists tried to escape from the European troops when they had a chance to do so. But the Russian and Ukrainian populations could relate many appalling crimes committed by these people. The proofs are not far to seek. Any soldier serving on the Russian front can corroborate these facts by his own experience.

The fearful power exercised by more than half a million Jews thus kept the so-called Soviet system in being. The statement of certain propagandists that the Bolshevik system does not suit the Jews because they cling to private enterprise is simply ridiculous. Wherever Bolshevism was established Jewry promptly changed its commercial and industrial key positions for those of public office. Thus the grocer became the police officer and the shopkeeper a state official. The partisan of the first stage (of the *Protocols*) was thus transformed into the professional soldier of the second stage.

All this was known by a few Americans. Hamilton Fish, a congress-man of New York, as early as 1933 referred to the Jewish character of the Soviet, and certain data and figures were published in the Congressional Records of February 29th, 1933. According to these the Soviet Government, including the governments of the provinces, consisted of 503 members of whom 406 were Jews. Out of the twenty-three members of the local Soviet in Moscow, nineteen belonged to the race of the world conquerors. Among the forty-two editors and publishers of the official press were forty-one Jews, led by David Zaslavsky, editor, and Ilja Ehrenburg, publisher of *Pravda*.

Douglas Reed, the eminent English journalist, reported in 1938 that press consorship in Russia was firmly in Jewish hands, and that a certain Epstein controlled film production.

Whenever any connection between Jews and Bolsheviks is exposed, western propaganda readily points out that now and again anti-Semitic tendencies are to be observed in Russia. But the truth is that until the end of the Second World War, Soviet Russia was the only State in the world in which " anti-Semitism " was declared a crime by law and in which the " criminal " often suffered the death penalty. All this logically follows from the teaching of Lenin that : " ' Anti-Semitism ' is the means of counter-revolution." This tenet, in a reversed sense, is an open admission that Bolshevism is, in fact, a form of Jewish domination.

Louis Levine, President of the Jewish Council of Russian Relief, visited the Soviet Union *after* the Second World War, and wrote a series of articles under the title *Soviet Russia To-day,* in which he testifies to the greatness and unchangeability of this domination. He writes, among other things :

" Special concern for the Jewish people has characterised the Soviet Union since its birth in 1917. A week after Tsarism was overthrown, the infant Socialist Government, headed by Lenin, abolished national

93

oppression, making it the first country in the world to declare 'anti-Semitism' a crime."

He also mentions with pride that many famous surgeons, generals and top officials of the Soviet are Jews.

This same Levine in the course of a speech in Chicago on October 30th, 1946, while giving a full account of his visit to Soviet Russia, said:

" Many of the high-ranking Government officials in Russia are Jewish. Many other Jewish officials did not look Jewish but they spoke to me privately in Hebrew or Yiddish.

" The Jewish people are unanimous in their love for Stalin. They regard him as the greatest friend of the Jewish people. They attribute to his understanding of national minorities and to his leadership the new exalted status of Soviet Jews."

Jewish rule is the sacred legacy of Bolshevism. Referring to those Jews holding key positions in the Bolshevik system, Lenin himself said:

" The rôle of Jewry will be most important in laying the foundations of the new world order. Jewry possesses adaptable characteristics together with outstanding intelligence and extreme cruelty. A Russian could never treat Russian counter-revolutionaries as cruelly as a Jew can." (*Lenin, God of the Godless,* by F. Ossendowski.)

In the modern dictatorship everything is under the control of a hidden power! More precisely, under the control of the person or group wielding the tommy-gun. The foregoing statement and the frank testimony of a leading Jewish personality shows clearly that in the Soviet Union this absolute power, which is based on the activities of one million Jews in key positions, is actually the power exerted by Jewry over Soviet Russia.

A Jew is a Jew more than anything else, even when actively engaged in promoting the cause of Bolshevism. First and foremost he is a Jew and only afterwards is he a Bolshevik, just as he is a Jew primarily before becoming a champion of Democracy. He regards the establishment of Jewish power and security as a matter of supreme importance; only upon its achievement will he impart a Jewish character to Bolshevism or to Democracy, as the case may be. Therefore, it can be truthfully stated that in fact Soviet Russia is not under Bolshevik dictatorship but under Jewish dictatorship.

Bolshevism like liberal democracy serves only as an excuse and a cloak. From Jewry's point of view, Bolshevism represents a higher phase of the development of Jewish power than Democracy does. In a Democratic government the danger always exists that at some time clear-sighted statesmen or skilled demagogues might succeed in exposing the illegal hidden power and in unmasking its holders. Though Jewry may control nearly everything in Democracy, there remains, perhaps, a two per cent chance of losing everything. But in the Soviet Union there is not even a half per cent chance of this. For here the power in the hands of the Jews is absolute. The Russian people are reduced to the status of bondsmen, cannon-fodder and slave-labourers to the Jewish power.

But let us have a closer look at that liberal democracy which, when it entered the war, became the ally of Russia, thanks to the efforts of Roosevelt and his brains trust. Are the United States still the America of Washington, Lincoln, and Jefferson? Whilst the capture of power in Russia was achieved with the help of the tommy-gun, the same feat can be repeated in the case of liberal democracy also, only by different means. Here Jewish leadership can be materialised through the monopoly of the Press, of gold and of currency-control and by secretly influencing public life.

As we mentioned earlier, when America entered the Second World War, out of Roosevelt's seventy-two advisers, fifty-two were Jews. According to *The Hidden Empire*, eighty per cent of the national income of the United States is controlled by Jews. Behind Roosevelt there were all the great world bankers with a financial network covering the whole of the globe. When Roosevelt came to power the State Department and the key positions of the Government immediately began to be penetrated. Parallel with this penetration a great purge began in the ranks of the officers of the armed forces, as a result of which officers with " nazi " tendencies were sacked, i.e. those who probably would not be too enthusiastic to fight Roosevelt's war.

Robert Edward Edmondson in his book *I Testify* (page 46) paints an original picture of the Roosevelt administration, depicting it in the shape of the Magen-David (six-pointed star). In the middle of the star Roosevelt can be seen with his administration surrounded on four sides by L. D. Brandeis, Felix Frankfurter, Bernard M. Baruch and Henry Morgenthau Jr. On the six points of the star the following names are to be found, showing those who have actual power, those who, in fact, are running the Government of the United States:

1. Rabbi Wise, Sidney Hillman, Samuel Dickstein, Herbert H. Lehman, James P. Warburg, Samuel I. Roseman.
2. Dave Stern, Henry Horner, Louis Kirstein, David J. Saposs, E. A. Goldenweiser, Rabbi Samuel Margohes.
3. A. Cohen, Gerald Swope, Adolf J. Sabbath, Isidor Lubin Jr., Mordehai Ezekiel, Moissaye J. Olgin.
4. Samuel Untermayer, Benjamin J. Cardoso, F. H. La Guardia, Dave Dubinsky, Jerome Frank, Robert Moses.
5. A. Goldman, W. C. Bullitt, A. J. Altenmeyer, L. A. Steinhardt, Albert Einstein, Rose Scheiderman.
6. H. Feis Ben Cohen, Nathan Margold, Walter Lippman, David E. Lilienthal, William M. Leiserson.

This is a terrible power, when we remember that it was supported by the entire Press, all the editors of which were Jews, led by Arthur Hays Sulzberger and by the whole radio network under David Sharnoff and also by the Hollywood cinema propaganda industry with its ninety-five per cent Jewish majority, led by Adolf Zukor. Neither must we omit the various political labour factions and unions directed by Sidney Hillman, Dubinsky and similar people, nor the various courts of justice in which by this time Jews pass judgment over the descendants of the early pioneers. Closely associated with this power we find La Guardia, the Mayor of the greatest city in the U.S.A., and around him legions of Jewish Communists, as well as Herbert H. Lehman, the Jewish Governor of New York State. Then there are Einstein, Oppenheimer, Leo Szilard and Lilienthal, the high priests of the new Atomic Sect reinforced by revengeful masses of refugees from Germany, Italy, Spain, Hungary, Rumania, Czechoslovakia and Poland coming to occupy key positions in American war production. They contributed propaganda for the War Office, ninety-five per cent of which was imbued with a hatred akin to that found in the texts of the Old Testament.

From these positions they prepared a war of revenge from which mercy and decency were excluded, not to mention the chivalry of past ages. Thus they degraded the war to the level of a series of bestial massacres. By means of U.N.O. they prepared to exchange

American key positions for ministerial rank in the cabinet of the future world government. Ben Gurion and Chaim Weizman stood by in readiness to revive and to re-establish one of the main pillars of world rule—the State of Israel. They issued their orders to the soldiers of Washington, and replaced the White Cross insignia on the steel helmets of the American 6th Division with the Magen-David (six-pointed star). They ordered the bombing not only of Germany but of all the monuments of European culture. They delivered arms **to the Soviet Union and gave her eleven thousand billion dollars** out of the pocket of the American taxpayer.

This Jewish nationalism bears no ill-will towards the Soviet Union. But if Hitler should win, or if the Christian nations should make peace among themselves, then that would mean the end of world domination. But if the warriors of the two different phases follow the plans of the Elders of Zion and join forces, they will surely establish their rule. Then the capitalist and Bolshevik leaders of the same nationalism will dominate the world. This is a gigantic coalition of the ill-informed American population and the 200 million mass **of Soviet Russia's enslaved peoples.**

The Stalin-Ribbentrop pact was itself a snare to entrap Germany. The scruples and misgivings of the German General Staff, trained on the doctrines of Clausewitz against a war on two fronts, had to be dispelled. It was thus easier to bring the Germans into the Second World War, which was actually declared on them by the Jewish Congress as early as 1933. When Hitler later found himself in the war up to his neck, suddenly Molotov, the husband of the beautiful Karpovskaja, appears in Berlin and places on the table the Soviet demands. Those Jews who had temporarily vanished through the trap door of the Kremlin in August, 1939, all re-appear on the scene once more. Hitler now had a terrible war on his hands on many fronts.

Meanwhile the new immigrants poured into the United States demanding vengeance. Immigration had, by this time, become an exclusive Jewish right and privilege. The Jewish Synagogue in 1930 had an active membership of 4,081,242. But according to the World Almanac of 1949 this number must have increased quickly, since in 1947 membership was up to 4,770,647. Jews were now making up a considerable percentage of the yearly immigration figures. In 1936 this percentage was 17.21%, in 1937 22.59%, in 1938 29.07%, in 1939 52.35%, in 1940 52.21%, in 1941 45.83%, in 1942 36.86%, and in 1943 13.83%. These Jewish newcomers, immigrants from Eastern European countries, did not settle at the bottom of American society, they did not live the wretched life of refugees. On the contrary they were fitted into jobs in the American Press, in offices, politics and the film world.

They were no longer traders and businessmen. They were the carriers of that hatred, vengeance and Bolshevism which destroyed Holy Russia.

All that rottenness which in the first place had called National Socialism to life and caused the downfall of the Weimar Republic now became firmly re-settled in America where according to the book *The Iron Curtain over America,* the term " Fourth Reich " became the nickname for those districts overrun and occupied by immigrants who had fled from Hitler. Their voices were to be heard in the broadcasts on American radio networks; they spoke in ten or fifteen languages. Their articles were read by millions in the national papers. The humanitarian methods of American democracy were not satisfactory to these people. So they praised the Soviet in America and strained every effort to threaten the destruction of American democracy should it be reluctant to help the Soviet Union sufficiently. For them, the real friend and liberator was not America but the Soviet Union.

In the issue of the *New York Herald Tribune* of December 22nd, 1938, appeared a letter from Mrs. Sarah Finkelstein protesting against an earlier article, in which it was alleged that out of the 400,000 Jews of Chicago very few became members of the Communist Party. Sarah Finkelstein says in her letter that she had lived in Chicago for thirteen years and thus knew by experience that 98% of the 400,000 Jews of Chicago were all convinced Communists.

And now simultaneously, Nemesis on mankind proceeded from both New York and the Kremlin. It was the Jews' war and the peace would be theirs too.

" Whoever wins this war—we will be the real victors!"

EIGHT

THE REAL VICTORS OF
THE SECOND WORLD WAR

WHEN America entered the Second World War many people believed that the greatest democracy in the world was going to fight for the principles of the Atlantic Charter.* Lying propaganda deceived the eighty-three per cent majority of Americans against the war into believing that Bolshevism was the same as Democracy, that Soviet terrorism was freedom, and therefore that it was absolutely necessary to cross the ocean and save " humanity ".

A certain part of belligerent Europe was also taken in by this propaganda. Those who organised the resistance movements and those reluctant to enter the war on the side of the axis-powers were all hoping that Roosevelt would not let loose the pest of Bolshevism on Europe. Every superficial sign seemed to indicate that after all American Capitalism and Soviet Bolshevism could never be brought together into a lasting alliance. It seemed beyond all belief that American democracy was waging ideological war against the " German form " of dictatorship, in alliance with the most cruel dictatorship of all.

But this appearance was misleading. For supranational Jewish " nazism " was the real cohesive force of the alliance, that force which, as we already know, played such an important part in the Roosevelt administration as well as in the Soviet system of Stalin

---

* A document containing eight points drawn up by Mr. Winston Churchill and President Roosevelt on a warship in the Atlantic in August, 1941. Although a very important document since it declared the intentions of Britain and U.S.A., It remained informal and was not in fact signed (to obviate necessity for approval by the U.S. Senate). The eight points were briefly as follows: 1, No aggrandisement. 2, No territorial changes without wishes of the inhabitants. 3, Restoration of self-government to those deprived of it. 4, Access to trade and raw materials by all peoples. 5, Improvement of labour standards and social security. 6, Freedom from fear and want. 7, Right to traverse the high seas without hindrance. 8, Disarmament of aggressor nations pending permanent system of general security.

and Kaganovich. For those behind the scenes there was one war-aim only—the establishment of their absolute world-domination. If this cannot be achieved, then according to the ancient principles of "Divide et Impera!" the globe must be divided; the Eastern Hemisphere to be ruled by the tommy-gun and the Western Hemisphere by gold, but tommy-gun and gold are to be in the same hands. *One World!*

Is it not written in the holy book of the Jewish "Führer":

"And thou shalt consume all the people which the Lord thy God shall deliver to them. . . ." *(Deut. vii.* 16.)

Let us not forget that all-out warfare was not invented by modern strategists and that *Torah,* the *Mein Kampf* of the Jews, points the way of those fighting for the "One World" principle.

"But thus shall ye deal with them; ye shall destroy their altars, and break down their images, and cut down their groves, and burn their graven images with fire." *(Deut. vii.* 5.)

". . . ye shall destroy their altars!" The Atlantic Charter is to be perceived here with its shop-window propaganda, the text of which was written by Samuel Roseman according to *Time* magazine, August 18th, 1941. Let American boys believe they are fighting for higher ideals. But, say the *Protocols,* the real plans will be known by us to the exclusion of everybody else! *"Violence and Hypocrisy."* Though the Atlantic Charter is what we promised, it is not freedom we are preparing for the world but absolute and total servitude. We will tell the Germans that we want to eliminate the "nazis" only, but our plans are ready and we are going to put them into effect.

And so in 1941, even *before* America entered the war, certain plans by Maurice Gomberg were published relating to "A New World Moral Order for permanent peace and freedom" (Maurice Gomberg, Philadelphia, February, 1942). See page 104 of E. J. Reichenberger's book *Europa in Trümmern* ("Europe in Ruins"). This is shown on a map printed in Philadelphia. *It is the most incriminating evidence against those who dreamed of exterminating whole nations and races before America was even at war.*

The work is presented in such a way as to appear to be a draft of a world map after the Second World War, when the United States (meaning, by then, the Jewish world government) would take control of the whole world and would establish *the New World Moral order* to ensure lasting peace, freedom, justice and security and to carry out reconstruction.

According to the map, Canada, Greenland, the Azores and the Canary Islands, as well as innumerable smaller islands between Japan and Australia, belong to the U.S.A. as protectorates. Sumatra, Java and Borneo are annexed to the British Empire. *The frontiers of the Soviet Union extend from Vladivostok to Cologne and the Rhine is the western frontier of Bolshevism.* " Our frontiers are on the Rhine!" did not Roosevelt say? Poland, Czechoslovakia, Hungary, Yugoslavia and Rumania are shown as member states of the U.S.S.R.

This map is another shocking proof that the aim of world Jewry is to rob small nations of their independence and drive the whole world under the yoke of its reign of terror. Austria and Germany, coloured on this map in red, are put into " quarantine ". China appears to remain an independent state, but Iran is shown on the map as part of the Soviet Union. France, Italy, Belgium, Holland, Luxembourg, Switzerland, Spain and Portugal appear on the map as members of the new United States of Europe. But the accompanying explanatory notes are even more interesting than the map itself, as we learn from them that a new " world moral order " must be built up. In this new moral order Talmudic morals will have the upper hand. This is the despotism of the Jewish world state. " It is from us that the all-engulfing terror proceeds," say the *Protocols,* and the organisers of the new world order are here evidently listing everything they have dreamed of and wish to put into effect. It will be quite sufficient to expose here the most important points of these plans.

The Soviet Union, collaborating with the U.S.A. to preserve freedom (!) and peace, will obtain exclusive control over Austria and Germany, in order to " re-educate " these states and afterwards to annex them as equal members of the U.S.S.R.

After the war the Holy Land, known at present as Palestine, is to be united to Trans-Jordania and adjoining territories by " historical right ", as well as on the ground of the necessity of having a demilitarised independent Jewish Republic to facilitate the solution of the refugee problem. This Jewish territory is marked on the map as " Hebrewland ".

As to war criminals, there was as yet no Moscow declaration in existence, since, apart from the Bromberg Massacres, there was no knowledge of any war crimes. Nevertheless, American world Jewry was already proclaiming Nuremberg in advance. Clause number 30 on the map states: "The criminal perpetrators and their partners in guilt of this hideous war shall be brought to justice and unforgetable punishment administered."

The plans for the murder and deportation of whole nations were also ready and were put into effect at Potsdam where the schemes worked out by world Jewry as early as 1940 were obediently signed by the Allied nations.

We learn from the notes on the map that Japanese subjects as well as persons of Japanese origin and therefore of doubtful allegiance, *are to be expelled from the Western Hemisphere for ever.* They are similarly to be expelled from islands under U.S. protection. Their assets are to be confiscated and put towards the cost of post-war reconstruction. All Germans and Italian subjects, as well as persons closely associated to them, who spread nazi and fascist ideology, are to be treated likewise. (It is revealing that the Government of the U.S. is unable even to-day to refund the seized German assets of 300 million dollars.) German, Italian and Japanese immigration to the Western Hemisphere as well as to all islands under the protectorate of the U.SA. is to be stopped indefinitely.

Here world Jewry again reverts to the ancient commandments of Torah, which aim at securing undivided Jewish rule over the Western Hemisphere.

". . . thou shalt smite them, *and* utterly destroy them; thou shalt make no covenant with them, nor show mercy unto them." (*Deut. vii.* 2.)

For the purpose of cleansing the axis aggressors of military chauvinism, of smashing their military power, or *recovering booty* and of *re-ducating* them to return to the family circle of nations, states Clause 36 of the world plan, German, Japanese and Italian territories are to be put in quarantine for an indefinite duration of time and are to be administered by governors under the supervision of the United Nations.

Well, here we find foreshadowed well before the outbreak of war, events which actually took place after 1945! And have we not seen the payment of Reparations made by Western Germany to Israel, together with the occupation of much of Europe by the re-educators, C.I.C agents and the dismantlers of the attempted but frustrated, Morgenthau plan, and finally the governing on behalf of Jewry of European territories by Russian and American "stooges"?

The magnitude of Jewry's world conquest is demonstrated by the fact that of all the war aims and promises, including the Atlantic Charter, the only plans achieved were those above mentioned together with some small adjustments.

All raw materials and industrial production of territories under quarantine, continues Clause 37 of the world order, will be used for post-war reconstruction

Other clauses explain that all persons born in East Prussia or the Rhineland will be expelled from the occupied territories and their estates confiscated for reparations. For potential military reasons, a plan must be elaborated to control the birth-rate of the territories in quarantine and thus reduce the numerical strength of the aggressor nations.

This is the very first instance in the history of mankind that a nationalist minority has openly renounced a law of nature and proclaimed its intention of destroying other nations.

"And thou shalt consume all the people which the LORD thy God shall deliver thee. . . ." declares Torah.

This is the opportunity, therefore, to expatriate the people of East Prussia, the Rhineland and other eastern countries. Twenty-five million displaced Christians must be expelled from their native lands, birth-rate control must be introduced and the Morgenthau plan, which could bring about the starvation of forty per cent of the German population, must be put into operation.

Never can world Jewry efface these terrible murder charges. The more so, since it not only prepared the plans but, as we will see later, executed them too.

The Gomberg Massacre plan, backed by most powerful American-Jewish organisations, and its methods are not new. Several thousands of years ago Moses had prescribed for this tribal "nazism" how a war must be conducted, as well as how to make peace:

"And when the Lord thy God hath delivered it [the city] into thy hands, thou shalt smite every male thereof with the edge of the sword.

" But the women, and the little ones, and the cattle, and all that is in the city, *even* all the spoil thereof, shalt thou take unto thyself. . . ." (*Deut. xx.* 13-14.)

The Atlantic Charter is still on display in the shop window of promises.

Samuel Fried, the well-known Zionist and pacifist, during the early part of the 1930's, while still in the flush of the First World War victory, does not hide the mass-murderer psychosis which is to be found in the drafts of the later peace treaties.

" People dreading the revival of German power will never again see the restoration of Germany's military might. We will nip in the bud every effort to restore it and finally, should the danger persist, *we will destroy this nation hated by everybody, both by partition and also by dismembering the country, as well as by ruthless mass-murders."*

In 1934, Samuel Roth characterised the intense hatred later manifested in the propaganda and peace plans of the Second World War. In his book *Jews Must Live,* edited by the Golden Press Inc., he writes as follows:

" We are still the seed of Abraham, Isaac and Jacob. We mix with the nations under the pretext that we are fleeing from persecution, *we, the most ruthless persecutors whose cruelty is unmatched in the annals of the history of mankind."*

Before 1945 there was a widespread belief that the so-called " Bolshevik Jew ", being filled with resentment and bitterness, had no chance to become cultured and thus turned into a sadist directly he got a tommy-gun in his hand. " But the cultured western Jews are different," went the popular dictum. They were humanitarians and philanthropists who contributed generously to the Red Cross and towards the funds of free meal relief. Only the bloody terror of Mandel-Rothschild, the French Home Secretary, foreshadowed in 1940 the fate Europe could expect once these humanitarians returned to the Continent as victors.

This Mandel-Rothschild executed several hundreds of French people in the name of national unity, demanding resistance from every Frenchman against the German peril. Later, when the French front collapsed, Mandel-Rothschild was the first to flee from France.

But by this time his hands were covered with the blood of hundreds of French people.

His political conduct was the first revelation of the intense passion and animosity hidden under the Western Jew's cloak of culture and humanity.

When at the beginning of the Second World War the voice of the Western press and radio became savagely distorted and slogans of a "humanitarian" world were broadcast (such as: "Make the Germans eat arsenic!" by a U.S. Columnist), evidence multiplied to show that this was no longer a warlike spirit, still less one of the Geneva Convention, but one of sheer murder. It is extraordinary to hear men of high intellectual capacity, such as writers, university professors and publicists, all suddenly speaking in the middle of the twentieth century the language of Old Testament prophets inciting to murder. It is a shock to realise that in the security of freemasonic lodges, " democratic editorial offices " and Zionist associations, books, articles, essays and political speeches are conceived and written, all proclaiming murder. These are not the unavoidable casualties of war but murders and cruelties planned for the ensuing peace.

Th. Nathan Kaufman, in his book *Germany Must Perish* (edited at Newark, see p. 104), wrote as early as 1941 that after the war Germany must be completely dismembered. Kaufman demanded that *the German population, both male and female, surviving the aerial bombings, be sterilised in order to secure the total extinction of the German race.*

The same hatred flares up in Maurice Leon Dodd's book *How Many World Wars* (New York, 1942), in which the author proclaims that no Germany and no German race must be left after this war. Charles G. Haertman in his book *There Must be no Germany after War* (New York, 1942), also demands the physical extermination of the German people. Einzig Palil, a Canadian Jewish writer, in his book *Can we Win the Peace?* (London, 1942), takes a similar stand demanding the dismembering of Germany and the total demolition of German industry. Ivor Duncan, another Jewish writer, in his article *Die Quelle des Pan-Germanismus* which appeared in the March, 1942, issue of *Zentral Europa Observer,* demanded the sterilisation of forty million Germans. He estimated the total cost of his scheme to be five million pounds sterling.

Douglas Miller, writing in the *New York Times* in 1942, states that seventy million Germans are too many. Exports and imports must therefore be so regulated that more than forty million Germans will starve.

In the library of the American House in Munich, on page 456 of an American book entitled *Joy Street,* by Keyes, written for the greater glory of overseas propaganda, we read:

" As Major David Salamon said:

' Could I have had the chance to choose my job in this war, I should have picked the same task I was actually assigned. Right through France, right into Germany *to destroy everything.* Never in history has there been such a war. *I am glad that I can tell my grandchildren that I was there and took part in the revenge. I thank God for this.*

' When finally we reached Germany we began to destroy and devastate everything. Then I realised that this was what I was waiting for, this was what I was living for. *My only regret is that I was unable to destroy and kill more as we had not much time left for it.* When we reached Wiesbaden our tempo became slower for there was nothing left we could attack, bomb or kill. We made such a perfect job that we had to stop for a while.' "

These are the " Atlantic Charters " of the ambitious men who are seeking to bolshevise the world and to destroy the nations, and they have been, to a great extent, realised. Thus the great vision of the *Protocols* lives through the war. At times it may appear to be sheer propaganda. But barbarism is contagious and eventually responsible officials are infected with it.

Behind Morgenthau, Harry Dexter White and other champions of culture drew up plans for the total destruction of Germany. The Atlantic Charter may promise freedom but the proposals of the world federalists are ready too. These are the dreams of the same unique supranational " nazism ". To abolish all national frontiers together with the freedom and independence of the nations and to establish world government—precisely as prescribed by the *Protocols.*

" In place of the rulers of to-day we shall set up a bogey which will be called the Super Government Administration. Its hands will reach out in all directions like nippers and its organisation will be of such colossal dimensions that it cannot fail to subdue all the nations of the world." (*Protocol* V.)

There is little doubt that the commands of the *Protocols* were obeyed by the United World Federalists during the war when they submitted proposals for a world government. These proposals were the exact opposite of those principles laid down in the Atlantic Charter.

" The nations must surrender their sovereignty to a world government because the age of independent nations is over," emphasised Robert Hutchins, Chancellor of the University of Chicago. " All armies, fleets, air forces and atomic bombs must be under the world government. The Panama Canal, Gibraltar, Okinawa, the Dardanelles, Aden, Singapore and the Kiel Canal must all be under the administration of the world government. The laws of immigration and citizenship must be abolished. A world court and a world bank must be established. The world government must be formed.

" The most important thing is to destroy that dangerous perversion called patriotism."

One world! One world government consisting of the fifty-two Jewish advisers of Roosevelt's brains trust. In the place of patriotic independent countries, there will remain but one country, a country belonging to the world conquerors. There will be one patriotism only: that of Jewish world nationalism.

Not only Jews take part in this feverish planning. Behind them are Fabian socialists, the freemasonic lodges, and even certain sects of the Protestant Church.

Only some time later did we learn from the investigations of the McCarthy committee as well as from John T. Flynn's book *The Road Ahead*, how powerful a certain sect of American Protestantism had grown during the Second World War, which *saw in the Bolshevik system the fulfilment of certain of Christ's ideals.* This was the same sort of aberration which bemused the Christian world about seven hundred years ago, when told of Genghis Khan's conquests. But the rumour spread that in the East a great Christian empire had arisen, not the empire of the Mongols but that of " Prester John ". He, it was said, ruled Christ's earthly kingdom which would be soon established in Europe thus fulfilling the ideals of Christendom.

This was one of the superstitions of the Middle Ages, whereas the rumour connected with the Soviet was nothing else but carefully planned propaganda originating from freemasonic lodges and Jewish circles. Marxists infiltrated into the ranks of the Council of Churches in America and started to spread the remarkable theory of " God's Kingdom ". According to Dr. Jones, America represents " best quality " in individualism, whilst Russia stands for " best quality " in collectivism.

But this " Kingdom of God " is not the Kingdom of Christ, which is " not of this world ". *It is the Kingdom of Jehovah, the Empire of Old Testament " nazism ".* This is the Kingdom of David foretold by the *Protocols* and represents absolute and unchallenged rule over the whole globe.

But many, many battles, much bloodshed, scheming and aerial bombing are required to achieve this. For though bloodstained and bombed, Europe still stands between Western and Eastern " co-operative " man, between the Western and Eastern Jew.

". . . Ye shall destroy their altars, and break down their images, and cut down their groves, and burn their graven images with fire." (*Deut. vii.* 5.)

The target of the bombing was by this time no longer German National Socialism but the Munich Pinakothek, the houses of the workers and the Monastery of Monte Cassino where the Christian culture of Europe was born. The two thousand years of Christianity were the target now, together with its symbol—Christ's Crucifix—which was spat upon by the Polish grandfathers of Morgenthau while passing over the plains of Poland. (Jan & Jerome Tharraud: *In the Shadow of the Crucifix.*)

It can be proved that Jewry thwarted all efforts during the Second World War to reach an armistice and establish peace and understanding. Roosevelt's brains trust was behind the demand for unconditional surrender, and by his own personal appearance at Casablanca, Morgenthau forced Roosevelt to be uncompromising in demanding it. *By this move Jewry succeeded in prolonging the war for two more years.*

Even were there no proofs of Jewry's aspirations, the notorious Morgenthau plan would still remain as an eternally incriminating document. It could not be proved, even in Nuremberg, that it was the intention of the Hitler régime to annihilate Jewry. Nevertheless

Jewry, in its blind thirst for revenge, wished to destroy forty per cent of the ninety million Germans.

The Morgenthau plan is a grandiose, undeniable historical proof of this. Jewry wished in cold-blooded premeditation to murder an entire nation. It is characteristic that the full details of this plan were never published in America. Perhaps this would have been too much even for American public opinion. But the plans of Mr. Morgenthau, Secretary of the Treasury in Roosevelt's administration, aimed at depriving Germany of her industry and of all means of livelihood; even the growing of sugar beet was forbidden!

"We will turn Germany into a pastoral country!" stated Morgenthau's broadcasting service.

The Quebec Agreement is another undeniable proof of this in writing:

"The purpose of this programme is to transform Germany into a mainly agricultural and nomadic state." (William L. Newman, *Making the Peace,* 1941-1945, page 73.)

Who is Morgenthau? McFadden, an American Congressman, had this to say of him in Congress on January 24th, 1934:

"Through marriage he is connected with Herbert Lehman, Jewish Governor of New York State, and through marriage or in some other way he is in relationship with Seligman, owner of the great international banking firm of J. & W. Seligman, who during a Senate investigation was proved to have attempted to bribe a foreign government. Morgenthau is related to Lewinsohn, the international Jewish banker, and also to the Warburgs who together control Kuhn, Loeb & Co., the International Acceptance Bank and the Bank of Manhattan, and have, besides, many other financial concerns and interests both at home and abroad. These bankers caused a shortage of three thousand million dollars in the U.S. Treasury and they still owe this sum to the Treasury Department and to the U.S. taxpayers. Morgenthau is also connected with the Strauss family and is either related to or connected with various other members of the Jewish banking world in New York, London, Amsterdam and other large financial centres."

During the great financial crisis Morgenthau was Under-Secretary to the Treasury. When Roosevelt ordered him to raise the price of gold to $35 per fine ounce, he obeyed with alacrity. And in the evening he made the following entry in his diary:

" Had the public understood how we fixed the price of gold they would have received a considerable shock."

Morgenthau suggested that Roosevelt should buy up 100 million ounces of silver above the current price, in order to capture the goodwill of senators representing the " silver states " of the U.S. and thus score Roosevelt's victory at the next Presidential elections. Whilst such a use of the taxpayers' money meant splendid business for the family group of the Morgenthau banking houses and also promoted the Presidential re-election of Roosevelt, it brought 450 million Chinese and 350 million Indians into a desperate economic plight. In China, as well as in India, silver is the only metal from which coins are minted, and the price of silver due to the above purchases rose higher and higher. After Roosevelt's silver buying transaction, China could export only by selling her products one-third cheaper than previously, and consequently her population suffered more from starvation than before. At that time whole provinces joined the camp of Mao-Tse-Tung, the Communist leader.

Morgenthau is, therefore, only second to Bernard Baruch as the most powerful leader of Jewry. He is supported by the press, the banking world and nationalist masses of the world conquerors, who are unanimous in their fervour and admiration for him. What Morgenthau does is done with the full approval of the whole of Western Jewry and he is supported by Eastern Jewry as well. Some time later, in the Press Club of Hamburg, Christopher Ennel, the well-known American radio commentator, made some very interesting disclosures about the origin of the Morgenthau plan. During the treason trials of Alger Hiss, it was shown that the Morgenthau plan was worked out by the Communists with the help of the Soviet Union.

Only after the McCarthy investigations was it possible to clarify the real facts.

Behind Mr. Morgenthau, the Western Jewish banker, there was another dark figure, Harry Dexter White, Assistant Under-Secretary of the U.S. Treasury Department. The latter was born in America, but his parents came from Russia, the land of pogroms, and so brought with them all the fanaticism and hatred of Eastern Jews. Later, as one of the directors of the International Monetary Fund appointed by President Truman to represent the U.S.A., he became one of the chief members of the spy ring working for the Soviet under the direction of Nathan Gregory Silvermaster, a government official in an executive capacity, appointed by Roosevelt. He was the author of the notorious Morgenthau plan. Morgenthau, who was then Secretary of the Treasury, took it with him to the famous Quebec Conference.

The memoirs of Cordell Hull (American Secretary of State, 1933-44) testify what this double-faced tribal nationalism intended to do. According to Cordell Hull " the Morgenthau plan aimed at the massacre, enslavement and liquidation of the German people."

" Shorty after the return of the President," writes Cordell Hull, " I told him angrily that the Morgenthau plan contradicts common sense and could never be adopted by the U.S. Government. I told him that the plan would wipe out Germany from the face of the earth for ever, whilst forty per cent of her population would starve to death as the land can feed only sixty per cent of her population."

The war propaganda was first concentrated on the necessity of defeating the " Nazis ". But when the Jews thought they had won the war, they wished to exterminate the whole nation.

At that time no Jew pointed out that the principle of collective punishment might, like the proverbial boomerang, return to strike the thrower.

When the Morgenthau plan was completed Jewry was able to repeat:

" The emblem of our people, the symbolic serpent, has closed its coils again! We are the nation wielding the power of a victorious ' nazism '. Winston Churchill, the Premier of the victorious British Empire, is still at Quebec. Possibly he still represents the real England and, at any rate, it was he who, in 1920, wrote a spirited ' anti-Semitic ' article, and whose better conscience is still in arms to prevent the peace that follows the war being turned into vengeance.

" This Churchill has no idea what everlasting hatred feels like. He still fondly believes that England has won the war, therefore we will show him that there is no real power or real victor any more in the Christian world which has been ruined in this fratricidal war, except ourselves, the people of Morgenthau! And should he be reluctant to believe it, then he too must be made acquainted with the might of Judah."

During the Quebec Conference, Morgenthau pointed the knife of Shylock at Churchill's breast.

He could either accept the Morgenthau plan or let Britain go bankrupt. He must either support Jewry's revenge, in which case Britain would receive a 6,500 million dollar loan, or else he must announce national bankruptcy—and that even before the war was over.

"What else do they want from me? Do they expect me to sit up and beg like a dog?" asks the old British stalwart indignantly.

But at his side sits the atom physicist, Lord Cherwell, his good friend, whose original name was Lindemann and who is of the same blood as Morgenthau. And he explains to Churchill that he has no choice but to accept the terms, so great by now is the victory of Morgenthau's nation—world Jewry.

Are all these things nightmarish dreams of Sadducees or are they plans of twentieth-century writers, publicists and statesmen? Are these people in consultation politicians or sadists? How the " peace " was prepared is told by the pro-Red Richard B. Scandrette, one of the members of the American Reparations Commission. His account was recorded in Congressional Records (June 7th, 1945):

" Germany will not exist any longer, only German provinces under Russian, American or British colonial governments. In these the living standards will be lowered to the level of the concentration camps and exile territories of Siberia. All classes of Germans will be ruthlessly forced down to the same level. As a final solution these territories will be governed by a Reparations Committee of the United Nations, and this Committee will decide how many Germans are needed in each of the provinces to secure the standard of minimum agricultural production. All German males not needed for this scheme are to be conscripted into compulsory labour battalions and sent to America or Soviet Russia, especially to those regions of Russia destroyed during the war.

" No regard is to be paid in the enslavement to the education, family connections, or dependent wives or children of the German deportees.

" No exemptions to be made of the clergy either. *Full under-*

standing was reached between America and the U.S.S.R. regarding the question of religion in Eastern Europe. The Russian Orthodox Church, after regaining the favour of the Kremlin, will be the ' official ' religion in the Baltic republics, Poland, Eastern Germany, Roumania, Bulgaria and Hungary. *The Roman Catholics will be cut off from Rome."*

" *The Society for the Prevention of World War III* ", the most fanatically Old Testament organisation of Morgenthau, especially demanded that the revengeful clause relating to the dismembering of Germany be carried out. All Germans should be expelled from neutral countries. American businessmen should be given no visa to visit Germany. For the next twenty-five years no German person may receive any visa to visit America. Marriage with German women is to be forbidden and German women may not enter the U.S.A. *Postal communication with Germany is not to be restored.*

All these stipulations were signed not by dictators, but by such brave champions of freedom as F. W. Foerster, Julius Goldstein, Isidor Lischütz, Emil Ludwig, Erich Mann, Cedrik-Forster, E. Amsel Mowre, Guy Emery, Shipler, W. E. Shirer, and Louis Nizer —

But they were not Bolsheviks. They were all civilised men of the Western World. That Jewry planned all this is proved, not only by the quotations above, but also by the German people themselves who saw this too and fought so fanatically against it.

" It is through me that kings reign," proclaims *Protocol* V. And in Quebec the *subdued* Churchill bows before Eastern and Western world power, before the earthly god, the power of gold.

"The new world state can now come. Now the glorious day of the ' Kingdom of God ' is at hand.

" Behold! From the East our victorious Bolshevik armies are attacking a rapidly shrinking Europe. There they are: Vienna, Budapest, Berlin and Breslau in flames. In a single night more than 300,000 East civilian refugees perish amid the downpour of bombs from our ' Liberators '. In our ' humanity ' we scatter graphite powder in the air. The air is burning. Mothers and their children are stifled. We fulfil Jehovah's commandment.

" ' *The graven images of their gods shall ye burn with fire . . . ye shall cut down their groves . . . and shall destroy them with a mighty destruction, until they be destroyed.'*

" Under a burning firmament our soldiers are attacking. They are the almond-eyed Mongolians and the semi-savage people of Turkestan and Central Asia with American tommy-guns in their hands and American rubber boots on their feet. Behind them come the American Sherman tanks. They are coming to liberate our future rulers from the concentration camps, to release our brothers!"

And Jews breaking out from the barbed wire enclosures of concentration camps embrace Soviet soldiers, quite understandably and with delirious joy:

" These are our liberators!"

And Europe, reduced in part to ashes and smouldering ruins, looks out from the debris and from the cellars to see Soviet Commissars, and the arrival of the Morgenthau boys in the wake of the American Army.

Europe scarcely dares to heave a sigh as she watches the real victors of the Second World War.

NINE

"REVENGE IS OURS"

ON May 9th, 1945, the revenge of Jehovah was turned loose over Europe. The 'planes of the British and American Air Forces were still called "liberators", but Eisenhower announced:

"We are not coming here as liberators *but as conquerors.*"

But were the Americans, in fact, the real victors? In the wake of the advancing American forces a sinister fifth column followed, the members of which in ninety-nine per cent of cases were not Americans. This revengeful army was made up of emigrants from Eastern European countries, of black-market operators from Brooklyn ghettos, of Czech, Polish and Hungarian Jews who took refuge in London and of criminal inmates from the liberated concentration camps. They filled all major and minor posts in the C.I.C., organised according to the Morgenthau plan; they swarmed in the O.S.S., in the various commissions searching for war criminals, as well as in the American security organisations. They became mayors of German towns and commandants of P.O.W. camps. They administered La Guardia's U.N.R.R.A. They occupied key positions in the American forces and thus exercised control over them.

There were only 2,524 German war criminals on the original list of the U.N., but soon the C.I.C. and the American conquerors were conducting a search for one million German "war criminals". At first the Soviets wanted to shoot 50,000 Germans summarily, then they proposed to bring 200,000 "war criminals" to trial at Nuremberg.

Simultaneously, the conquering flood began to move eastwards. A mass of several hundred thousand released from the concentration camps surged towards Poland, Hungary, Roumania and Yugoslavia, to become officers in the Communist police forces and other terror organisations and to assume judicial powers in the people's tribunals and so be able to pass sentence upon innocent people in an orgy of revenge. They were welcomed with open arms by the Soviet M.V.D.

who were in control of the Eastern European countries. The pattern was everywhere the same. In the forefront there was either an American, a Soviet or a French general but in each case *a Jewish deputy dogged his heels.*

Actually, Europe did not fall under the Russians, British or Americans, but *under Jewish occupation.* Everything that had rightly or wrongly belonged to Europe for 2,000 years now disintegrated. The avengers continued doing (but more cruelly) the very things they had set down as crimes against Hitler. This was no occupation by the forces of American democracy or Bolshevism but by those of a victorious Jewish nationalism glowing with hatred. Ensconced in key positions among the occupying powers, they were able to punish everyone, whether innocent or guilty. In their eyes there was but one crime—to have opposed, or to be in a position to oppose, *Jewish nationalism.*

To be a Jew in Europe became a greater privilege than any enjoyed by even reigning princes of the Middle Ages. The railway stations were guarded by special Jewish police and an identity check of Jews could be carried out by Jewish police only. They received their food ration cards without queueing. For a while, immediately after the war, only Jews received travelling passes, thus securing for themselves free movement and the unrestricted monopoly of the black market. In the refugee camps they were the chief caterers for U.N.R.R.A. as well as the privileged beneficiaries of this relief. Thus, they snatched the best rations from Poles, Ukrainians and Czechs, their former fellow-prisoners in the concentration camps. At the same time, on the roads, military policemen overturned cans and spilled milk to deprive German children and hospital patients of their diet. In German cities, working-class families were turned out of their homes by the tens of thousands, thus rendering vacant the nicest workers' settlements. The victims had to leave behind everything — furniture, kitchen equipment and cooking utensils, clothing and even linen, thus forcing the German people to recompense three times over in the form of Wiedergutmachung (reparations) the actual value of the goods confiscated from the Jews. Uniformed Zionist guards were posted at camp gates and, at first, for a while, even the Military Police of the victorious American Army could not enter Jewish camps. Victorious Jewish nationalism was granted

116

similar rights in the East, in Slovakia, in some parts of Roumania, in Hungary and Bohemia. They took possession of the flats and furniture of the Gentiles, occupied key positions in government offices and in editorial posts of the national press. Concurrently, former Jewish journalists returned to Germany and took complete charge of the newspapers of the occupied zones, and began to incite revenge upon the German nation on its own soil.

" It is from us that the all-engulfing terror proceeds . . ." wrote the Protocols fifty years ago. And now, backed by Soviet and American arms, the most dreadful terror descended on Europe, often without the Americans and English being aware of it. Hitlerism and the war was finished with but neither peace nor law and order or justice or democracy were restored.

The Western and Eastern Jew set out hand-in-hand to liquidate the Christian upper classes who had succeeded in escaping to the West from Bolshevism. These were considered unreliable people. Vlassow's Cossacks, for instance, wanted to fight against Bolshevism. But whoever resists Bolshevism is actually fighting one section of the Jewish world-kingdom. These Cossacks knew very well who were the commissars of the collective farms (kolkhoz) before whom the Russian peasant had to go down on his knees. In 1940 they had seen the " Russian " M.V.D. entering Latvia, Estonia and Lithuania and thus knew the Jews almost exclusively organised the deportation of tens of thousands of unfortunate people from these small Baltic states. These people were dangerous because *they had witnessed certain things. These witnesses must be slain!*

How can one account for the fate of Vlassov's Cossacks otherwise than by Jewish nationalism operating behind the visible power. How else could such inhumanity be accounted for when British democracy allowed armed military police to deploy against thousands of unarmed Cossacks.

" I was calling on Vlassov," writes Laszlo Gaal, a Hungarian journalist, " when a lieutenant wearing a German uniform and whose forehead was bathed in blood, burst into the small country cottage and reported direct to the general standing amongst his three staff officers :

"'Sir, everything is lost! We are to be handed over to the Bolsheviks!'"

You who are reading this book did not see the P.O.W. camp with its fourteen feet high wire fencing and its wooden barracks. You never heard that cry of despair when the white-belted and white-helmeted military police came to hand the Cossacks over. Tear gas bombs had to be thrown into every room. The Cossacks hurriedly knotted their shirts into ropes to hang themselves before the military police could force its way in. They barricaded the doors, then broke in the windows and fought for every piece of broken glass in order to cut open their veins. Old friends tried to cut each other's throats. Those unable to die this way tore off their shirts, offering their bared breast, shouting: " Shoot here, for I am not going back to Soviet Russia." (*Pittsburgi Magyarsag,* July 2nd, 1954.) (Also *Magyarok Utja,* edited in Argentina.)

The clamour of the same executioners was heard throughout Europe from the English Channel to the Black Sea. It was not nazism that had to be liquidated now, but *the leaders of the Christian nations irrespective of political creed or party.*

Those who rounded up " war criminals " by the ten thousand and tortured both guilty and innocent in their jails were, almost exclusively, Jews. The commandants, captains and secret agents in the jails for " war criminals " at Salzburg and other places, as well as in the notorious Marcus Camp were, almost without exception, Jews dressed in American uniform. According to a Jugoslav refugee who had been in the camp at Klagenfurt, its British Commandant, who handed over " war criminals " and compelled them by force to return to Communist dictatorship, proudly put a notice on his desk sporting the inscription " I AM A JEW!"

The Jews handed patriots over to the gallows and to the common grave. They handed over 100,000 gallant soldiers of the Croatian Army to the partisans of Tito and to Mojse Pijade, who summarily executed them all.

The caves and abandoned trenches of Slovenia were utilised as common graves. Vlassov is a symbolic figure in this great tragedy, in the slaughter of millions. He was the last person capable of rallying an army of several million men under his flag against the Stalinist dictatorship. So, naturally, this symbolic personality was handed over by the Western democracies to the Bolshevik terror régime. To the Jew, Lavranti Beria, was given the pleasing task of organising

Vlassov's public execution in Moscow. And because all this happened with the approval of America, *an incurable wound was inflicted on the soul of Europe.*

Everything that took place in Eastern Europe can, perhaps, be explained away by the cruelty of the Bolsheviks, although we know very well that the agents of Jewish nationalism were its real instigators. At the end of the war the casualties of the German Reich amounted to 8,300,000 dead. 3,300,000 German soldiers were killed in action; more than 2,500,000 of these in the fight against Bolshevism. 1,200,000 civilians, amongst them many women and children, were killed in air raids. More than 1,400,000 men perished or were murdered in captivity by the Eastern and Western allies, mostly in Soviet P.O.W. camps. 2,400,000 Eastern Germans were butchered by the Soviet occupation forces invading East Prussia, or killed by an aerial warfare blindly extended to include the civilian population. To all these things hypocrites can retort: " Well, after all, this is what is called total and all-out war!" But nobody could explain away by referring to " total war " what happened in Czechoslovakia on the day of the armistice. When the last Wehrmacht units left Prague, Jewish Communists, led by Slansky-Salzman, returned from Moscow to the Czech capital where they proceeded to gather together the revengeful ex-prisoners of Hitlers concentration camps—the " liberating " partisans.

" The Czech Communists made very clever use of those unfortunate Jews," wrote *Vilag* on March 15th, 1953, " who came out of the extermination camps half dead. They put these Jews in charge of the expatriation of Sudeten-Germans and Hungarians. The idea was not at all new as Lavranti Beria did the same when he used Polish and Ukrainian Jews to hunt down the Ukrainian and Polish ' anti-Semites ', i.e. those who *could be supposed* to have collaborated with the Nazis."

And because they believed that this supposition could be extended to include nearly everybody, they began a campaign of revenge unprecedented in the history of mankind.

When Edward Benes, the great humanitarian, the " bel espirit " and master of freemasonry, entered Prague on Sunday, May 13th, 1945, German citizens were burned alive in his honour in St. Wenceslas Square. (Document No. 15 concerning the expulsion of the Sudeten Germans.) Many Germans were hung up by their feet from the big advertising posters in St. Wenceslas Square, then when the great humanitarian approached their petrol-soaked bodies were set on fire to form living torches.

Six hundred thousand Sudeten Germans were killed during the massacres in the earthly hell of the death camps of Czechoslovakia. The Sudeten German White Paper records these horrors with full details on more than 1,000 pages, horrors for which there is no precedent in the history of mankind. Armed Czech women and Jewesses continued hitting the womb of expectant mothers with truncheons until a miscarriage followed, and in one single camp ten German women died daily in this way. (Document No. 6.) In another camp, the inmates were forced to lick up the bespattered brains of their fellow-prisoners who had been beaten to death. German prisoners were forced to lick up infectious faeces from the underwear of their fellow-prisoners suffering from dysentery. (Document No. 17.) The Czech and Jewish doctors refused all medical aid to German women raped by the Russians. Hundreds of thousands died by these means or sought salvation in suicide, as, for instance, in Brno (Brun), where on a single day 275 women committed suicide.

Naturally, the Western "humanitarian" press, the American radio network and the B.B.C. commentators took good care never to mention these facts, although they themselves were in the first place responsible for this campaign of revenge to which they instigated the members of their own nations. They were thus guilty of poisoning the soul of Christendom by the hatred they induced.

But Czechoslovakia was not the first state where horrors of this type occurred. Anna Rabinovich Pauker returned to Roumania as early as August, 1944, and under the orders of the Eastern Jews who arrived with her, massacres began there too.

According to authentic Bulgarian emigrant sources, 30,000 members of the professional classes were murdered in the trail of the invading Soviet armies by Bulgarian "proletarians", led by those "ladines" whose forefathers had been expelled from Spain by Catholic Ferdinand. Similarly, in Belgrade and Southern Hungary the name of Mojse Pijade is connected with bloody "purges" the victims of which were Serbian intelligentsia, prosperous German settlers and the most intelligent Hungarian peasantry. When, in October, 1944, the German and Hungarian armies left the territories of Yugoslavia and Southern Hungary an unprecedented wave of mass-murders broke over the unprotected population. Thirty thousand Hungarians, mostly peasants and smallholders, died in this bloodshed, under the savage terror régime of Mojse Pijade's partisans. The Katyn Wood murders are a modest, amateurish effort in comparison with it. According to documentary proof in our hands, Hungarians, Germans and Croatians alike, died slow and horrible deaths wracked with agony. Besides the 30,000 Hungarians, nearly 200,000 Germans died in the death camps of the " liberators ", where powdered glass was mixed with the children's food and where with the finesse of Chinese executioners those to perish in the biological class-warfare were despatched, in order that their places as civic leaders and police officers could be taken by the revengeful representatives of Jehovah.

In this classic age of race murder, the case of Hungary is quite extraordinary. This unfortunate nation, even in its dismembered state after the 1920 Parish treaties, had provided 560,000 Jews with peaceful and safe homes. The Hungarian nation did not take vengeance on Jewry even after the first Communist dictatorship of Bela Kun in 1919-1920, despite the fact that Jews, almost exclusively, were the commissars and leaders of this Communist régime.

During the era between the two World Wars, 1,100,000 acres were owned by Jews out of a total of 9,000,000 acres of arable land. A Jewish minority of six per cent possessed fifty-one per cent of house property in Budapest, thirty per cent of the total national income and twenty-five per cent of the total national assets. When, after the German occupation, the state authorities listed the property and assets of Jewry amassed in less than a hundred years, it was estimated that it possessed the equivalent of nineteen wagon loads of gold, silver and jewels, whilst the total gold reserve of the Hungarian National Bank could have been loaded into twelve wagons easily. Later, *the American authorities returned all this amassed wealth to Jewry.*

As late as 1943, Hungary was the last refuge of the Jews in Europe. Despite this, when the war was over and the country overrun by Stalin's hordes, the revengeful spirit of the Old Testament inflicted horrors on the innocent Hungarian people without precedent in the history of mankind. Under the protection of Soviet bayonets the Muscovite emigrants returned, all of them Jews without exception.

Closely behind them followed many thousands of young Maccabbees, released unharmed from the labour divisions of the " fascist " régime. They soon became terrorist colonels and police officers of the M.V.D., as well as party secretaries and police chiefs of the provincial cities. From the ghettos of Budapest 200,000 Jews were released almost without loss — Jews whom the Hungarian nazis had been unwilling to hand over to the Germans.

One million Hungarian women were raped by the Russian Bolshevik troops, usually led by Jewish commandants. Six hundred thousand prisoners of war, as well as 230,000 civilians, were dragged off to extermination camps in the Soviet Union. At the most modest estimate, 500,000 people were murdered by the Jews in the cells of 60, Andrassy-ut, Budapest, in internment camps or in the open streets. All the characteristic features of *biological class-warfare* can be distinguished in this campaign of revenge. The Hungarian middle classes, the intellectuals and the national leaders had to be slain so that their places could be taken by another middle-class by the Jews! And, moreover, those who presided as judges in the revolutionary tribunals were almost all Jews.

In Western Europe, a Hungarian-born " American ", Colonel Martin Himmler, directed the campaign of vengeance against 300,000 Hungarians who escaped from the Bolsheviks. Was this man a Communist? Or was he an American democrat? At all events, in its issue of April 30th, 1954, the *Uj Kelet* (New Orient), a Zionist Tel-Aviv paper, let the cat out of the bag — he was neither; he was a Jew!

. In the commentary reviewing Martin Himmler's work and career he is highly praised as one who came forward to " revenge the shedding of innocent Jewish blood ".

One wonders whether Cardinal Mindszenty was also " a Hungarian nazi murderer " who during the war rescued and protected persecuted Jews, and who after the war tried to protect and rescue persecuted Christians. Cardinal Jozsef Mindszenty was not a victim of the Communist terror but of racial revenge, because he had demanded an amnesty for tens of thousands of tortured Hungarians during the great massacres and gruesome pogroms directed against Christians.

Jozsef Mindszenty in his earlier capacity as Bishop of Veszprem, vehemently opposed the Hungarian Nazi Government of the day.

He rescued Jews whom the Germans wanted to deport by giving them Papal safe conduct passes. After the Szalasi Government came to power he protested against continuing the fighting. In the end the Hungarian Nazi Government was compelled to intern him at Sopronkohida as an enemy of the Germans and the greatest protector of Jewry.

Shortly after that the tables were turned. The armies of the Soviet barbarians occupied Hungary. Jozsef Mindszenty was released from captivity at Sopronkohida and, as Archbishop of Hungary, rapidly became one of the leading constitutional figures.

Whatever his private political views may have been, he felt that, as a Catholic and leading exponent of Christianity, it was his duty to protect Hungarians against Jewish persecution, just as he had protected Jews against German persecution. In his letter written to Ferenc Nagy, Prime Minister after 1945, he pointed out clearly that " anti-Semitism " could only be successfully eradicated were " war criminals " to be granted a general amnesty and were the campaign of revenge against the Hungarian nation to be called off forthwith.

From this moment Jozsef Mindszenty, Cardinal of Hungary, who wished to check the campaign of revenge against the Hungarian people, became an " anti-Semite ". Peter Fuerst, a Zionist writer, made murderous accusations against him.

According to Fuerst, it was generally known in Budapest that Cardinal Mindszenty was an " anti-Semite ". The printed " anti-Semitic " leaflet edited by him was in the possession of the Jewish Centre at Budapest. During the Mindszenty trials several Jewish organisations asked if it were a fact that Mindszenty was known in the West as " pro-Semitic ". Bertha Gaster, correspondent of the London *News Chronicle,* met Cardinal Mindszenty. During one of her interviews, Gaster was surprised to hear the Cardinal using strong terms concerning the conduct of Hungarian Jewry. At the end of the interview Miss Gaster rose, thanked him for the statements he had made, but, at the same time, let him know that she was a Jewess herself and an active member of the London Jewish Community. he " Jewish Clarion " of February 1949, asserted that Jozsef Mindszenty was, in fact, a notorious " anti-Semite " because *he demanded an amnesty for " war criminals ".*

At the same time the *Jewish Chronicle* wrote in its issue of February 4th, 1949:

" Hungarian Jewish organisations have learned with great surprise that Western Jewish organisations took the side of Mindszenty, whom these statements show up as the arch-enemy of Hungarian and East European Jewry."

It was enough to brand the " pro-Semitic " Mindszenty, who saved the lives of many thousands of Jews, with " anti-Semitism " for the most sinister campaign of revenge to start against him immediately. The hatred of Eastern Jews was picked up by Western Jews so that soon, from both East and West alike a campaign was in progress against a Christian high priest whose only " crime " was to remain human and to raise his voice against the persecution of his own people.

It was Matyas Rakosi-Roth, the Communist dictator, who entered the lists against him, whilst " ideologically " this campaign was led by Jozsef Revai, Minister of Education, whose real name was Moses Kahana. Amongst his own priests who betrayed him the first was Istvan Balogh — alias Izrael Bloch. Those who produced faked evidence were Ivan Boldizsar, alias Bettelheim, a press chief; Reissman, chief of the publicity department, and Gera, alias Grunsweig, deputy propaganda chief. Hanna and Laszlo Sulner who prepared " his " forged manuscripts were also Jews.

Colonel Kraftanov, the Soviet hangman, was brought specially from Moscow. Benjamin Peter-Auspitz, the chief interrogator, put him through the third degree; the Jew Karpati-Krausz, a wrestling champion, was his torturer; Imre Zipszer, the Jewish prison governor, sat next to him all the time, even during the court hearings; and finally, Balassa-Blaustein and Emil Weil administered stupefactive drugs to him.

The Primate of Hungary and the protector of Jewry thus became the victim of the Jews because he wished to prevent a campaign of revenge against his nation.

About this time, even such a well-known Communist as Laszlo Rajk, whose first wife was of Jewish origin, fell victim to the same tribal " nazism ". He used abusive language about the Jewish descent of Erno Gero-Singer, Chief Communist Commissar in the 1936 Spanish Civil War and from this moment he was considered an " anti-Semite ". It was in vain that he helped to murder the best part of the Hungarian ideological *élite* when he was Minister of the Interior. During a party conference he frankly told Matyas Rakosi-Roth that "Communism would not spread because there were too many Jews amongst its leaders". From that moment his doom was sealed. He ended his ignominious life on Rakosi's gallows.

The great Hungarian patriot Laszlo Endre, who finished his life on the gallows of tribal "nazism", wrote the exact truth in his farewell letter of March 21st, 1946, the day of his martyrdom.

"The contents of the *Protocols of the Elders of Zion* are true. . . . The means are in their hands by now to accomplish world-hegemony and they will destroy everything that might impede them in building this new world state. Therefore all that is now happening concerns in no way the administration of justice but only prevention and revenge. This entails the destruction of not only those who have done something, but also of those who might do or could have done something."

All these cases so far reported concerned defeated states. But let us see whether the position was any better in the states which won the war after sacrificing the lives and blood of their sons and risking their very existence.

Neither Germany nor her allies were the first victims of the revenge of Jehovah but rather victorious France, where, after the departure of the German troops, the fateful purge started. The blood-bath of the Commune of Paris in 1871 was nothing in comparison to what took place in victorious France during the summer of 1944. Twenty thousand French lives were lost during the terror régime of the great French Revolution; eighteen thousand French people died on the barricades of the Commune of Paris. But now one hundred and fifty thousand French citizens perished in more horrible circumstances than ever before. During the great French Revolution there was at least some pretence of trial by courts or tribunals. But in 1944 French people were shot dead like rabbits. The victims of the Great French Revolution, the Dantons and the others, were at least able to mount the stairs to the guillotine with straight features and an unimpaired body. But in 1944 fifty per cent of these French victims were half dead from torture before being killed. Their bodies were lacerated, their nails plucked out with pincers and their flesh burned by red-hot irons or cigarette butts. Behind General de Gaulle a Polish Jew called Thomas, one of the leaders of the Spanish Red Brigade, was the chief perpetrator of these monstrosities. He organised common criminals from the jails together with ex-prisoners from the concentration camps into storm-troops to wreak vengeance.

" *The whole massacre was brought about by the propaganda of Jews on the B.B.C.,*" wrote the German paper *Der Weg,* " *who let loose the bloodthirsty devils of revenge.*" " Nazi collaborators " were not primarily the victims of these massacres, but peasants with large farms and the French intellectual *élite.*

In Belgium and the Netherlands the same retribution continued, though with more regard to preserve some kind of semblance of legal formality. The charge of " collaboration " was brought against 480,519 people and out of these 1,208 were sentenced to death. All those who volunteered for work in Germany were convicted.

The basic motives of this campaign of revenge were not only induced by the terrible sight of the ruins but also by the guilty conscience of Jewry. The real war criminals had a foreboding that one day they might be called upon to render an account for what they had done in planning the war as well as for its barbarism. They had to produce an even greater criminal. To justify their revenge they had to find something apparently even more horrible than the 300,000 dead bodies of Dresden or the Katyn Wood murders or the massacres of Bromberg which could be used as an eye-wash to mislead public opinion. The massacres of 1945, on the other hand, could not be justified by anything else than by the magnification several hundred times over of cruelties committed by the Germans. Not only revenge as such had to be justified, but the post-war attitude of Jewry itself which shocked a good many members of the Jewish community.

Sussmanovics, a Soviet Jew, Commandant of Budapest in 1945, summoned the author, Gizella Molinary, to his office and said to her :

" Why bother me with your complaints that you are ignored and let down by your former Jewish friends? Look down on the street from my window here ! The war is still raging, the Red Armies have not yet reached the outskirts of Vienna. In the German concentration camps belated efforts are being made to exterminate the Jews, yet— look out of this window and see what is going on down there in the street ! The Jews here have little thought for their brothers pleading for their lives in distant countries. Have any of them any intention of fighting to save them? On the ruins of gutted and burned shops, in the doorways of houses and even on graves, the small pair of scales and a big poster appear: '*Gold is bought and sold*', says the poster. Here, the soldier throws away his rifle and the writer his pen for everyone is sitting on graves buying and selling gold. Why do you look at me like that? Because I am aware of these things? Of course I am! I am a Jew myself and I am filled with bitter rage and contrition." (From *In the Shadow of the Mindszenty Trials* by Aladar Kovach, page 131.)

A special technique of psychological terror had to be employed, therefore, to cover up all these things. Quite a number of Jewish witnesses gave evidence at Nuremberg that though they lived in the vicinity of crematoria they were not aware of their existence. Nevertheless, radio commentators and " judges " taunted the German people with: " You all knew of these! You are all murderers!" If anyone, even a bishop or a cardinal, tried to raise a word of protest and state the truth, he was silenced with the threat of " Nazi "! Perhaps he was also threatened with being handed over to the Russians. Thus not only the German people but the whole of cultured Europe was intimidated. Thus a stage was reached when nobody dared to tell the truth or state the basic facts for fear of appearing to defend murder and atrocities.

The foul propaganda campaign brought about a state of affairs in which the lie appeared as the truth, revenge as administration of justice and a truthful utterance as a condonation of war crimes. This propaganda tried to convince the ill-informed Gentile masses that the Jews were the only victims of this war and that no other nations suffered any losses whatever. It remained silent about the common graves dug for ten millions of Gentile victims and not a word was said about the massacred Hungarians, Roumanians, Bulgarians and Frenchmen. At the same time the story of Jewry's sufferings was exaggerated beyond all measure. In so doing, the privileges enjoyed by Jews in U.N.R.R.A. and I.R.O., as occupation authorities, in receiving the lion's share of the food rations and in holding the black market monopoly, were also justified. Thus they attempted to justify the outrage of handing over the *élite* of Central Europe to the Soviets—or those of them they had not murdered themselves.

A new age had now dawned in which Jewry could escape the

consequences of any deed, however dastardly, and the whole of Christian Europe became a happy hunting ground for Jewry's revenge. It was enough to speak Hungarian in the streets of Munich to be immediately picked up and handed over to the Communist hangman by the Military Police, whom the Jewish executioners called in promptly. Thus an atmosphere was created in which the allied military authorities not only became unable to check Jewry's revengeful excesses, but also in which their own existence was jeopardised if they showed any reluctance to offer themselves as instruments of Jewry's aims.

What, in fact, happened in Europe between 1945 and 1950 was nothing else but an uncanny materialisation of the prophecies of the " forged " *Protocols*.

In this way the victorious Western allies lost their independence. And in the shadow of the National Flags associated with Magna Carta, the Declaration of Independence and the Code Napoleon, the Nuremberg trials began.

TEN

NEW PURIM AND NUREMBERG

WHO knows about those ancient teachings on which the Jewish doctrine of revenge is based? Who knows the real meaning of the feast of Purim? Who has seen this feast? Who has seen the Jews getting drunk in their synagogues? For, although they are at other times often teetotallers, on this day their religious duty is to get inebriated. Who, among all the " Bible-reading " Gentiles knows that Purim is celebrated by Jewry to. this very day as a feast of rejoicing to commemorate one of the greatest mass-murders in the history of the world?

Nearly 2,500 years have passed since the first Purim, but the descendants of Mordecai and Esther still bake their cakes decorated with the lion of Judah. The male members of the Jewish community still become drunk on the fourteenth day of the month Adar, remaining in an ecstasy promoted by a sense of revenge. And when in the synagogues the book of Queen Esther is read, Haman-sticks are taken out of caftan pockets; for orthodox Jews must symbolically strike them on the synagogue bench whenever the name of King Ahasuerus's chief minister is read out in the text. In the synagogues of the East also, drunken Jews who have consumed unlimited quantities of wines and spirits are seen reeling about on this day. In Belz and Sadagora, Palestinian dancing girls perform their lustful eastern dances. This feast is to be enjoyed; it is to celebrate a mass-murder and a great revenge.

Let us see what the Jews are taught in the Book of Esther. What happened at the first Purim?

The Book tells us that Ahasuerus, the Persian King, fell out with his wife, who was also a lady of Persian descent, and decided to find himself another. The new Queen whom he chose happened to belong to the Jewish community which had been carried into captivity by Nebuchadnezzar. But Esther did not disclose either her origin or her nationality to the King and the royal household.

Mordecai, her uncle, forbade this. Thus Mordecai laid the foundation stone of a new political school. He marked out for future generations the policy of having Jewish women selected for the royal chamber and thus influencing kings, emperors, presidents and other statesmen, in order to achieve at a high level the aspirations of Jewish nationalism. Though these Jewish women repudiated the Mosaic commandment, nevertheless they furthered the cause of their nation.

At this time Haman, son of Hammedatha the Agagite, was advanced by King Ahasuerus to the highest office, to the post of prime minister of the Empire The reason is not recorded in the Bible, but Haman was the " enemy of the Jews ' and accused them before the king as follows:

". . . There is a certain people scattered abroad and dispersed among the people in all the provinces of thy kingdom: and their laws are diverse from all people; neither keep they the king's laws. . . ." (*Esther iii.* 8.)

According to the Book of Esther, the King ordered in his edict that on the thirteenth day of the month Adar the Jews must be killed. But old Mordecai learned of the king's plan and sent a message to his niece to go to the king and " make supplication unto him, and make request betore him for her people.". Thereupon the queen invited the king and Haman to a banquet.

" And the king said again unto Esther on the second day at the banquet of wine, What is thy petition, Queen Esther? and it shall be granted thee: and what is thy request? and it shall be performed, even to the half of the kingdom." (*Esther vii.* 2.)

It is clear from the Book of Esther that by the time the queen began to accuse Haman, the "hater", the king was under the influence of wine. Ahasuerus in a rage left the banquet and went out into the palace gardens to cool himself; meanwhile Haman began to beg the queen for his life. The application of the Nuremberg methods can here be clearly recognised; lies and slander! When Ahasuerus returned, the queen accused Haman of attempting to rape her while the king was out. Thereupon the king ordered that Haman be immediately hanged.

The taking over of power was achieved before the prime minister's

* One of several Mede and Persian kings mentioned in the Old Testament, specifically in the Book of Esther, generally identified with Xerxes. Xerxes (circa 519-465 B.C.) king of Persia was the son of the first Darius.

body was cold. On the order of the beautiful Jewess the king promoted Mordecai to the post of prime minister and simultaneously bloody massacres broke loose from India to Ethiopia, perpetrated by Jews who had actually suffered no harm whatever. After all, Haman's plan remained a plan only, never being carried out and Haman, the person responsible, was hanged. Then, as always, whenever power fell into Jewish hands, they celebrated their victory by bloody massacres. The husband of the Jewish queen, the ancient symbol of the puppet statesman, graciously permitted the Jews " to take revenge on their enemies ".

Since the first Purim Mosaic nationalism has consistently bathed in the blood of victims slain in achieving perpetual revenge.

" The Jews had light, and gladness, and joy and honour!" (*Esther viii.* 16), says the Old Testament.

The Book of Esther gives a detailed account of the victims of this mass slaughter who were executed with exceptional savagery. It recounts that all the ten sons of Haman were killed, whose only sin was that their father was an " anti-Semite ". In the city of Shushan the Jews first killed 500 men, then slaughtered another 300 and finally in the provinces ". . . slew of their foes seventy and five thousand . . ." (*Esther ix.* 16) without any plausible reason.

To be able to assess the magnitude of these massacres correctly, we must not consider these figures in relation to the present-day population of the earth. The armies of Alexander the Great which conquered India consisted only of 47,000 men. The total strength of the Persian army at Marathon was 5,000, and Hannibal fought the battle of Cannae with 20,000 soldiers. Therefore the figure of 75,000 massacred Persians was statistically an exceedingly high number.

All this happened

"on the thirteenth day of the month Adar; and on the fourteenth day of the same rested they; and made it a day of feasting and gladness." (*Esther ix.* 17.)

"Because Haman, the son of Hammedatha the Agagite, the enemy of all the Jews, had devised against the Jews to destroy them and had cast Pur, that is, the lot, to consume them, and to destroy them." (*Esther ix.* 24.)

" But when Esther came before the king he commanded by letters that his wicked device, which he devised against the Jews, should return upon his own head, and that he and his sons should be hanged on the gallows." (*Esther ix.* 25.)

" Wherefore they called these days Purim after the name of Pur. Therefore for all the words of this letter, and of that which they had seen concerning this matter, and which had come unto them." (*Esther ix.* 26.)

" The Jews ordained, and took upon them, and upon their seed and upon all such as joined themselves unto them, so as it should not fail, that they would keep these two days according to their writing, and according to their appointed time every year." (*Esther ix.* 27.)

" And that these days should be remembered and kept throughout every generation, every family, every province and every city; and that these days of Purim should not fail from among the Jews, nor the memorial of them perish from their seed." (*Esther ix.* 28.)

No nation has ever kept a pledge better than the Jews have kept the feast of Purim for more than twenty-four centuries. Year after year they have celebrated the anniversary of the revenge and massacres. The frenzy induced by blood and wine and the triumphal exultation of satisfied revenge soared from city to city and from village to village. In the small thatched village synagogue as well as in the impressive domed metropolitan temple Purim became both a religious and *national* feast day.

The writer of these pages, when in a provincial town in Hungary, happened to witness the caftan-clad troops reeling out of the synagogue in fours. It was the feast of Purim.

Passers-by commented casually: " Hello, the Jews are having their holidays."

This same eternal hatred burns behind the teachings of Marx and of the Illuminati. *It has turned Marxist Socialism into a creed of hatred.* The apostles of this hatred have stood in the background of revolutions and Communist uprisings; they came to power with Bolshevism. Perhaps one day the history of the modern Hamans will be published—the story of those politicians, clergymen, statesmen, writers and journalists who were bold enough to see in the hatred demonstrated during Purim, a threat to the Christian world—and an account written of how they were persecuted, how their families were

132

ruined and how their children were plunged into destitution, and lastly, how " the haters " were hanged.

Jewry's greatest holiday is Purim: the feast of hatred. The greatest holiday of Christianity is the birth of Christ — the birth of love. At Nuremberg, Purim was dressed in the robes of legality. Revenge was wrapped up in legal paragraphs. A brand new " legal title " was created for the purpose of carrying out mass slaughters, whilst the real aim behind it was far more ambitious and sinister. Christian and Roman law and, generally speaking, *Law itself,* was to be nullified. The aim was to humiliate the vanquished nations, to intimidate the minds of the people, and through the " new law " to secure the political possibility of attaining total and complete world rule.

Was the farcical procedure to furnish " war criminals " at Nuremberg an example of democracy in action? Was there really an unbiased court under the United States of America, Great Britain, France and Soviet Russia or was the procedure nothing but the sword of Jehovah smiting a defeated people? Were the " new laws ", i.e. the basis for the verdicts, Christian in character? Did justice or revenge prevail?

The Nuremberg verdicts were pronounced to punish crimes committed against humanity. But on the bench sat the mass murderers of Katyn together with those responsible for the bombing of Dresden. The war propaganda of the allies always protested with extreme vigour against the principle of collective guilt. Nevertheless this principle of collective guilt was sanctioned by the Nuremberg tribunals when the ignominious theory of " guilty organisations " was invented. The radio networks everywhere lectured frequently at this time about " the law ", yet at Nuremberg one of the most important legal principles was thrown aside, i.e. that no one can sit in judgment on his own case. American and Soviet flags were displayed together on the tribunal, but the most basic legal principle of the American constitution and judicature was ignored, i.e. *Nulla Poena Sine Lege,* which means that no one can be convicted for acts which were not punishable by law when committed. In the courtroom sentences were pronounced against barbarism, while concurrently in the basements of the court buildings the Prison Guards of Robert Kempner, the Public Prosecutor, brutally tortured prisoners. The principle of fair play was observed formally only, as the sentences

133

were based on incriminating or forged documents. Any crimes committed against humanity in the concentration camps should have been brought under the jurisdiction of an international court consisting of judges delegated by neutrals, and under conditions in which the court could judge not only the barbaric acts committed by the defeated parties but also those committed by the victorious states. Had this happened, the real criminals could never have obliterated the black stigma branded on them. But by adopting Jewish revenge methods, martyrs were made of certain guilty persons who in any case would never have been acquitted by an impartial court.

In the tribunal at Nuremberg, American, Russian, French and British judges sat, but a single victorious power prosecuted and judged: *Judah!*

Now we know what actually took place behind the scenes. Robert M. Kempner, a Jew of course, and formerly an " oberregierungsrat " in Germany, had been working behind General Taylor, the Chief Public Prosecutor. Morris Amchan assisted Kempner. In the court buildings of Nuremberg, excepting the judges and the accused, there were hardly any other people but Jews. The staff of the Ljudljanka and the M.V.D. was not any different from the personnel of the courts of Nuremberg, Dachau and other places dealing with " war criminals ". It consisted of Jews almost exclusively. The majority of witnesses were Jews as well, and of these Maurice Bardeche writes that their only concern was not to show their hatred too openly and, at least during the hearing of the witnesses, to try to give an impression of objectivity. It is characteristic of this kind of " administration of justice " that the number of witnesses called to give evidence in court was 240 only, yet 300,000 written affidavits were accepted supporting charges without this evidence being heard under oath. It is needless to say that the majority of these depositions were not true.

The accused prisoners were subjected to exactly the same kind of tortures as in Soviet prisons. Julius Streicher was flogged until he was covered with blood and was forced to drink water from the W.C. Then the Jews wearing U.S. Army uniform spat into his mouth in turn and forced him to kiss the feet of a negro. In the prison of the Schwabish Hall the young officers of the Adolf Hitler guards were flogged until they were soaked in blood, then they were forced to lie prostrate on the ground while their torturers trampled on their sexual organs. As in the Malmedy trials the prisoners were strung up in turn and then released until they signed the confessions demanded of them. On the grounds of such " confessions " extorted from Sepp Dietrich and Joachim Paiper, the Leibstandard Garde was convicted as a " guilty organisation ".

Oswald Pohl, a general of the S.S., was manhandled with savagery during the trials of the personnel of the S.S. Paymaster's Office. His face was smeared with fæces, and he was beaten until he signed the desired confession submitting to false accusations. These Jews, clad in the uniform of the American forces, had similarly tortured Weiss, S.S. Obergruppenfuehrer, at Frankfurt-am-Mein and in Dachau. In the Malmedy trials Jewish torturers in American uniform likewise extorted confessions from private soldiers. McCarthy, the American Senator, when dealing with these cases, gave the following statement to the American Press on May 20th, 1949:

" I think the world expected us to give proof of American legal principles and judicial practice by using them when dealing with our defeated enemies. Instead of this, Gestapo and M.V.D. methods were used. I have heard evidence and read documentary proofs to the effect that the accused persons were beaten up, maltreated and physically tortured by *methods which could only be conceived in sick brains*. They were subjected to mock trials and pretended executions, they were told that their families would be deprived of their ration cards. All these things were carried out with the approval of the Public Prosecutor in order to secure the psychological atmosphere necessary for the extortion of the required confessions. If the United States lets such acts committed by a few people go unpunished, then the whole world can rightly criticise us severely and for ever doubt the correctness of our motives and our moral integrity."

In addition to the tortures, forged documents were also produced to convict the accused persons. Mitigating circumstances were not allowed to be considered against incriminating proofs. This in itself is a falsification of truth and justice. A periodical called *Madrid* reported the hearings of the Nuremberg trials, that some American business Jews had converted some of the concentration camps into museums and in return for cash were conducting tours to these camps to show American tourists, journalists and other invited people the horror spots. With the help of wax figures, the entrance to the camp "gas-chamber" was reconstructed. Wax figures representing horribly distorted human forms were used to demonstrate the alleged tortures in these camps. If a camp had no "gas-chamber"—and in most of the camps there were none—then they built an improvised one with expert studio methods as we will see later.

Not only did the propaganda of the World Jewish Congress and of similar other Jewish organisations utilise film trick photography but the Public Prosecutor's Office, headed by Robert M. Kempner, former German-Jewish emigrant, operated with "proofs" of a similar value. In a film about Funk, Minister of Economy, great piles of gold teeth, spectacle frames and pince-nez were to be seen, which were supposed to prove that they came from Jews exterminated in these camps. It is generally known to-day that American Jews brought these films with them when they arrived at Frankfurt, a few days after the city was occupied, in the wake of the American troops. The notorious film called "Todesmuhle" (The Mill of Death) which was shown in the courtroom during the Nuremberg trials with the purpose of turning public opinion against the accused prisoners, is also a forgery.

The Jews stuck to their old tactics of remaining in the background, with the "Gentiles" in the forefront. Though the judges were presumably Christians, they entirely lacked the spirit of Christ. The most incriminating evidence—forged films, documents, affidavits and extracted confessions—was produced by the Jewish prosecutors, C.I.C. agents, false witnesses and others, working in the background. The judges were afraid of the Public Prosecutors. General Taylor, the acting head of the Public Prosecutor's Office, together with Robert M. Kempner, organised and ran a sort of "intelligence service" for spying out and controlling opinions expressed by judges, which had leaked out from their private discussions. Sixty per cent of the staff of the Public Prosecutor's Office consisted of persons who had to leave Germany when the Hitlerian racial laws came into force. Earl Carrol, an American lawyer, stated that, according to his observations, not ten per cent of the Americans employed at the Nuremberg courts were actually American by birth.

It was an American judge, Justice Wenersturm, who exposed the real background of the Nuremberg revenge campaign. He was

President of one of the tribunals which tried the cases of certain German generals who had held commands in the South East and were charged with "war crimes". Wenersturm gave up his appointment at the Nuremberg court and took the risk of returning to America. Half an hour before his departure he gave a statement to the reporter of the *Chicago Tribune* (a paper in Gentile hands), under the strict condition that it should not be published before his 'plane grounded in America. His statement contained the following points:

1. The high ideals prescribed for the Military Court of Nuremberg had never materialised in the practice of the Nuremberg Courts.

2. The fact that the victors alone were trying the losers did not promote true justice.

3. The members of the department of the Public Prosecutor, instead of trying to formulate and reach a new guiding legal principle, were moved only by personal ambition and revenge.

4. The prosecution did its utmost in every way possible to prevent the defence preparing its case and to make it impossible for it to furnish evidence.

5. The prosecution, led by General Taylor, did everything in its power to prevent the unanimous decision of the Military Court being carried out, i.e. to ask Washington to furnish and make available to the court further documentary evidence in the possession of the American Government.

6. *Ninety per cent of the Nuremberg Court consisted of biased persons who, either on political or racial grounds, furthered the prosecution's case.*

7. The prosecution obviously knew how to fill all the administrative posts of the Military Court with "Americans" whose naturalisation certificates were very new indeed, and who, whether in the administrative service or by their translations, etc., created an atmosphere hostile to the accused persons.

8. The real aim of the Nuremberg trials was to show the Germans the crimes of their Führer, and this aim was at the same time the pretext on which the trials were ordered. But the only fact the Germans were shown was that they had fallen into the hands of rather brutal and hardened conquerors. Had I

known seven mouths earlier what was happening at Nuremberg, I would never have gone there. (*Das Letzte Wort über Nurnberg* — The Last Word about Nuremberg — Der Weg's edition, page 57.)

When some one posed the question:

" Why did Justice Wenersturm not have his statement published until after his personal arrival in America?" an English press observer remarked shrewdly:

" Justice Wenersturm was well aware of the fact that air crashes are not uncommon in American civil aviation."

Thus it can be seen that even American lives are not safe from the revenge of Jehovah. It is enough for us to conclude that Nuremberg was not the work of either American or British mentality, but that of typical Jewish tribal " nazism ". It is a clear demonstration of the fact that once administration of justice falls into the hands of Jews there will be no justice since, according to Jewry's double morality, against Gentiles everything is permitted.

So, for the public prosecutors of the Nuremberg trials, procedure was governed by no code except that of the *Protocols* only.

That the revenge of Jehovah took its course at Nuremberg is not only demonstrated by the mentality displayed there, but also by statistics. Out of 3,000 people employed on the staff at Nuremberg Court, 2,400 were Jews. This figure speaks for itself! But, in the background of the Nuremberg tragedy there is another far-reaching aim discernible: *the terrorisation of the whole world through the Nuremberg sentences.* It was to silence all opposition, to brand as " war criminal " anybody daring to criticise Jewry, and on the Soviet pattern, to punish with death all those who might become embarrassing witnesses.

Besides the above-mentioned aims, a further and even greater one was completely achieved: the prevention of any reconciliation between the Gentile nations. The aim was to arouse the hatred of the Germanic people against America. World Jewry reckoned that a time would yet come when America might sorely need the aid of German divisions against Bolshevism. As most of the sentences were announced in the name of America, they had therefore to be worded in such a manner that no European nation would ever be prepared to take up arms to support America.

Jewry's aim was achieved, and this was reflected by German public opinion which, between 1945 and 1951, placed America on the same level as the Soviet Union.

It was not Washington's America nor England of Magna Carta fame nor the France of Descartes which carried out this revenge. It was the spirit of Purim that sat in judgment at Nuremberg, ". . . and slew of their foes seventy and five thousand . . ." says the book of Esther. Haman's false accuser, Queen Esther's ghost, had returned to hire false witnesses in Christian Europe, to manufacture forged affidavits, to produce faked films, to torture innocent people in prison dungeons and to *falsify history itself*.

The glorification of treason and the rewarding of traitors was one of the horrible consequences which will afflict the world to-day. Nuremberg acquitted everybody who had betrayed his country and convicted all those who had kept their oath of allegiance. Thus the gulf between patriotism and treachery disappeared. Which country is to be betrayed? Hitler's of course, but probably Washington's country as well. The verdicts acquitting people such as Julius Resenberg and the atom spies-all had their precedents at Nuremberg. When, in spite of everything, traitors were occasionally Jewish, anti-American demonstrations showed that, from Jewry's point of view, treason committed against other nations was wholly justified. The British Military Code demanded unconditional loyalty from the British soldier, while at the same time German soldiers were sentenced to death for obeying orders. The traitors were rewarded. By doing these things all those traditions of loyalty that upheld states were demolished.

The Nuremberg Court became not only the symbol of revenge but an emblem of moral depravity as well. The Nuremberg Court building itself was the centre of black market activities in a starving Europe devastated by war. Mark Lautern draws a shocking picture of this sink of iniquity engulfing the Court of Nuremberg. "They have all arrived: the Solomons, the Schlossbergers and the Rabinoviches who, as members of the Public Prosecutor's staff, in the intervals between two death sentences or between two executions, deal busily in American cigarettes, valuable chinaware, silver, gold, furs and works of art."

Mr. Salamonson specialised in watches; Mr. Sterling smuggled paintings; Mr. Cohen ordered coffee by the wagon-load or American cigarettes.

"But it was not the black market only," writes Mark Lautern, "that converted the surroundings of the Nuremberg Court into the very sink of Europe. Even more horrible was the moral degradation originating here. The orgies of the foreign employees carried on in private flats and hotels often caused indignation in the whole district. The number of young women employed at the Court grew steadily. Amongst them were Germans and allies alike, drawn into the whirl of depravity and corruption. Sexual incontinence and the most revolting perversion prevailed in these circles, and unlimited scandals supported by ample evidence, provided certain papers and magazines with material for years. (*Das Letzte Wort über Nurnberg,* p. 68.)

Sentenced to death or life imprisonment stood the new Hamans before Queen Esther's people; they were privileged to hear their haters, the black marketeers, the perverts and torturers, singing in chorus an improvised Nuremberg march twisted from Lehar's *Merry Widow*:

> Da geh ich in PX,
> Dort bin ich bis halb sechs!

At midnight on October 16th, 1946, eleven European "war criminals" set out for the gallows at Nuremberg. And then a miracle happened. *At the very portal of death the vanquished scored a victory over their conquerors.* It did not seem to be a scaffold they mounted but the pedestal of a morality which might save Europe yet. Joachim von Ribbentrop died first in silence. General Wilhelm Keitel stepped after him under the gallows, his uniform smart, his boots shining. Before dying, he said:

"Two million German soldiers died for their country. I am going now to follow my boys!"

It was then the turn of Dr. Ernst Kaltenbrunner:

"I loved my country and my German people with all my heart! Good luck, Germany!"

Silently, with set face and an immense contempt, Dr. Alfred Rosenberg confronted the hangman, being followed to the grave by Dr. Hans Frank, Governor-General of the Polish territories. These

140

two men were held responsible for Jews said to have perished in the East.

Dr. Wilhelm Frick, Minister of the Reich, was the next victim:
"Germany for ever!" he shouted, before the trapdoor opened.

Julius Streicher succeeded him on the gallows. He belonged to that small circle possessing the power of vision. He had been captured by a New York Jew named Blitt, who, with the rank of major, specialised in exterminating "anti-Semites". Perhaps Streicher had foreseen the gallows awaiting those leaders who dared defend themselves and their nation. Regarding the spectators with contempt he sarcastically announced the whole truth about Nuremberg:

"It is the feast of Purim of 1946!"

Dr. Fritz Schaukel came next with the words:

"I die guiltless. I respect American soldiers and their officers but not American justice!"

With head erect, General Alfred Jodl stepped under the gallows, Arthur Seyss-Inquart followed:

"I believe that this execution will be the last act in the tragedy of the Second World War!" he said.

It was perhaps a symbolic fact that even the military executioner, John C. Woods Short, was a Jew. He took 143 minutes to hang the "war criminals".

"This smart job," he said proudly, "deserves a good long drink!" Meanwhile, the reporters of *Life* took his picture, rope in hand, so that this well-known magazine could, in the most doubtful taste, reproduce the photograph on its front page. All this may indeed deserve a good long drink. But a prophecy of Julius Streicher loomed ominously over the heads of judges and hangmen alike. They had heard him pronounce from the gallows:

"Remember! Your turn will come next! You will be hanged by the Bolsheviks!"

Hermann Goring, having taken potassium cyanide smuggled into his cell half an hour before the time of execution, was dead. British, American and Russian agents were looking feverishly for Hitler's body in the ruins of the Führer's shelter. Goebbels perished, together with his family; he first killed his six children and then committed suicide. Bormann disappeared. Himmler committed suicide with cyanide when he fell into the hands of British-Jewish interrogators. Robert Ley committed suicide in Nuremberg prison.

In Milan, Mussolini, who had already been shot dead, was hanged by his feet, upside down. The last scene at Nuremberg depicted aeroplanes taking off to scatter over Germany the ashes of the " war criminals ". This deed symbolised the fear induced by a guilty conscience on the part of both judges and participants awakening from the drunken frenzy of Purim.

In France, the old grey-haired General Petain, already on the edge of the grave, was sentenced to life-imprisonment in a fort, out of gratitude for defending another fortress, Verdun, against the Germans. Then Pierre Laval, the French Premier, boldly faced the firing squad. He too had taken cyanide, but for two hours doctors fought desperately to save him—for death. And, in the end, he stood there confronting the guns, while the judges appointed to be present at the execution took cover behind the prison van, unable to look at the scene which was the consequence of their judgment. Laval, though wrecked physically by the horrible effects of the poison, refused the offer to be executed sitting in a chair. Though staggering, he braced himself to say:

" A French Premier dies erect! "

He himself gave the order to fire, but the bullets missed their target. Finally the French Premier had to be killed by a revolver shot through the back of his head.

In Norway, Prime Minister Quisling was executed in the prison yard of Akershus, and the members of the firing platoon were deeply impressed by the courageous and dignified manner with which one of the oldest enemies of Bolshevism faced the guns.

The Hungarian Leader Ferenc Szalasi was executed together with his ministers. Miklos Horthy, the previous Head of State, only escaped Nuremberg by becoming one of the chief witnesses for the prosecution and by denying he had anything to do with the so-called " Jewish Laws " which he himself had sanctioned. Ferenc Szalasi gave a military salute to his fellows, the members of his Cabinet, who had already been executed on the gallows, when he was passing by to take his turn, and he died with such bravery that the Soviet-made film of his execution had soon to be banned from all cinemas, to such a degree did his heroic conduct command the respect and admiration of the whole nation. Laszlo Bardossy, Bela Imredy, Dome Sztojay and Jeno Szollosi, the four ex-Prime Ministers of Hungary, died with similar bravery on the gallows or tied to the stake. Those who made retrospective laws against them or sat in judgment over them belonged almost without exception to the world conquerors. It could not even be said against Laszlo Bardossy that he was an " anti-Semite ". His only crime was that he had declared war on Bolshevism. When he looked down at the dense mob released from the ghettos and saw the revengeful spectators crowding the place of execution, he cried out as his last prayer:

" O God! Deliver Hungary from these bandits!"

In Roumania, Marshal Antonescu, one of the greatest Roumanian heroes, was executed. In Yugoslavia, the leader of the patriotic partisans, Drazsa Mihajlovich, was handed over to the butchers of Mojse Pijade. Dr. Joseph Tiso, both priest and Prime Minister of independent Slovakia, also died on the gallows on April 18th, 1947. The revenge did not stop at the persons of church leaders. Even the Pope himself could not rescue Christ's priest from the hands of Eduard Benes, the great freemason who grimly said:

" Tiso must hang!"

In eight or nine countries the heads of state, prime ministers and leaders, were executed during the new Purim. But they are not war criminals in the eyes of their peoples but symbols of their nation's martyrdom. They were followed by anonymous martyrs, by soldiers loyal to their oaths, by intellectuals, journalists, farmers and church-men. Thus, not only the " anti-Semitic nazis " and " fascists " were murdered but also anybody representing quality who might be un-pleasant witness against perpetrators of outrages. For example, Ferenc Orsos, the Hungarian university professor and European authority on forensic medicine, was a " war criminal " because he signed the report on Katyn confirming that it was not the Germans but the Bolsheviks who massacred the officers of the Polish army.

Possibly the Americans are already beginning to feel that the time is approaching when Streicher's prophecy may be fulfilled:

" Remember! Your turn will come next! You will be hanged by the Bolsheviks!"

The greatest service that can be rendered to America would be for somebody to have the courage to explain that all these outrages were not the acts of Americans but of world Jewry, and that *Nuremberg represented no new law but the terror of Purim.* After all, not only the vanquished and the collaborators were murdered at Nuremberg. One of the first martyrs of Jew Finance was America's epic hero, General Patton, Commander of the U.S. Army invading Germany, the " knight of the armoured divisions ". A descendant of the American pioneers, he thought of Nazism as a satanic evil. The propagandists, journalists and statesmen said so, anyway, so far as he was aware. He arrived in Germany hating it. He believed that the nazis must be punished. Then, a German dairymaid living in the neighbourhood of his H.Q. happened to come his way, and during a casual conversation she told him about the things happening behind the " villa of the commandant ", i.e. his house. She described how the milk intended for the cities was dumped in the roads by the military police on the order of the Morgenthau boys, how, no longer Nazis but ordinary German soldiers were detained in crowded internment camps just because they did their duty, how the workers had been expelled from thir homes out of revenge by the former inmates of the concentration camps, and how Jewish doctors in the hospitals recommended that every fourth newborn baby should be killed with an injection because there was not enough milk.

And General Patton set forth like the medieval knight-errant to see with his own eyes whether the German peasant woman's account was true or not. Without displaying his rank, in the uniform of a private, he toured all parts of this earthly hell; the prisons, the internment camps and the prison camps where he saw for himself that those torturing Germans teaching the theory of collective guilt and meting out collective punishment were not American boys but sons of Jehovah. From that moment the officers of the U.S. Army received strict orders to give sufficient food to the prisoners of war, already half dead with starvation and the Military Police was forbidden to dump the babies' milk on the roads any more. General Patton was not prepared to put the Morgenthau plan into effect, although he had fought for America — and, alas, also for Judah. But another general was only too willing to serve the Morgenthau plan: his name was Dwight Eisenhower.

It was not possible to convict the " knight of the armoured

divisions" at Nuremberg. Patton was therefore convicted and sentenced to death behind the scenes. But the people who sat in judgment upon him were the same as those who had convicted the German leaders at Nuremberg. In spite of having been hushed up it is well known to-day that on the order of C.I.C. agents, an "American" car drove into Patton's. As a result of this "accident" General Patton was injured. He was promptly transferred to an ambulance, but on its way to hospital the ambulance collided with a large American heavy lorry and this time he was killed. At the same moment something disappeared from his pocket which the world conquerors had every reason to fear.

"I have a little black book!" the General had said earlier, "and when I get back to the U.S.A. I am going to blow hell out of everything."

But before closing his eyes for the last time, his eyes surely saw the same enemy as did Keitel, Jodl and Streicher when they stood under the gallows of Nuremberg.

Nevertheless, certain people were never brought to trial at Nuremberg. The members of the Frankfurt *Research Institute for the Investigation of the Jewish Question,* and the representatives and staff of *Welt Dienst* (World Service) were never touched although they were the first to be captured by Jewish members of the American C.I.C. They were the first to be brought to Nuremberg and to be threatened by the hangman *before* he despatched the ministers of the Reich. But these people simply retorted to their interrogators:

"Very well then! We are ready to stand trial at the Court of Nuremberg, but with the help of our hidden documents we will prove that world Jewry is the real perpetrator of the war crimes. At the same time we will be compelled to disclose that 'World Service' was not a nazi organisation at all. The members of twenty-three nations contributed to its columns. Amongst them was an American ex-President, officers of the Swedish General Staff, several of the worthiest members of the English aristocracy and a Cabinet Minister of the Union of South Africa."

The leaders of these German organisations, although detested by the world conquerors, were never even indicted. They were freed in a hurry and anyone reading the Nuremberg sentences will see

Note: C.I.C. stands for Counter Intelligence Corps.

that neither the Frankfurt Research Institute nor " World Service " are to be found mentioned among " Guilty Organisations ".

It would have been most unpleasant for the world conquerors had the leaders of these groups submitted their " defence " in court.

Union, an English paper, in its issue of January 19th, 1952, writes that it had just received news from Germany which seemed to show rather bad taste on the part of the authorities of the American Occupation Zone. The first Jewish synagogue had been dedicated in the Court Palace of Nuremberg in the very place where Goering and the other National Socialist leaders were sentenced to death. Were any more proof needed to convince German public opinion that their leaders were murdered by the schemes of world Jewry, this synagogue dedication would be sufficient.

And so the Nuremberg courtroom will ever remain a symbol of the new Purim, for here, in 1952, a new synagogue was established to the glory of Jehovah and as a token of the fact that Judah and not the allies, sat in judgment at Nuremberg.

ELEVEN

WHAT HAS BECOME OF
SIX MILLION JEWS?

IN the Second World War Jewry, which declared itself to be a belligerent party, suffered unknown losses in dead. Other nations mourn their dead, erect monuments to them and keep anniversaries to cherish their memory. The majority of Jewry made good business out of their dead and used their bodies to serve as a step towards world domination. It regarded them as a political investment and a means of achieving power. Whilst over the graves and war memorials of other people's heroes sweet flowers of remembrance blossom, around the graves of the Jewish dead the loudspeakers of propaganda are, even to-day, still roaring at full blast. The survivors of other nations bring floral tribute to the graves of their mothers. But around the graves of Jewish mothers are only to be heard profaning shouts of: " Give *me* an U.N.R.R.A. parcel too! My mother also was killed by the Nazis!"

For the survivors, the graves at Auswitz and Bergen-Belsen represented no symbol of eternal protest again barbarism. Hollywood made a splendid business out of them and the Gentiles stood around the Jewish graves in consternation. Jewry did so also equipped with film cameras, loudspeakers and every kind of photographic apparatus. On learning of the concentration camps the spontaneous comment of the shocked Christian world was: " Some shameful outrage has been committed!" But the headlines of Jewish nationalism blared: *A world sensation!* The survivors have earned the pity of the world, as well as the right to revenge, to quick emigration and, of course, to *world domination!*

All this is without a parallel in the history of the world.

Compassion, shock and indignation were the reactions of the Christian world. But the Jewish survivors said:

" *We demand privileges!* My mother, my sister and my father all fell victims to the Nazis." The martyrs rested in their common graves, while the New York millionaire and the small Brooklyn chandler were carrying on business with the halo of martyrdom around their brows and displaying an expression of sadness which could not have been bettered had they themselves been lying in the camp of Bergen-Belsen.

Other nations also have their dead and their martyrs, perhaps many more than the Jews. Six million people were starved to death in the Ukraine as victims of the food-dumping plans of the Kremlin Jews, but the world never awarded privileges to the Ukrainians. Nobody ever gave double rations to the dependents of the victims buried in the common graves of Katyn Woods. Nor have the survivors of Brno death-march ever received any compensation. Not one of the perpetrators of the Bromberg, Prague or Yugoslav massacres was hanged at Nuremberg.

" Six million martyrs! " announced the Jewish newspapers, the Nuremberg judges, the films and the radio network.

Six million!—the Gentile world recoiled with horror and nobody dared to raise a dissident voice even when it became apparent that this alleged figure had become the centre of a world blackmailing manœuvre.

Six million! cried the Germans in consternataion, who knew nothing about the concentration camps until the day of the armistice and over whose heads the scourge of collective punishment was poised menacingly.

But were there, in fact, six million victims?

When General Taylor, the Chief Public Prosecutor at Nuremberg, was asked where he had got this figure of six million, he simply replied that the figure was based on the confession of S.S. General Ohllendorf. During the Nuremberg enquiries, Ohllendorf allegedly said that this was the number of Jews killed. Later it became known that American Jews had extorted this " confession " from Ohllendorf under torture. Oswald Pohl and Berger, both S.S. group leaders, were similarly tortured. Forged affidavits were also used to support this unprecedentedly high figure of Jewish " martyrs ". This figure is also given by Dr. Wilhelm Hoettl, a rather strange person in the service of the American C.I.C., the author of several books written under the pen name of Walter Hagen. He appeared in Nuremberg as a witness for the American prosecution. We learn from *Der Weg* (3rd number, 1954, p. 203) that his evidence was the only " proof " regarding the supposition of the murder of six million Jews. *He was also engaged by the Soviet for espionage,* working with two Jewish emigrants from Vienna, Perger and Verber, as U.S. officers during the preliminary inquiries of the Nuremberg trials.

The intention of exterminating the Jews is usually supposed to be
announcement made in the course

e peace treaties will not find any

how did he intend to solve the

plan to Goering for the *expatria-*

d practical," said Goering, " and
pport. If it becomes practical I
(Sven Hedin: *Ohne Auftrag in*

amphlet form by the party, was
nation without a country must
tine would not be able to take
pean Jews, and the revival of
be a source of perpetual trouble,
rld. This has indeed been the

most reliable evidence regard-
e war, it published statistics
ing the world's Jewish population, and admitted that Hitler allowed 400,000 Jews to emigrate from the Reich. Had he cherished the intention to exterminate the Jews, these emigrants would never have been allowed to leave Germany.

The World Jewish Congress admits in its publication *Unity in Dispersion* (page 377) that: " *The majority of German Jews succeeded in leaving Gemany before the war broke out. . . .*"

World Jewry knew and foresaw clearly that the Second World War, especially in the case of a Bolshevik defeat, would take a heavy toll of Jewish lives, but did absolutely nothing to further emigration while there was still ample time for it. World Jewry badly needed victims in order to be in a position to blackmail the world with the story of six million Jewish martyrs. It was evident to the Jews that here was a rare opportunity of obtaining an excellent psychological weapon to silence " anti-Semitism " and to capture world power. After the events of the Kristallnacht (crystal night) in Germany, forty-eight states, led by America, France and Great Britain, held a conference, the only topic of which was how to save the Jews threatened in Germany. Although it was clear to all parties concerned that in the case of war the position of European Jewry would be precarious, the conference ended without any positive results. Great Britain was not prepared to take in the German Jews. Though America was ready to grant German Jewry admission, certain Jewish forces working behind the scenes sabotaged this solution. They knew very well that this would have meant the end of anti-nazi propaganda. It may sound paradoxical, but the anti-Jewish character of German National Socialism came in handy for world Jewry. World Jewry required a Second World War, despite knowing that this would cost a certain number of Jewish lives.

After the outbreak of war all such expatriation plans became unpractical. But did the Germans really wish to destroy the Jews in their hands? This is hardly credible. After the occupation of Poland, photographs of the Polish ghettos were published by the German picture magazine *Signal*. That these Jews were living separated, for reasons of security, is *quite understandable in time of war*. But had the intention of the Germans been to exterminate them, then under no circumstances would their pictures have been published by official German propaganda agencies, showing them working at various tasks, such as packing and doing other light jobs for the German Army, and thus earning regular wages. The *Signal* also published a reproduction of the special currency notes introduced in the ghettos to prevent speculation. The interior administration of the ghettos was in the hands of Jewish councils elected by themselves. It may be a question of opinion whether this arrangement was right or wrong. The ghetto is perhaps a humiliating social establishment, but it is not barbaric. It is not an organisation for the destruction of a race. Let us not forget that the United States interned Germans and Japanese citizens, while England put the

Mosley fascists and many others in internment camps. This number of *Signal* was obtainable all over Europe at that time.

" World conscience " raised no objection against these ghettos then.

What was meant by talk of a solution for the Jewish question? The book *Nuremberg on la Terre Promise*, by Maurice Bardeche, answers this question when discussing the Nuremberg trials:

" It is clear from the documents of the trials that the solution of the Jewish question, as approved by the leader of National Socialism, meant simply to concentrate all Jews in one place set apart for them and *this place would be known as the Jewish reservation.*

" This would have been a special type of European ghetto, and this intention can be recognised by various ministerial executive decrees and by inter-departmental orders emanating from higher authorities of the Reich. There is nothing else to it! Those accused at Nuremberg could state repeatedly with a clear conscience that during the whole war they knew nothing of mass-executions or of Auswitz or Treblinca, and that they first heard of them from the Public Prosecutor."

How, then, did the German concentration camps come into being?

According to accounts in the *Munchen Illustrierte* appearing in 1958, a very interesting answer was given to this question at the Nuremberg trials. Raymond H. Geist, a Jew and First Secretary of the American Embassy in Berlin, when National Socialism took over in 1933, made a statement under oath. In this statement he said that during the first few days following the taking over of power, the victims of the Gestapo reached a figure of *several hundred thousands.*

But Hermann Goering, the chief defendant at the Nuremberg trials, when questioned about this, replied to the American judge:

" In the beginning there were naturally certain abuses of power and, of course, sometimes innocent persons suffered, but in the light of the magnitude, both of the action taken and of the whole movement, this German impulse to independence constituted the most *bloodless and most disciplined revolution in history."*

At first only the Communist leaders were sent to concentration camps. After learning that Thalman, the leader of the German Communist Party, had been manhandled in " protective detention ",

Goering gave orders that Thalman be brought before him and then said to him:

"My dear Thalman! Had you seized power, you would not have been beaten up, but on the other hand, I have no doubt you would have ordered my prompt execution."

"Naturally!" retorted the Communist leader.

This incident proves better than anything else that in the beginning there were no Jews in the German concentration camps and that the National Socialist leaders themselves prevented the ill-treatment of the internees.

The real aim was the establishment of a special territory for Jews in the East. This was the project referred to, and the journals and magazines containing German war propaganda published pictures illustrating it. These were the modern ghettos and in each one the Jewish population of a whole district lived and worked. The Germans were convinced they would win the war and then they wanted to expatriate the Jews from Europe. The Eastern ghettos, therefore, did not represent the permanent Jewish homeland but a temporary reservation only. Well, to what extent was this right or wrong? The British can, perhaps, give the best decision, who, during the Boer War, interned all the women and children of the population so that more women perished than men.

However, under no circumstances could the British be charged with wanting to exterminate the Boers. They simply put into effect certain safety measures. It is even more understandable that the Germans should wish to carry out such safety measures, for the Jews never denied that they opposed the Germans with fanatical hatred and that they had no scruples in resisting them either by partisan warfare or by acts of sabotage. Moreover, there was ample bases for these measures under international law, since Jewry declared itself to be a belligerent party.

Have the Germans ever had any intention of exterminating Eastern Jewry? There is indirect proof that the Germans never had any such intention. During the air raids and "saturation bombing" of residential districts, churches, hospitals and workers' settlements, irresponsible people in the war-worn population often voiced the demand that all Jewish workers in the Reich should be regarded as hostages. The "man in the street" in his simple, decent way, argued that if Western Jews ordered air raids against innocent women and children, then this outrage made it justifiable for innocent Jewish women and children to be sent to perish also under the carpet-bombing. But the party and the leaders never gave way to these demands, though the execution of this policy would only have required giving notice through the radio that the inmates of the Jewish camps would be transferred into the residential districts and non-military targets most frequently bombed, so that they would perish first in the saturation bombing.

In the Eastern territories, i.e. in Poland, in the Ukraine and Lithuania, Jewry suffered its greatest losses. But up to 1943 nobody knew anything of the so-called mass murders. These losses were suffered in the Ukrainian partisan warfare, when the Germans were compelled to take hostages. Amongst these hostages there were a good many Jews, as it was commonly known that the Jews sided with the partisans. The great question was whether an army in the field has the right to take hostages during gruesome and murderous warfare against partisans. From the point of view of humanity this is very doubtful. In any case, in the course of the Nuremberg trials several witnesses testified that an order written and signed by General Eisenhower was found in the Harz Mountains. This order directed that for every American soldier killed twenty German hostages must be slain. It is also noteworthy that during the Korean war the Americans were compelled to adopt "German methods" against the partisans. Whole villages were razed from the face of the earth because it was suspected that partisans might be hiding there. On page twenty-five of *Colliers* magazine of August 26th, 1950, several photographs were published depicting captured partisans and hostages. The caption under the photographs says: "The events of the war show that in Asia very little regard is shown for human life. Southern Koreans suspected of treason were loaded into trucks to carry them to the place of execution. (In some cases their backs were broken before they were shot.)"

In these pictures the Korean partisans are guarded by American soldiers. Thus it can be seen that Eisenhower, as well as McArthur, found it justifiable to take hostages. Yet members of the German security forces were sentenced to death for obeying orders of exactly the same nature.

It is most interesting to compare events of to-day with those of the Second World War. We can read almost daily in any newspaper how the British are killing Mau Mau without the least sentimentality. One day 130 die and on another 34 members of Mau Mau are executed. But "world conscience" by now merely dismisses these horrors by nonchalantly acknowledging that Britain has to employ these drastic measures to establish order. But there is no doubt that the rebels in the Warsaw ghetto were at least as ruthless and fanatical as the murderous members of Mau Mau, and Jewry had declared itself a belligerent party and acted as such all over Europe. But Western and Soviet radio networks never missed a chance to stir up the fanaticism of European Jewry. The Jewish speakers of the various broadcasting stations bawling into space from the safety of bomb-proof shelters, called down, in fact, the fate suffered by Jews in German hands.

The human lives lost in partisan warfare do not prove any intention to exterminate Jewry. The camps were under the constant supervision of the sanitary authorities and regularly inspected up to the time of the invasion of Europe, i.e. up to June, 1944. A minimum space of four cubic metres was calculated for each inmate. Belsen camp, near Bremen, accommodated 15,000 internees. This camp was actually a substitute for a prison. The internees were under regular medical care. Those seriously ill were transferred to hospital. The lighter cases were medically treated in the camp. Internees of foreign origin could also receive parcels, just like the Germans. The office of the Public Prosecutor conducted thorough investigations in each case, and those found innocent were sent back to their own country. But those found guilty were sentenced to death by the military courts and executed. The average number of natural deaths was 200 monthly in 1944. But when saturation bombing paralysed the transport and communication system of the Reich, the rationing system became more and more chaotic, and in consequence epidemics broke out. The behaviour of the camp guards towards the internees became stricter and the mortality rate rose. But despite every handicap Belsen was not an extermination camp. Why was it, then, shown as a terror spot in the propaganda film prepared by American Jews? What sort of horror propaganda was this? Who is responsible if, as a direct consequence of allied bombing, a famine resulted? Was it the Germans or the Allies? Which of them caused the highest casualties in the camps?

Shem, the underground paper of Jewish nationalists in France, on July 8th, 1944, published a noteworthy article describing conditions in the internment camps of Eastern Germany. We should regard these reports as reliable sources of information, for they were given by Jews to Jews and they were based on direct experience. They deal in detail with conditions in the camps of Byslowitz, Chrszno, Kattowitz-Birkenau-Wadowitz, Meisso, Lager Oberlagenbielau, Waldenburg and Theresienstadt. Life in one camp might appear to be rather hard for the internees, whilst in another it appeared to be more tolerable and in a third there might be quite good conditions. Generally speaking the inmates everywhere received strict but fair treatment. The women had to do light household work. The men worked on road buildings and construction, but skilled workers were employed in their own occupations. There is not a word in the report of this Jewish paper about extermination or maltreatment of the internees. Neither is there a word in these accounts about gas-chambers, extermination camps or infanticides. On the contrary! *Shem* reports that the very young children between two and five years of age were being sent to various kindergartens in Berlin to enjoy the care of the German Red Cross and Public Welfare Department.

How, then, was the world deceived by the fiction of the extermination of six million Jews? Where were the gas-chamber scenes and the dead bodies shown in the propaganda film *Todesmuhle* (Mill of Death) actually photographed?

At the end of 1945 new inmates appeared in the concentration camp of Dachau. But these were no longer Jews but some of the defeated German people—the " war criminals ". They were ordered subsequently to build various additional auxiliary buildings with the greatest possible speed. But first of all, the horticultural beauties of the camps had to be destroyed because it would be rather difficult for the American cinema-going public to believe that the Jews were suffering amid nice gardens and flower-beds, especially when they came to the cinema in the anticipation of seeing horrors. Thus the workers received orders to dig a blood-pit with a drainpipe for draining off the blood, because it must be made to appear that here

Jewish blood had been flowing in streams. The shower-baths, dressing-rooms and reception halls had to be rebuilt so that they should appear like gas-chambers. For the sake of achieving this appearance a special separate concrete structure was built with small porthole-like openings, and these contraptions are still on show to-day purporting to demonstrate that the killing " death gas " was let in through these portholes. The captive workers also received orders to build *" a special execution yard purporting to show where the victims were shot through the back of the neck "*.

Philip Auerbach, who became Under-Secretary of State in the Bavarian Government, as well as the leader and acting head of German Jewry freed from the concentration camps, had the bright idea that there should be a " hanging tree " in the camp too. A big fir tree standing in the park was tidied up and embellished, and moreover, to the great luck of Auerbach, this tree had a stout branch projecting horizontally. So the end of this branch was cut off and the remaining stub rubbed with ropes for a long while until it appeared highly polished and capable of providing evidence that every day hundreds of executed Jews had been hanged from this tree.

The Jews converted this camp into a chamber of horrors and a memorial plaque was unveiled, the inscription on which says that 238,000 persons were cremated here. But the crematorium had only two furnaces. In order to cremate the alleged 238,000 bodies, these furnaces would have to have been kept going for three years without ever stopping, and in this case about 530 tons of human ashes would have been recovered.

Relying on the information received from a bribed Pole in 1949, an American Jewish C.I.C. officer started excavations on a large scale in the camp vegetable garden. But despite all his tireless efforts and expense no ashes or Jewish bodies were found. Small wonder! Since one of the two furnaces of the crematorium had been built *after* the war for shooting the scenes from *Todesmuhle*.

Cardinal Faulhaber, the German archbishop, informed the Americans that, during the air raids on Munich in September, 1944, thirty thousand people were killed. The archbishop himself requested the German authorities at the time to cremate the bodies of these victims in the crematorium of Dachau. But, unfortunately, this plan could not be carried out. *The crematorium, having only one furnace, was not able to cope with the bodies of the victims, nor could it have accommodated the alleged Jewish bodies either.* The only bodies cremated were those of inmates who passed away naturally.

To complete the story of Auerbach, he was convicted in 1952 and sentenced to a term of imprisonment for forging documents purporting to show he had paid out huge sums of reparations to non-existent Jews.

The other " proofs " were similarly concocted. Jews in U.S. Army uniform showed the Chief Constable of a large German city a photograph and said to him: " Look here, we understand that it was you who ordered the killing of nearly 20,000 Jews whose bodies can be seen in this photograph!" The photograph showed a macabre sight, hecatombs of horribly distorted human bodies. But the Chief Constable retorted curtly: *" These are not Jewish bodies. These are the bodies of the inhabitants of this city killed in the air raids. These are all Germans.* By the way, I can prove that I myself ordered this picture to be taken when I was head of the police force."

Thousands and thousands of similar proofs can be produced to-day showing the fantastic methods and tricks utilised to spread the fictitious story of six million exterminated Jews, concocted by Jewish propagandists, film producers, journalists, C.I.C. officers and torturers.

Well, what really did happen to those six million Jews, the erection of a memorial to whom is being planned in Manhattan?

The *Baseler Nachrichten* on June 12th, 1946, published the news that a press conference was held at Geneva by leading members of the Jewish World Congress, at which Dr. M. Perlzweig, the delegate from New York, made the following statement: " The price of the downfall of National Socialism and Fascism is the fact that seven million Jews lost their lives thanks to cruel ' anti-Semitism '. The number of Jews surviving in Europe to-day stands at one and a half million."

But in its next issue the *Baseler Nachrichten* was compelled to give space to the report of an American correspondent, challenging the authenticity of this propaganda figure in the strongest terms. This report points out first of all that if this figure were correct, *the losses of Jewry in the war* would be greater than the total losses of *Great Britain, America, Australia, Canada, New Zealand, France, Belgium, Holland and Denmark all added together.*

The most remarkable thing about all this is that, in 1933, the total number of European Jews, excepting those in the Soviet Union, was 5,600,000. This figure was well known by the American Jewish Congress from statistics published in the *New York Times* on January 11th, 1945. From this 5,600,000 one million must be deducted for the number of Jews remaining in East Poland beyond the Molotov-Ribbentrop line, to whom nothing happened until June 21st, 1941, when the German-Soviet war broke out. According to statistics of the *Baseler Nachrichten,* five million Jews were living in Europe, not counting those in Soviet Russia. But from this five million, the *number of Jews living in neutral countries must be deducted since nothing ever happened to them.* According to the statistical figures of the 1942 World Almanac, the number of Jews living in Gibraltar, the British Isles, Portugal, Spain, Sweden, Switzerland, the Irish Republic and Turkey was 420,000.

The number of Jews, therefore, within the reach of National Socialism was never more than 4,500,000. The same neutral source of information, the *Baseler Nachrichten,* in referring to available Jewish statistical data, establishes that between 1933 and 1945, 1,500,000 Jews, emigrated to Great Britain, Sweden, Spain, Portugal, Australia, China, Indian and Palestine, not to mention the United States, where eighty per cent of the immigrants arriving with German, Australian, Polish or Czechoslovak passports consisted of Jews. According to the report of the *Baseler Nachrichten* half a million Jews escaped to Siberia before the German armies launched their attack on Soviet Russia. Therefore, the number of Jews remaining in Hitler's sphere of influence could not have been more than 2,500,000. But in 1946, again excepting Russia, there were still 1,559,600 Jews living in Europe!

" But to-day one thing is certain: *the presumption that Jewish losses* were between five and six million (a presumption adopted even by the Palestine Committee) is absolutely absurd. The maximum conceivable number of Jewish victims could be estimated as being between 1 and 1.5 millions, since there were no more Jews within the reach of Hitler and Himmler, and we can reasonably estimate that the actual losses of Jewry are well under this figure."

The American occupation authorities in Germany carried out a post-war investigation to ascertain the number of persons who perished in the concentration camps. According to their report published in 1951, 1.2 million people died in these camps during the whole period of their existence. This number includes Jews, Gypsies, Ukrainians and all other nationalities, i.e. all prisoners who died a natural death in the concentration camps. At the highest possible estimate the number of Jews who perished cannot, therefore, be put higher than 500,000 or 600,000 persons. In comparison with this, Christian nations suffered immeasurably greater losses. Let us consider the small Hungarian nation whose total population is about the same as that of world Jewry. Hungary's war losses in dead, including the victims of air raids and those frozen or starved to death in Siberian death camps, reach at least one million. And what are Germany's losses? Three million six hundred thousand German soldiers died in action in the war forced on the Reich by world Jewry. One million two hundred thousand civilians were killed in the saturation bombing, while two million four hundred thousand East Germans, together with six hundred thousand Sudeten Germans and two hundred thousand other people of German origin were massacred at the end of the war. One million four hundred thousand Germans perished or were murdered in the jails, P.D.W. camps and internment camps of the Allies, and the Soviet Union.

Against the horrible truth demonstrated by these facts and figures the real war criminals had to build up a legend of Jewish martyrdom and this gigantic lie-propaganda was assisted by all Jewish official organisations, all Jewish world papers like the *New York Times,* etc., and all Jews, whether leading statesmen or small black-marketeers in the shady side streets. The *New York Times* in its issue of May 1st, 1946, published its notorious statistics according to which the number of Jewish victims was over six million. In *Die Neue Zeitung* of February 4th, 1946, a semi-official organ of the American occupation forces, the Joint Distribution Committee published its statistics and according to these the number of Jews who perished during the Second World War is estimated at 5,012,000. Both these statistics are masterpieces of juggling and the result of a collection of false-hoods. Their compilers apparently relied on the ignorance of the rest of the world.

Churchill has said that there are two sorts of lies: brazen lies and *statistics.* But these lies represent and combine both sorts. It is revealing that in order to reach the required result, the Jews simply raised their numbers living in Europe in 1939.

But the chief question remaining to be dealt with is whether the number of survivors is reported correctly by Jewry. The various Jewish papers written in Hungarian and edited in different parts of the world continuously emphasise that six hundred thousand Jews perished in Hungary. In contrast to this, the statistics of the *New York Times* puts the figure of the Jews who died in Hungary at two hundred thousand, whilst the Central Statistical Office of Budapest, which was from 1946 in sole control of Jewry and the people's democrats, states that the losses of Hungarian Jews were one hundred and twenty thousand. But even the figures of the Hungarian Statistical Office were obtained only by comparing the data of legal death declarations with the statements of Jews returning to Hungary. It is remarkable that in the section relating to Hungary, a dotted line with no figures attached appears opposite Hungarian displaced persons. From this it can be deduced that no Hungarian Jewish D.P.s were left in Austria or Germany. But the truth is that 35,000 Hungarian Jews never returned to Soviet-dominated Hungary. So if this figure is taken into consideration the losses of Hungarian Jewry would not be 120,000 but 85,000. The *New York Times* remarks that 25,000 Hungarian Jews who reached Russia as members of labour divisions and were captured there later, are not taken into consideration in the list of lost Hungarian Jews. These all returned later to Hungary in the best of health. Thus a fairer estimate of the losses of Hungarian Jewry would be about 60,000 persons.

Similar statistical frauds can be detected concerning French Jews as well. The Public Prosecutor representing that part of the indictment relating to France during the Nuremberg trials, stated that 120,000 Jews were deported for racial reasons. The *New York Times* states that out of 320,000 French Jews there were 180,000 survivors only. Thus 140,000 had perished. But how? the reader may ask—when, according to the French Public Prosecutor himself there were 120,000 deported. Furthermore, quite a large number of these survived too. We can read in the book *Your France,* by Bradley, of the horrors committed against the French people by Jews released from concentration camps.

But greater and even more glaring frauds are to be seen in the statistics concerning the largest blocks of Jewry, i.e. in Poland and Russia. According to the tales of the Joint Distribution Committee and the *New York Times,* out of three million two hundred and fifty thousand Polish and Russian Jews there were only eighty thousand survivors. The most flagrant fraud is that according to the "Poland" column *there are no Polish Jew D.P.s left in Western Germany or Austria.* On the contrary, they swarm there by thousands in the black markets! But, unfortunately, a very unpleasant surprise came to spoil the world-wide belief that there were only eighty thousand survivors left from Polish Jewry. One hundred and fifty thousand Polish Jews suddenly arrived in the West fleeing from Polish pogroms. They were spirited away with all haste to Palestine and America. Their emigration was carried out in a record short time.

Here is another noticeable point. In the statistics of the Joint Distribution Committee, Soviet Russia is not mentioned at all. What is the position of Russian Jewry? The Committee gives the following information only: "Other countries of the Continent" — "Losses: 139,000 persons." But the *New York Times* corrects this figure and says that, including the Jewish population of Estonia, Latvia and Lithuania, out of 3,550,000 Russian Jews only 2,665,000 survived. This means that 885,000 Baltic and Russian Jews perished.

There is no doubt that in these territories Jewry suffered considerable losses and not only in partisan warfare alone. The German troops in the East did not commit atrocities against the Jews. *The Ukrainian population killed a few thousand Jews but they killed them not as Jews but as Bolshevik oppressors and tormentors.* In Odessa the Roumanian troops staged a massacre as a retribution for an attempted attack on their headquarters. But the intervention of German troops suppressed these incidents.

As the paper *Der Weg* proved, the so-called "interrogators" were sent to Europe early in 1945. These "interrogators" consisted of up to one hundred per cent of American Jews and of German Jews who had emigrated to escape from Hitler. They began their enquiries in 1945 and when their records were summarised, it appeared that twelve million Jews were killed by the Germans in the gas chambers. This result was apparently a bit too much even for the Jew Walter Lippman, who warned the Jews in the columns of the *New York Herald Tribune* that by using such manifestly forged figures they would only harm themselves. As a result of his leading article the figure for Jews " murdered " by the Germans was suddenly dropped to six million.

The question can always be asked as to whether it would have been physically possible to destroy as many Jews as the propagandists state were destroyed. Had the Germans enough time for it? Did they possess adequate facilities for it? And then, why was it necessary to build additional crematoria so quickly for shooting scenes in propaganda films? Is it possible that the Jews built these additional crematoria to make their unbelievably high statistics more credible? Was it necessary for the Germans to destroy the Jews systematically, when they were at all times short of manpower and could use the Jews very well for purposes of war-production?

The alleged " extermination " would not have begun before the early part of 1944. Is it credible that during this short time, i.e. from early 1944 until the end of the war, the Germans could destroy six or five or even three million Jews, as the various " sources " state? After all, it is a well-known fact to-day that the German population knew nothing of the existence of the Jewish camps. It is therefore unthinkable that the Germans could have staged massacres on the scale of those committed by their enemies on the public squares of Prague. There were only small units on guard duty in the camps and these were later replaced by camp police, often partly consisting of a few Jews, who kept order and watched over the prisoners. Such an enormous gathering of Jews equal in number to the total German armed forces can hardly be conceived. At a time when the Germans faced the most difficult problems concerning the transport of ammunition, food and petrol, is it likely that they would have transported and concentrated Jews only, instead? Can it be reasonably supposed that the mass-destruction of millions on such a vast scale could have been kept secret? Why did the Russian radio remain silent? And why did Western propagandists say nothing about these would-be exterminations? Since they knew the most intimate secrets of the German General Staff and of the National Socialist party through spies and traitors, they would surely have known of these " exterminations ". Why did they begin to speak of these horrors only towards the end of hostilities?

The real truth about the extermination of six million Jews must

organisations such as the Catholic Welfare Conference or the World Church Service. Some came with their papers in order, others with forged passports. Jewry had a larger share in the D.P. quota than all the other nations together. But this did not satisfy Herbert H. Lehman, the New York Senator, who stated that the Displaced Persons' Act was "anti-Semitic". But the immigration authorities at the ports of New York and Boston and the officials at American Consulates were far from being " anti-Semites " for they were, almost exclusively, Jews.

According to the latest statistics the total number of world Jewry is about fifteen million. But if this is the case it is absolutely impossible for either six million, or even one million, Jews to have been " destroyed ". The number of American Jewry has risen by almost two million since the war. Before the war Jewish synagogues had only 4,081,242 active members. The atheists, agnostics, converts and communists who regarded themselves as Jews on political but not religious grounds are not included in this figure which, in any case, must be regarded as unreliable, since it was prepared with the sole view of furthering Jewish interests. But we can demonstrate the tremendous increase in the number of the American Jewish population from the figures contained in the linguistic statistics, which, in any case, are more reliable than those relating to creed and religion. According to these 2,270,000 persons speak Yiddish in New York alone, and the 1950 statistics of the Jewish World Congress tell us that the total number of Jews in the world only amounts to 11,473,353. But despite this statistical figure it appears to be quite definite that the Jewish population of the United States has reached the figure of seven million. It is likely, however, that Dr. Cecil Roth, Jewish historian and reader at Oxford University, has reached the most accurate conclusion. This courageous historian and Jewish leader read a lecture in the B'nai B'rith Jehuda Synagogue at Kansas City on March 18th, 1952, in which he stated that *two-thirds of the world's Jewish population lived in the United States. According to Cecil Roth, the total of the Jewish world-population, including secret members, is ten million.* (Edmondson: *I Testify,* page 57.)

The Jewish " dead " as represented by the faked figures of the Nuremberg sham-statistics are, in fact, living either behind the Iron Curtain of the Soviet or behind the purple plush curtains of

Rooseveltian politics. Thus these fraudulent statistics multiply by ten the *actual figure* of Jews who perished in the Second World War. The U.N. never dared to hold an impartial enquiry into the case of the alleged six million Jewish victims, and Germany, while she lived under military occupation, had no chance to publish the official statistics in German hands relating to the concentration camps from which the true facts could be ascertained. Nevertheless the lists containing the names of the inmates of the various concentration camps, together with all other proofs, are there in the archives of the Federal German Government. *Why is it that the Germans dare not publish them? Because if they did the world conquerors would thereupon bring about an immediate crash of Germany's fantastic financial recovery.*

This propaganda figure was needed to secure the sympathy of the world. By raising the number of martyrs world conquest was rendered easier and the Gentile peoples could be terrorised more.

Had world Jewry stated the plain truth and given the correct figures of the Jewish victims, it would have scored a moral victory in this debate. But with its lies, it has dissipated its greatest moral asset and gambled away the sympathy of the world. Hundreds of thousands were tortured in a frenzy of revenge for the ill-treatment of Jews. *Yet the number of Jewish victims in Europe to-day is much higher than the number of Jewish martyrs under the Hitler régime.* A day will come when history will decide who were the real tormentors of Jewry and who treated them most barbarously.

On April 6th, 1951, in *Aufbau,* the New York Jewish paper, the following appeal was published in German under the title: " Israel is looking for witnesses." " The Israeli Ministry of Justice in Jerusalem is looking for witnesses in the cases of several persons under investigation for having committed grave crimes against humanity and against the Jewish nation during the Second World War. Almost all of them are charged with crimes committed against internees (Jews)." And the following names were given: Andre Banek, Mordechai Goldstein, Ria Regina Hanzova, Jacob Honnigmann, Pinkus Pshetitzky, Moses Puesitz, Dr. Joshua Sternberg and Trenk Elsa. Of these eight people seven are Jews.

" How can this be possible?" the man in the street may ask, who has only been informed of the alleged atrocities of the S.S. " How could Jews commit atrocities on other Jews in the concentration camps? Is this not some yarn cooked up by the Nazis?"

The Hungarian Daily Journal (*Magyar Jovo*), a New York Jewish Communist paper, on April 27th, 1951, reprinted an article from the pen of Sandor Grossman, originally published in the Zionist paper, *Hatikva*, edited in Buenos Aires, which went as follows:

" The attention of the world press is taken up by reports published in Israeli papers. According to these reports the court of Tel-Aviv is devoting long sessions to throw light on the activities of certain members of the KZ Police (KZ = concentration camp). Thus it was learnt that a Jewish doctor of Chedera had treated deported persons with great cruelty. *He killed Jews by giving them lethal injections.* He refused to give medical aid in many cases, with the remark: ' You will perish in any case like a dog!' Of another doctor witnesses said even worse things in their evidence. A third ex-member of the KZ Police manhandled and tortured his Jewish brethren and caused the death of many of them.

" These late charges preferred against ex-members of the KZ Police brought to light many unbelievably cruel and horrible acts of violence. . . . It is the crime of a decade of official Jewish leadership that a social class has been permitted to develop whose members are ready to undertake anything, however unscrupulous, *surpassing even the most horrible mental aberrations of the fascist thugs, and to gratify their selfish instincts by torturing and crippling their own blood-brothers and sisters.* We have not to go far either in Hungary or in any of the other fascist countries to find the chief culprits—the educators of the KZ Police and their predecessors. These men were always well in the forefront of Jewish religious communities and offices and of Jewish social organisations."

No biased " anti-Semites " are writing this, but a Jewish nationalist in the columns of a Jewish paper. And though the complete list of similar cases is not in our hands, it will be worth our while to note one or two of them here.

On page four of the December, 1946, issue of the Social Democratic paper *Nepszava* of Budapest, the following article appeared. It was entitled " The Horrible deeds of Flogging Nelly " and continued:

" The People's Prosecutor indicted Mrs. Mor Klein, a clerk in the people's court. According to information received as a result of the enquiry made by the people's prosecutor, the accused, Mrs. Mor Klein, was known by the eight hundred unfortunate people under her charge in Bergen-Belsen by the nickname of 'Flogging Nelly'. She always took good care to conceal both her name and origin and caused the death of all those who could unmask her. According to the indictment, 'Flogging Nelly' was a block-commandant, and committed her outrageous deeds in this capacity. In the depth of winter she ordered the women to line up naked in front of the bath-house and made them wait several hours both before and after their baths. By this exposure she caused the death of many women under her charge. She ill-treated one of the deportees—a girl called Magda Lowi, who was not in her block and thus not under her charge—by flogging and hitting her for half an hour continuously, until the girl was hardly recognisable, being covered with wounds all over her body. Flogging Nelly often poured scalding drinks over the unfortunate internees so that they suffered in consequence from severe scalds and burns. Instead of distributing the food issued for her block, she stole it, and thus the number starved to death was several times more than in any of the other barracks. She failed to distribute those provisions most required during the cold winter of 1945, allocating them instead for her own gain."

Mrs. Mor Klein was sentenced to death by the people's court and so was *the only real war criminal who paid the penalty for her crimes.*

Another Budapest paper, *Vilag* (The World), gave an account in 1947 of a similar case under the title: " She flogged her comrades in Auswitz." The paper records that " Tigress Klara " was captured in one of the fashionable restaurants. The account continues: " This sadistic woman was the commandant of Barracks No. A/7 at Auswitz Camp. According to the depositions of several witnesses, this woman, who was twenty-five years old, went about with a cudgel in one hand and a whip in the other. She flogged the deported women mercilessly and for the smallest misdemeanour ordered them to lie prostrate and have a heap of bricks loaded either on their breasts or on their backs. She also compelled hundreds of young girls and older women to remain on their knees for hours until they fainted."

As was proved at Nuremberg, the S.S. guards were detached from the internment camps towards the end of 1943 and in the early part of 1944. In the camps, apart from the Commandant's personal staff, only the Jewish KZ Police and the block-commandants were left.

If the time ever comes when the truth is told, the world will learn who were the real torturers of Jewry and what happened to the six million " wandering " Jews.

TWELVE

SPIRITUAL AND ECONOMIC PERSECUTION

SIX million ghosts, a grandiose legend of murdered Jews, served as a great capital investment for the world conquerors. We do not wish to whitewash anybody or anything, and we willingly acknowledge that even if the number of Jews who perished during the Second World War were only 600,000, this would constitute as big a crime as if the number had been six million. But then, the Prague murders of Sudeten Germans, the killing of the Roumanians of Moldavia, of the Greeks, and of the Hungarians, etc., etc., were also big crimes.

These crimes became really sinister when a propaganda tale multiplying the actual figure of the Jewish victims by ten, was used not only to carry out an Old Testament revenge but also to serve as an excuse for renewed world terror. For this terror to become firmly established it was not enough to merely kill physical bodies at Nuremberg, because *the spirit had to be murdered too*. Not only the spirit of German "nazism" but the spirit of Christianity. In the "spiritual Nuremberg", the real accused were not Goering Rosenberg and the other leaders, but the person of *our Lord Jesus Christ himself*.

In 1946 a Jewish conference was held in Switzerland, and on its agenda, amongst other things, was a proposal to amend the New Testament in those parts where it pictures Jewry unfavourably, and it was suggested that all the available copies in the world be confiscated. (Maurice Bardéche: *Nuremberg or the Promised Land*.) At the same time Amsterdam Jews wanted to stage a re-trial of Christ before the court of Jerusalem in order to "rehabilitate" Him And just about this time a new attraction was being prepared at Hollywood. The world Press reported that a new film of Christ was being shot with the bandy-legged Charlie Chaplin in the title rôle. Meanwhile Jewish rabbis were demanding that the singing of

169

Christian religious songs in the schools of the U.S. be forbidden because their sensibility was hurt. Anna Rosenberg, the Assistant Under-Secretary of War, would not allow crosses to be placed over the graves of soldiers killed in action during the Korean War if these cemeteries contained any Jewish dead.

The deaf and half-blind Knut Hamsun, one of the greatest European writers of our age, was a typical victim of the spiritual terror. Although eighty-five years of age, this celebrated and widely respected man was silenced by confinement in a lunatic asylum. Knut Hamsun sided not so much with nazism as with German ideology, for he himself was descended from pure Germanic ancestry. But the very fact that a world-famed intellectual authority endorsed the conceptions of National Socialism, was intolerable to Jewry. In any case, it was not possible to present Knut Hamsun to the world as an uneducated, ignorant lout, and similarly the other great German genius, Sven Hedin, could not be passed off as an S.S. man or a gutter-snipe. Therefore the grey-haired eighty-five-year-old Knut Hamsun was dragged before the " Norwegian " court on a charge of " treason ". He was sentenced to thirty days jail, together with his wife, just for the sake of branding him. He who is not a servant of the world conquerors is a guilty man. He is guilty because behind him looms the shadow of six million Jewish martyrs! But the great writer, undaunted, speaking on behalf of the prosecuted and hanged Christian European *élite,* defiantly stated:

" I can wait for another occasion and for another court. The day may come either to-morrow or, perhaps, in a hundred years, but I can wait. I have time enough. It makes no difference whether I am alive or dead. But I can and I will wait."

And when, half blind, he still tried to write and earn his daily bread so as to help his grandchildren, he was locked up in a lunatic asylum.

" I can wait! " echoes his voice from the heights of immortality, vibrating with the unbroken faith of a dismembered Europe.

Similar, almost in detail to Knut Hamsun's, is the tragedy of Ervin Guido Kolbenhayer, one of the greatest German writers, the author of the Paracelsus Story. He was evicted from his house, and an emigrant Jew presided over the " German " court sentencing him. He was forbidden to follow his " calling ", as if a writer could be

170

forbidden in the name of freedom and democracy to fulfil his divine mission by using his God-given talents. Yet, faced with the Morgenthau spirit of persecution and destruction, Kolbenhayer also stated the truth:

"Everybody who tries to defend or excuse himself is considered guilty!"

It is a well-known fact to-day that the black-lists compiled against intellectuals were brought into Germany much earlier than the lists relating to the S.S. men cited as war criminals. Those world conquerors who returned from the United States and who were mostly fanatical Communists, compiled and brought these lists with them when they arrived in the capacity of Press and theatrical entertainment officers of the U.S. Army. Though they wore American uniforms they did not represent Jefferson's America, since they portrayed only the intolerant and revengeful spirit of Jewish Chauvinism. This mob, consisting of Jewish intellectual fanatics, was a baneful present from the land of liberty, and it repudiated all Jewry's earlier doctrines concerning humanity, philanthropy and progressiveness, i.e. all those principles put forward as a mask while Jewry previously donned the cloak of democracy. These people had one goal only: to destroy all competition from the intellectual social classes and professions, and to remove the intolerable superiority of the Christian outlook.

It was said that on the battlefields as well as on propaganda levels, a fight was being waged for the freedom of mankind and of the human spirit. Yet now, black-lists, censorships, the barring from professions, the muzzling of truth and threats of terror, were brought from the America of Roosevelt to the Continent of Europe, wherein lay the centre of human culture.

This spiritual terror, carried on under the shield of the American flag, dishonoured America and forever discredited the slogans of American freedom, since *up to the present day America has made no official amends for permitting this persecution.*

On the black-list were the names of Sauerbruch, Europe's greatest medical genius of the present century and Wilhelm Furtwängler, the greatest conductor in the Western world. These black-lists of Jewry further contained names such as Richard Strauss, Luise Ulrich, Emil Jannigs, Herbert von Karajan, Clemens Krauss, Julius Patzak, Walter Gieseking, the world-famous violinist, Vasa Prihoda, Paul Linke,

Werner Krauss and hundreds more. Fredl Weiss, the noted comedian, who often made jokes at Hitler's expense, was also brought before the court. This Jewish terror did not hesitate to stamp such an intellectual genius as Gerhardt Hauptmann "suspicious", because he dared to write a few sad lines about the ruins of Dresden. Leo Slezak was branded a "nazi", and Max Schmerling was described as a concentration camp leader. Even some of the dead were included in these lists, such as Heinrich George, who died in a Soviet forced labour camp, and Paul Linke, the great composer, who was dead long before the "Hollywood liberation" took place.

Gerhard Eisler was the leader of this spiritual extermination band. He was a typical figure of Jewish Chauvinism, really a Communist whom Mrs. Eleanor Roosevelt smuggled into America, and from whence he later returned to enter illegally the Eastern Zone of Germany. With him also returned a great number of Press and theatrical officers in American uniform. The emigrants quoted in *Aufbau,* the New York Jewish paper, together with a pen-pushing mob of character assassins, settled down in Western Germany. They were not satisfied with the extermination of the *élite* of German National Socialism. They wanted to hold the entire spiritual life of Germany collectively responsible. Simultaneously Communism began to spread. The prescription is as old as the hills: an American democratic uniform for show, with Bolshevism rampant behind the scenes. It is the Eastern Jew in a Western mask. According to the files of the McCarthy committee of investigation, Cedic Henni Belfrage, agent of the New York Intelligence Service, was chief Press executive. He was, of course, a crypto-Communist. James Aaronson, another Communist, prescribed to the German journalists what they must do in order to build up German democracy. This man worked out a Press programme for General Eisenhower, who, with the political experience of a soldier, signed everything the excellent Aaronson or, later, Kagan, put before him without asking any questions.

But it was not only in the strangling of European spiritual life that this spiritual world conquest became manifest. On the positive side, what was called re-education followed. Jewish Press officers filled the libraries of the "American Houses" in Germany with Communist works, written, of course, by Jews for the re-education of the German nazi people. In the name of liberty and democracy the publishing of papers was restricted by licence. But at first only racially persecuted immigrants and German Communists were granted licences to publish daily papers. The Western Jew who had established so many contacts with the Eastern Bolshevik Jew (as we showed earlier), now tried by wrapping himself in the Stars and Stripes, to " re-educate " the German people, i.e. to make them Communists. The world conquerors felt that American democracy was not enough security for them. The Soviet sub-machine gun with its open terror would be more satisfactory in covering up the crimes they had committed against humanity. Jewry tried to *establish* an exceptional state of affairs in which a Jew could do anything he pleased. This process began in fact with the Nuremberg trials, where it was not " war crimes " that were punished but where acts committed against Jews were revenged. World Jewry here declared almost openly that *the Jews regarded themselves as the sole victors of the last war.* This outlook became manifest in the codes, jurisdiction and proceedings of the so-called people's courts in the various States subjected to Bolshevik rule. The Code and the Criminal Procedure Act in Hungary was drawn up by a Jewish lawyer, István Ries, Minister of Justice, and by his under-secretary, Zoltán Pfeiffer, who was married to a Jewess, and according to these laws *even the smallest and pettiest things against Jews constituted crimes against the State and the people.* The People's Code and Criminal Procedure Act states that all members of any unit in the armed forces are responsible if one of their members does anything against the Jews. In this way, hundreds and thousands of innocent persons were hanged or imprisoned. One individual was committed for trial on the " serious charge " that he allegedly smiled when a Jew was deported. He was sentenced to prison for two years. According to the Code, " if a person did not prevent " preparations to assault Jews, or actively committed assault against them, the penalty was death in both cases.

The establishment of special rights and privileges for the Jews is especially apparent in Austria and Germany. In this respect the gravest measures were instituted against the Germans. *Out of at least sixty million victims of the Second World War, the Jews alone enjoy personal reparations.* The Jewish assets, though already redeemed and bought off in cash by the Hitler régime, had to be paid off again by the Germans after the Second World War. Not one of those twelve million people expatriated and expelled by the Potsdam Convention received reparations; neither did any member of the nations which were ravaged, raped and plundered by Russian Bolsheviks, not to mention intellectuals who became Stateless. Millions were robbed of their assets, land and houses. Millions were expelled from their homelands only taking with them one hundred pounds of luggage. But nobody, neither Uno nor the League of Human Rights, ever suggested that these victims should be compensated. The Arabs expelled from their homes in Israel never received any reparations either. Those prisoners of war who, against all conventions, were kept in captivity or as ordinary slave labour for eight, ten or more years after the end of the war, received no reparations either. In contrast to this, the I.G. Farben Industrie was closed down and the heir to Krupps was punished for having on their pay-rolls, on normal rates of pay, so-called displaced workers, amongst them a few Jews, whom they had to employ in their factory under the order of the German Government.

But Jewry received compensation in plenty, not only by the multiple repayment of losses actually suffered but by the systematic plunder of the defeated people. The legend of the six million dead Jews gave Shylock the rights to his piece of flesh, but this was to be cut out of the body and national finances of the defeated nations again and again. Those Jews freed from the concentration camps had occupied the houses of the German people as early as 1945. They plundered and wasted the contents of these model apartments in the beautiful German Workers' Settlements. Then, on the basis of the Reparations Act, they extorted a multiple of the costs of their own flats from the poverty-stricken German people. They picked up the cash grants from I.R.O., from U.N.R.R.A., from the defeated nations and from the victorious nations, which were paid out to the persecuted. The greater part of the costs of the Israelite war against the Arabs was met through selling the stocks of U.N.R.A.A. and I.R.O. on the black market. Thus they defrauded those non-Jewish Ukrainian, Russian and Polish refugees who, like themselves, were displaced persons too.

But· with all this they have not reached the end of blackmailing the world. The Israeli Government obliged the West German

174

Government to undertake to pay as reparations three and a half billion marks to Israel, *a State non-existent during the Second World War*. The Israeli Reparations Committee adamantly demanded the redemption of Jewish assets confiscated before and during the war. Possibly the Germans themselves do not know *how many times these Jewish assets were redeemed and paid for*.

Schäffer, ex-Minister of Finance of the West German Federal Government, said recently at a public meeting during the early part of 1958, that *the Jews had lodged a new claim of twenty-seven billion German marks* for reparations against the West German State. If Germany paid this enormous sum, he went on, it would assuredly ruin her monetary system, and consequently bankruptcy would follow. In this case Western Germany would fall into the Soviet trap.

But perhaps this is the true aim of the world conquerors!

But Schäffer said something else which lead to an exposure. He said that as apparently forty to fifty per cent of the reparations being paid out only covered legal fees, nearly half the reparations went to lawyers. This whole question came to a head in connection with the 41,000 D.M. reparation awarded to Sarah Katz. One of her lawyers, a Mr. Greve, received out of this sum 9,069 D.M. for his fees. The trouble started owing to the fact that this Mr. Greve was not only one of the lawyers in the case but also the president of the "Reparation Committee" in the Bonn Parliament. He belonged to the Social Democrat Party (S.D.P.). Jakob Diel, a Christian Democrat M.P., began inquiries into the activities of Mr. Greve, and thus it came to light that this brave Marxist patriot had so far collected 30,000 D.M. in fees, in connection with Jewish reparation cases handled through his office. All over the world and especially in America, certain lawyers ganged up by forming their own "kolkhozes", with the aim of squeezing more money from the West German State. These lawyers and solicitors all enjoyed the support of Jewish world organisations and were thus in a position to inspire terror and exercise pressure on the German authorities.

The rest of this scandal consists of the fact that Jews could claim reparations by simply signing an affidavit under oath, and so thanks to many forged affidavits the West German State is being robbed of many billions of marks.

When a journalist asked one of the leading officials of the

175

Reparations Commission what kind of injury, illness or bereavement had to be suffered to enable a person to receive, say, 10,000 D.M. in reparations, the official answered:

" Including blood-circulatory disorders, we pay up for every possible illness even when the sick persons have not been persecuted at all."

Jakob Diel, the Christian Democrat M.P., found out in the course of his inquiries that *reparations were even being paid out to those Communists and professional criminals who had been sent to prison for ordinary crimes.*

It will be difficult to hush up this scandal now, for Jakob Diel also emphasised that the Social Democratic Party of Germany wishes to drain away the money allotted to cover the training and equipment of the divisions West Germany undertook to contribute to the North Atlantic Treaty Organisation.

Thus the plan of world Jewry becomes clear and understandable: to blackmail the West German State with false affidavits and, by means of very high legal fees, to rob the Germans of the funds which should serve for the re-armament of the new divisions. Thus the German worker will become an eternal payer of taxes to world Jewry, the unification of Eastern and Western Germany will be prevented, and the way paved for inflation and Bolshevism.

Naturally, world Jewry lost no time in stamping Jakob Diel as an " anti-Semite " for unmasking the greatest blackmail of all time.

The " reparations " blackmail is not the only type of extortion practised; there are many others.

The German newspaper *Der Weg,* edited in Argentina, in issue No. 6 of 1954, furnishes shocking statistical details concerning the horrible robberies committed to the detriment of Germany. Up to May, 1945, the allies destroyed goods and property to the value of 320 billion D.M., and the German population suffered a loss of 15 billion D.M. from looting. Under the pretext of denazification, various assets were confiscated to the tune of 108.5 billion D.M.,, whilst by means of the many forms of indirect confiscation, as well as through the activities of an American export organisation known as J.E.I.A., and further by seizure of the German commercial fleet, further damage was inflicted in the region of 1,381 billion D.M. Moreover, through the currency reform the German population suffered a loss of 198 billion D.M. The "occupation bank notes" issued by the allied powers represented a further loss of 46 billion D.M. which the German taxpayers had to shoulder. On the dis-annexed territories the losses of German citizens reached the sum of 457 billion D.M., the dismantling of the German factories represented a loss of 10 billion D.M., whilst the ruthless deforestation of German forests by the French resulted in a loss of 14 billion D.M. The artificial price fixed for coal has resulted in a loss for the Germans of another 84 billion D.M. But the most characteristic damage inflicted was the robbing of patents. German inventions fell almost exclusively into the hands of the Jews, and American Jewish firms made a haul of 78.5 billion D.M. by exploiting German patent specifications, the files of which filled 2,000 waggons. The amount of wages owed to prisoners of war are estimated to be as high as 11.5 billion D.M., whilst the Germans shouldered transporta-tion expenses of 72 billion D.M. During the period of the occupa tion there were 305,000 half-caste babies born whose keep has so far cost the German taxpayer 135 billion D.M. The confiscated German assets abroad represent a loss of 18 billion D.M., and al-though the Germans had to repay any Jewish assets confiscated by them several times over, the U.S., on direct intervention by Jewry, refused recently to return seized German assets. In acting thus, the U.S. repudiated its professed principles relating to the "inviolability" of private property. The Germans had to pay also more than 15 billion D.M. on old debts originating from the Versailles treaties and they were charged 8.6 billion D.M. on the Marshall Plan. The West German State has so far paid the Jews 9.5 billion D.M. "re-parations".

The big American Jewish capitalists yearly pocket a profit of 2 to 3 billion dollars out of the proceeds of German patents alone. More than 100,000 (at one time half a million) Jews received 300 D.M. monthly for sitting in concentration camps during Hitlerite times. As proceedings against Aurbach proved, this compensation was paid out in many thousands of marks to Jews who in fact did not exist at all.

This blackmailing and looting of the nations under a semblance of legality, will be carried on as long as the parasite State of Israel needs money, and so long as Gentile nations refuse to restore international law as it was practised in 1945 and before.

But it is not only in respect of the laws relating to private property that Jewry has created dangerous precedents. It wishes to establish on all levels a *supranational and privileged status for the Jews.* This became manifest in the so-called " welfare " activities after the last war. U.N.R.R.A. supported Jews and Communists almost exclusively, and anyone who dared to utter a word against this discrimination was silenced or gagged as a " nazi ". U.N.R.R.A. did not concern itself about the welfare of Gentiles who had been in the same camp as the Jews. I.R.O. usually made the emigration of Stateless persons dependent on what they thought about the Jews. The regulations of I.R.O. were made to serve such questions as : " Had he helped persecuted Jews?" " Had he sabotaged the work of his own Government?" " Had he ever made any ' anti-Semitic ' statement?" or " Had he ever written any ' anti-Semitic ' article?" The screening of the emigrants was mostly carried out by Jewish consuls and the consular office staff. They did their utmost to keep the number of Gentile immigrants to the United States as low as possible. The work of I.R.O. was the manifestation of perfect collaboration between Eastern and Western Jews. It was found out later that several officers acting in an executive capacity in I.R.O. centres were actually secret Soviet agents of the M.V.D. I.R.O. in the name of " humanity " handed over to Soviet hands several refugees against whom there were no charges whatever, but whose only " crime " was that they belonged to an intellectual *élite* which had to be exterminated.

Jewry has established a most dangerous state of affairs regarding civic rights and the laws of naturalisation, especially since Israel came into being as a separate State. In the defeated States of Germany, Hungary, Slovakia, and Roumania, etc., Jews were promptly granted full citizenship, without satisfying any legal conditions at all. Many had never belonged to these States and had absolutely no legal right to apply for citizenship. In the States behind the Iron Curtain only Jews received exit permits to enable them to emigrate to Israel. These same States were forced to take back these emigrant Jews if decided to return, either to avoid military service, or because they were not satisfied with conditions in the new Jewish State. There is a definite attempt in the American Immigration Acts, as well as in the laws and regulations of several other nations, *to establish supranational world citizenship for Jews.*

Dangerous precedents were also created by the Nuremberg court. Maurice Bardéche points out that *the concept of having a native country was discarded.* Everybody, or more correctly, every Jew, is a world citizen. The Jewish migrant from Zhitomir is as much a citizen of your country as you are. He has equal rights to your land. You agricultural workers must respect the rights of negroes on the land and you must make room for him at your table. He will march in and take office in your city or rural council, so as to make you familiar with outside "world conscience". His sons will, perhaps, become masters over you and *they may sit in judgment over your sons.* They will rule in your own city and they will re-sell you your own land, for "world conscience" entitles them to do so.

This is no joke! Dr. Levy, a Jewish doctor, wished to take up residence in the German city of Offenbach, although he had never been a German citizen. When the civic authorities refused to appoint him to the post of Public Health Officer, the so-called "democratic" newspapers threatened the City Council with intervention on the part of the occupation authorities. In America fictitious information lodged by a single Jew is sufficient to prevent a person's immigration. If the Jew says that the intending immigrant is an "anti-Semite", then the Attorney-General of the U.S. can declare that this immigrant is an undesirable person who "would endanger national security". And this means that America depends on the opinion of Jewry as to who will be accepted as citizens of the United States.

But the countries of the Western world, though perhaps often unaware of it, have actually adopted the Soviet system by the establishment of Jewish privileges as part of their constitutions. As we pointed out before, no Soviet citizen may be referred to by the adjective "Jewish". This would be punished by death or by deportation. Immanuel Birnbaum mentioned this matter with great satisfaction in *Aufbau* on March 17th, 1950, and his article emphasised that this law is in force at present. In the Soviet, where allegedly no one has any privileges, the Communist laws secure that Jews may exercise their powers and protect themselves from being pointed out as Jews. *" Secrecy is the character of our power,"* say the *Protocols*

179

of the Learned Elders of Zion. So the origin of Malenkov can be discussed but not that of Khaganovich!

With the help of U.N.O. a new international law was made to preserve Jewry's supranational status. This new law immortalises Nuremberg. It is called the *"Genocide Convention"*, i.e. the law relating to the systematic extermination of racial and national groups. The time appears to be very opportune to bring in this Act when millions of people, even whole nations, are vanishing in the forced labour camps of the Soviet. But the genocide law is not made to punish those particular crimes.

The Act terms it racial murder to bring about the partial or total extermination of a nation, or of an ethnical, racial or religious group, or even to have the intention to do so. But this convention also rules that physical or spiritual violation of, or insult to, members of any of the aforesaid groups falls under the heading of racial murder. Of course, it was only natural that U.N.O. should have forgotten to apply this new law in connection with the Hungarian uprising and fight for freedom on October 23rd, 1956.

With this genocide convention all liberty was suppressed, including freedom of speech and the right to hold public meetings. If anybody objects to the terrorism of the Jewish Communist leader or does not hold a good opinion of Jewry's world government or of the public activities of Mendes France, Frankfurter or Morgenthau, he can be promptly convicted under the genocide convention for spiritual violation of, or insult to, the respective ethnical or racial group. This is termed racial murder and is punishable with five years of prison in any part of the world. This, of course, supposes that it is the protection of the Jews which is in question, for naturally *Chinese, English or Arabs, etc., can be violated or insulted "spiritually"* with impunity. This law offers unlimited possibilities for terrorism. The city of Cincinnati (Ohio, U.S.) adopted Munich as her sister city. American Jewry protested immediately against this, stating that Munich was a hot-bed of Hitlerism. Thus the beneficial action of Cincinnati welfare organisations would amount to a "violation of Jewry". Therefore, according to the genocide convention, Cincinnati must be wiped off the face of the earth like Sodom and Gomorrah, or perhaps like Dresden and Hiroshima.

On the basis of the genocide convention Ahasuerus and Shylock can be banned from literature and Dickens' story of Oliver Twist in both its book and film forms must be prohibited, for it incites to murder against " usurers ", and " spiritually " insults the sensibility of Jewish nationalists. Auerbach, the Jewish commissar, with whom the German people were saddled and who, when unmasked, took refuge in suicide to escape from the crimes he committed, had banned the Ahasuerus story from German school books, for its " anti-Semitism ". The reason given was: " After Auswitz, this untenable Biblical Jewish legend cannot be tolerated." Gentile children may only be taught what the Jewish censorship passes as appropriate.

The genocide convention, though supported by Felix Frankfurter and Robert M. Kempner, the Jewish public prosecutor at Nuremberg, nevertheless encountered grave criticism. Certain clear-sighted people in American public life drew attention in public meetings to the fact that *the genocide convention was not only tyrannous and treacherous but also constituted a sort of permanent war against the American people*. Mervin K. Hart pointed out that, genocide convention or not, Palestine Zionists murdered all the men and women in the Arab village of Dair Yassin and got off scot-free without any charges being raised because they were Jews. He emphasised that once the genocide convention were enacted, " the slightest reference to a single member of a certain racial or religious minority would constitute a criminal act ". James Finucane, a delegate of the National Council for the Prevention of War, said that: " *Quebec, Yalta and Potsdam were racial murders under the American flag.*"

The fact that the genocide convention was the work of the Morgenthau group serves as the best proof that this Racial Murder Law was intended to be nothing else but an exclusive privilege for Jewry, as well as a means, approved by U.N.O., of exercising world terror. " A permanent war against the American people! " Agnes Wather described it. A permanent fight against spiritual freedom. A privilege, in the shadow of which Arabs, Frenchmen, Germans and Roumanians, etc., can be murdered with impunity.

The genocide convention—not applied, of course, against leaders of countries behind the Iron Curtain which are run by the Jews—must be viewed against a sinister background of events showing how Jewry attempts to silence all dissenting opinion. It is generally known to-day that black-lists compiled by Jewry are lodged even with so-called Gentile publishing houses. Thus no work can be published by an author " whose name is not good " from the point of view of Jewish nationalism. Anyone appearing in a film or play disliked by Jewry will never be able to appear again in any rôle, however talented an artist he or she may be.

Veit Harlan the director of " Jew Süss ", was acquitted by all the courts. Nevertheless, Jewish organisations still prevent his showing social films which could damage them. Many Jewish organisations protested against the showing of the English film " Oliver Twist ". At the same time the Jews accused certain American religious organisations of " anti-Semitism ", because they wished to ban the showing of Ingrid Bergman and Rosellini's blasphemous film about Christ. Jewish organisations again protested because an American publishing company edited Dostoievsky's political essays. Amongst these are a few masterpieces dealing with the Jewish problem. Gieseking was expelled from the " land of liberty " because he gave concerts during the Hitlerite era. Ernst Dohnanyi, the composer, could not appear for years in the Carnegie Hall just because Jewish war veterans proclaimed him a " fascist ". Heinrich Gulda, the world-famous pianist, was sent to Ellis Island for having been a member of the Hitler-Jugend when he was ten years old!

Here we can recognise the spiritual world terror in its completeness. Consistent and persistent, it goes right back to Christ Himself. German writers whose works were neither " anti-Semitic " nor nazi nevertheless received sentences in German courts. It was sufficient for them to be suspected of having " anti-Semitic " leanings, to be punished by being banned from their occupation or by the confiscation of their property, regardless of the fact that they were politically harmless persons, such as artists, writers or actors. Lajos Docvenyi Nagy, the author of the novel *The Khaganoviches*", was sentenced to be imprisoned in Hungary. Alfons Luzsénszkya, the translator of the Talmud, was imprisoned for five years. Lajos Méhely, one of the leading European biologists, was sent to prison for seven years at the age of ninety-three. Aloysius Dolány-Kovács, whose crime was the preparation of a few dry statistics showing the distribution of national wealth in Hungary, was also sent to prison. Similar sentences were passed in Roumania, in Czechoslovakia and in the other countries behind the Iron Curtain.

The newly formed State of Israel greatly helped in the establishment of world terror in the Western hemisphere. Five years after the war the Israeli Parliament passed a resolution according Israel the right to punish " war criminals " and to demand their extradition from any other State. *This is quite beyond the limit of any sort of legal justice.* A State here claims the right to be judge of so-called " war crimes " which were said to have been committed before that State existed. Here we are faced not only with *post facto law* but with a State directly benefiting from it. Every form of criticism or purely theoretical literary activity can be prosecuted. Israel has the right to extradite and hang Swedish. Chinese or Argentine intellectuals.

The special feature of this law is the fact that *while it tries to place all Gentiles under Jewish law, it intends to exempt all Jews from the laws of Gentile States.*

In Henry Ford's book *The International Jew* we can gather much information concerning special Jewish courts in New York, and indeed at the present day we know of cases which could only be heard by special Jewish courts. In 1950 a certain Mayer Mittelman was charged in New York with beating to death a fellow-Jew called Benjamin Krieger, in one of the German cencentration camps during the war. New York Jewry saw to it that this unpleasant case was not brought up before an American court. The American Jewish Congress convened a special court to try this murder case. The trial ended by acquitting the accused and finding that he did not commit any murder after all.

So here again we confront a double morality enforced by terror. The Argentine paper *Der Weg* published a very interesting article by Felix Schwartzenborn, under the title: " World tyranny from 1955 on?" which describes the plans relating to the establishment of the Jewish world kingdom. The U.N. is regarded as the supreme organiser of this world terror. The American weekly *Common Sense* also confirms the existence of such plans.

" The plans for the establishment of Jewish world domination are progressing well towards realisation," it writes. " It is probable that the future world government will be what is known at present as the United Nations Organisation " The world is now divided into two hemispheres by two opposing great power groups. One is ruled by Muscovite Jews under the "seal of Solomon" (the five-pointed star), whilst the other is under the flag of the U.N. Bernard M. Baruch was commissioned to accomplish the unification of the economic forces of the U.S.A., which actually meant the handing over of American power and economic resources into the hands of the Wall Street Jews. The internationalisation of raw materials, the European Army, the European Parliament in Strasbourg, and the Schuman Plan (drawn up really by David Lilienthal), are all intended to drive the non-Communist world under the economic terror of the Jews. And now one thing only is lacking: the welding of the two giant blocks, ruled under the red star and the blue and white U.N.O. flag, into a "super State", i.e. a State over all States. Once this is accomplished, the American stars and stripes and the Muscovite red star will be replaced by King David's six-pointed star. According to the latest plans all atom bombs, hydrogen bombs, armies, fleets and air forces must be handed over to the U.N. for, as it is said, "it would be too dangerous to leave them in the hand of a single power or power group". Finally, U.N. armed forces and U.N. atom power, with its operational centre in Jerusalem, will be able to suppress with ease all "uprisings" of the Gentiles. The U.N., governed by the Jews, will be the supreme power of the world, and on the basis of the genocide convention, drawn up by the Polish Jew Raphael Lemkin, professor of Yale University, everything that can be called "anti-Semitic' will be punishable by death or imprisonment.

Mankind is now living under a menace the like of which has never been known before. World terror has indeed begun to march and the sinister shadow of world tyranny envelopes the globe.

The plans of the world conquerors are greatly facilitated by a process which is partly natural and partly artificial and which can be described as the reduction of the masses to the level of herds of cattle.

THIRTEEN

BIOLOGICAL CLASS-WARFARE AGAINST ALL NATIONS

ORTEGA Y GASSET wrote his book *La Rebelión de las Masas* in 1929, and it can be regarded as a basic work relating to the nature and problem of the masses of human society. But the importance of the masses was recognised long before the great Spanish socioligist wrote his work. *The Protocols of the Learned Elders of Zion* mention as early as 1897 that they had " replaced the ruler by a caricature of of a government ", i.e. " by a President, taken from the mob, from the midst of our puppet creatures, our slaves ".

" *Our puppet creatures, our slaves!* This definition has a decisive importance in assessing the problem of the Jewish world conquest.

No doubt capitalism, with its higher standard of living, improved social conditions, prolonged expectation of life, reduction of death-rate, etc., has greatly increased the numbers of the masses. Hegel, Malthus and Marx all noticed this increase of the masses and the menace of over-population, which by itself is nothing but a simple biological and statistical fact. Neither Jewry nor Bolshevism has anything to do with this biological phenomenon, which can be regarded as an example of the natural fecundity of life. Then, first Marx, and later the *Protocols,* recognised the sinister possibility of " melting down " large crowds of people so as to form a characterless mass. *To make a herd-like crowd out of the people is the surest way not only towards achieving Jewish world power but towards achieving power for any minority group.*

" Without an absolute despotism there can be no existence for civilisation . . ." state the *Protocols,* for: " What we have got to get at is that there should be in all the States of the world, besides ourselves, only the masses of the proletariat, a few millionaires devoted to our interests, police and soldiers."

" The division of society into masses and *élite*," writes Ortega y

Gasset, " is not so much a social differentiation as a classification of people into categories which do not necessarily coincide with the ranks of the higher and lower social classes. *Strictly speaking, each social class has its masses and its élite."*

It is not difficult to recognise that ceaseless striving towards increasing the masses at the expense of the *élite,* which has been in progress throughout the century. To this result, no doubt, certain biological and hereditary factors contributed. These are dealt with by the American professor Lothropp Stoddard in his book *Rebellion Against Civilisation.* He ascribes the present crisis of humanity to the biological degeneration of the various races and to the disproportionate increase of world population — especially of the lowest and most worthless specimens. *But world Jewry did its utmost to speed up this process* during the century that has elapsed since the Marxist manifesto. Proletarians such as those composing the assault troops of Béla Kun or Sidney Hillman, who never bothered to consider what were the real aspirations of their leaders, became natural storm-troops of the masses. The theory of the class struggle, a typically destructive Jewish invention, tends in itself to increase the number of the mob. It levels downward and lops off heads above the average. The Press, and later, both radio and television, reinforced by the Jewish mentality of the Hollywood film industry, also contributed to the production of men with robot-like minds. Moreover, the mercenary spirit will neither educate the masses nor raise their intellectual status. On the contrary, by descending to the low intellectual standard of the average person, it will improve conditions for traders. In countries already conquered by Bolshevism, the breeding of colourless, leaderless masses, under the sole control of the " chosen ", is proceeding according to carefully worked-out plans. The Russian aristocracy, the middle classes, the intellectual *élite,* the landed peasantry and those workers who could be regarded as the *élite* of the working class, were all executed. The independent landed peasantry were robbed of their lands and deported to Siberia. Individual and independent smallholdings were replaced by the kolkhoz system, and the " liberated " proletarians were enlisted in the workers' divisions of the factories were they had *no leaders any longer but lords and masters only.*

The Jews sitting in Stalin's brains trust were always aware that the "ruthless despotism" of the *Protocols* can only be exercised over herd-like masses. The greatest menace of Bolshevism is its creation of a herd-like mentality in the people, which thinks in terms of the lowest intellectual levels, which destroys all initiative in the individual and kills all differentiation of taste and personality. There are no Russian people left but Russian masses only, and in thirty years' time the same statement will apply to all the other enslaved States behind the Iron Curtain. There will be just masses all the way from Vladivostok to Stettin. The colour of their skin may be usually white, sometimes yellow, but their distinguishing characteristic will be the negative one of belonging to the masses. This will be a mass-produced, homogeneous and characterless human pulp that has been churned out on the assembly lines of the camps and in the retorts of Communist education propaganda. This is the youth produced by Communism and trained to have no individual thoughts or ideas of their own. They have ready-made slogans only, coined by propaganda. This is a herd of anthropomorphous beings, shepherded by Jewish commissars armed with tommy-guns. One sees no longer the glittering billions of single water-drops but only muddy and turbid flood waters.

So-called civilised man of the Western world is still unaware of the meaning and importance of these anthropomorphous masses which have lost all knowledge of the outside world, of the beauties of life and of the value of personality. The Iron Curtain hermetically sealed them off from living thoughts and ideals. They possess less knowledge of the outside world than had the people of the Middle Ages. They know nothing about history, culture or present-day life in the West. They live in a distorted dream-world produced and projected for them by Ilia Ehrenburg and David Zaszlavszky.

But unfortunately the proud citizens of the West are little better off in this respect. Their knowledge, general outlook and political ideas are similarly mass-produced, controlled and directed by their Jewish entertainment monopilies. The personality of Western man has atrophied and his national heroes have been forgotten. Their place was taken by that most ridiculous figure of Western democracy, *the "man in the street"*, i.e. by the average half-educated, ignorant human being who is unable to think for himself. To-day this person states his opinion in the Press, answers the questions of the Gallup poll and represents public opinion and *"world conscience"*, in the name of which the scandal of Nuremberg was staged and the massacre of Katyn was hushed up. What does this "sharp-witted" individual, this constant reader of picture-comics and detective stories, know about the "Elder Statesmen" performing behind the screen of the political parties, about the plans of the "initiates", about decisions of the lodges and about the lies of the Press? He simply reiterates everything hammered into his head by journalists and newspaper kings of Galician Jewish origin. And the columnists of democratic and republican organs alike will, of course, only spread such "opinions" as favour the world conquerors.

Thus we can readily understand how it is that the so-called statesmen who appear to rule the world are, on the one hand, puppets of powers behind the scenes, and on the other, slaves of the mob. Politicians do not act any more according to the rules of common sense, but are obliged to rely on the taste and mood of the masses. They think in terms of the masses and they allow themselves to be carried away by the masses. The statesman of the past, after working out a clever programme, submitted it to the electors, hoping to convince them to do the right thing, i.e. to adopt his proposals The present-day politician first tries to find out the general trend of public opinion and then adjusts his own views to this. But when Jewry, disposing of all the modern media of propaganda, made the masses its sounding-board, statesmen dependent on the masses fell a ready victim to the will of Jewry.

The most successful politician in these days of "peace" is he who can drive the largest crowds to the polling booths, to prop up by votes the policy he has broadcast previously through radio and television.

Even war itself no longer serves as a last resort in the pursuit of higher ideals; it has one purpose only, which is the extermination of large masses of people. The A-bombs, H-bombs and carpet-bombs are no longer weapons of war between nations, but between *masses*. A lurid murder, or social scandal connected with a film star, makes headlines nowadays, but 300,000 dead in Dresden or 70,000 in Hiroshima can be ignored or perhaps dealt with in a small news item of five lines.

We have already mentioned that world Jewry, in order to increase the number of destitute masses, utilises mankind's natural urge for revenge. After the last war, many people thought that the increase in the number of destitute masses was the work of Bolshevism, and thus Yalta and Potsdam were debited to Stalin's account. However, after a certain time, it transpired that during the Potsdam conference, held under triumvirate of Stalin, Truman and Attlee, world Jewry in the form of the Morgenthau Plan and the Gomberg Plan stood by all the time in either democratic or Bolshevik guise. The purpose of both was the extermination of the *élite* and the reduction of the people to destitute, herd-like, characterless masses.

The Potsdam Agreement made twelve to sixteen million people Stateless. The Eastern European independent landed peasantry, and the skilled craftsmen and artisans of the Sudetenland were reduced to a destitute proletarian mass thrown across the frontiers with a hundred pounds weight of luggage per head. The nazi professors were forced to do the job of street sweepers and the nazi street sweepers were thrown out of their jobs. The Transylvanian Saxons were carried off to Siberia, while the highly cultivated German settlers of Southern Hungary and Northern Yugoslavia were sent to Tito's extermination camps, where glass powder was mixed into their food. Sixteen million people were torn from their country and made into a rootless, Stateless, destitute, hungry mob. They were driven like cattle towards Western Germany in the name of humanity.

Previously, Beria had liquidated the Polish intellectuals and national leaders in the Katyn Woods. Eleven thousand officers, mostly doctors, professors and artists, were called up from their civilian professions, were exterminated, and more than a million Poles were carried off to Siberia. Who were responsible for this? According to the official records of the U.S. Congress Investigating Commission, Father Braun reported concerning his Russian adventures (Reports of Investigations, page 197) that he had seen the secret police at work between 1936 and 1937, during the days of comrades Jeshov, Jagoda and, more lately, Beria (all three of them Jews— AUTHOR). They were successive chiefs of the secret police. He had also seen the Russians (Jews) murdering their own countrymen in cold blood. In view of the fact that internees were murdered by the thousand in the concentration camps of the Soviet Union, and that these atrocities were regarded as merely routine work not worthy

189

of mention, it can be understood that the extermination of influential Poles such as doctors, writers, professors, teachers and civil servants, etc., was similarly regarded. The report adds that *this was just a part of their general plan which was the systematic extermination of racial and national groups.*

Are Jeshov, Jagoda-Herschel and Beria the only culprits haunting the common graves of the victims of the Katyn Woods? Goriczki, a Polish witness who escaped from the mass-executions, told the American Committee investigating into the slaughter of Polish prisoners at Katyn: ". . . when the groups were ready to march, two officers of the political police, Colonel Urbanovitz and a Muscovite Jew, Commissar Sirotky, were standing near me. I overheard Sirotky remarking to Urbanovitz: 'Yes they are happy and laughing now, but if they knew what is coming to them . . .!'" (Reports of Investigations, page 176.)

So it appears that not only did the Jews organise and carry out the Katyn Wood mass-murders, but that through Robert Kempner, the American public prosecutor at Nuremberg, they tried to conceal the truth from the world.

Thus, in a few days or perhaps in a few hours, they exterminated the *élite* of the Polish nation and with it most of the intellectual class.

The colourful, free Hungarian *élite,* so individual in outlook, was similarly annihilated in 1945 with the help of the People's Tribunal Act, when the list of "war criminals" was handed over to the Americans.

And so *biological class warfare,* based on Talmudic commandments, progresses relentlessly. The Marxist theory has now reached a higher rung of the ladder. For the physical extermination of the Christian *élite,* there are Soviet prisons as well as the gold-diggers' camps in the Arctic Circle where, according to recently returned prisoners of war, five million people are forced to slave. World Jewry, whose total strength is about 15 million, is clearly aware that it can become the sole ruling class of all nations, once it succeeds in exterminating those social layers whose calling, on account of their intellectual faculties and integrity of character, is to be the leaders of their respective nations. With this end in view, the ignorant masses, "pink" intellectuals and other bribable characters are invited to serve the ends of the world conquerors to the extent of betraying their own race and nation. The conditions prevalent behind the Iron Curtain show more clearly than anything else that the fifteen million Jews could soon become a supranational middle-class, ruling over entire nations and whole continents. A ruling class which no longer needs to do any inferior or subordinate work. Their next generation can safely occupy the leading positions in all States. They wish no doubt to repeat the feat accomplished in Soviet Russia, where Jewry moved up from the bottom to the top of the social ladder.

And to attain this aspiration it is quite enough to carry out the Talmudic commandment:

" Kill the best of the Goyim!"

Gunnar D. Kümlien has written a very interesting article about biological class warfare in the *Rheinischer Merkur* of October 4th, 1957. This paper is closely connected with Chancellor Adenauer. In this article he records a conversation he had in Moscow recently with a Russian intellectual just released from one of the Siberian slave-labour camps. He could only speak in the greatest secrecy with this intimidated, scared man, because it was the forty years of the Bolshevik " revolution " they were discussing.

" That section of society which retained an ideological independence," said the Russian, " does not count any longer to-day. Its strength twenty years ago was as high as about twenty per cent of the population. It was still ten per cent about ten years ago. Supposing it was to have been reduced one per cent per annum, you can imagine how much is left of it."

A Swedish journalist who reported recently on living standards in the Soviet, gave a shocking picture of proletarian masses crowded in slums. The party keeps them in such poverty and in such low living conditions that the whole of their life consists of a ceaseless fight to keep themselves alive, and thus they have no time left to deal with political problems or to have any thoughts of their own at all.

Should the biological class struggle be applied to the spiritual leaders of Jewry, the Jews would call it " anti-Semitism " at once. Yet the cold-blooded, systematic slaughter of the *élite* of the Russian people and of the nations behind the Iron Curtain is not anti-Russian, anti-Hungarian or anti-Chinese! Nevertheless the consequences of tnis biological class struggle would remain permanent features even after the downfall of Bolshevism.

For the systematic extermination of the *élite* entails a good many alarming consequences. Due to the fact that the most cultured individuals, the most capable workers, the most intelligent farmers and the most skilled tradesmen and artisans were destroyed in the countries behind the Iron Curtain, *the quality of production in all trades has sunk accordingly*. There is no taste or " finish " applied to the various goods manufactured. Ornamental skill has become a a luxury; chair legs will not be planed or given a smooth surface, and the most common consumer goods are no longer available. The " new intellectuals ", mass-produced through " potted " courses, are nothing else but the slaves of the masses and are thus unable to direct trade, finance or agriculture The level of the sciences is reduced to the minimum; the doctor becomes a mere quack, and the ordinary scientist has little more knowledge than a foreman. On the soil of the Ukraine, the most fertile land on earth, the yield of wheat is lower now than ever before (eight cwt. per acre); the world-famous vineyards of Tokaj are in ruins and the plants dried up, the standard of the fruit-growing has regressed 100 years. The wheatfields of the Banat (in Southern Hungary and Northern Yugoslavia) where, due to the industry and skill of the German settlers, finest agriculture on earth flourished, are overgrown to-day by weeds, and the houses of the Sudetenland are in ruins. The population lives and starves in misery. The shapeless felt boots and the standard quilted and padded jackets are the only articles of clothing available to the enslaved masses. Whoever can look ahead can but visualise an appalling future : civilisation buried under the quicksands of the desert or overgrown by the jungle. Owing to the extermination of the *élite*, this menace hangs over the civilisation of all Christian nations as well as over the culture of all races.

The great martyred Hungarian patriot, László Endre, prophesied from his prison : " Proletarianised Europe will face them [the Jews] with such debased and brutalised instincts that the most savage means, necessary to suppress the most savage revolt of slaves, will have to be used to keep the people in bondage."

There will be no more revolutions or wars of independence, but slave risings only. What a future!

192

At this juncture somebody may point out that when this stage has been reached, then in all probability the world conquerors' power and privileges will also come to an end. Perhaps they will! But the world conquerors do not like to look into the future. They sit in the seats of the mighty.

FOURTEEN

THE JEWS HAVE THE ATOM BOMB

ON August 6th, 1945, Harry Truman, President of the United States, surprised the world with the following announcement:

" Twenty-four hours ago a U.S.A.F. bomber dropped a single bomb on Hiroshima. The effect of this bomb was greater than that of 20,000 tons of trinitrotoluol (T.N.T.). This was an atomic bomb."

Two years later, the thirty-one-year-old Rabbi Korff, one of the leaders of the Stern terrorist organisation, lead a march of 600 fanatical rabbis to Washington, where as their spokesman he demanded that on account of events in Palestine, the United States should drop another atomic bomb—on London. Rabbi Korff openly threatened Washington's successor with the power of world Jewry. (*The Jews Have Got The Atom Bomb,* page 3, edited by Gerald K. Smith.)

Two years later President Truman made another announcement. On September 23rd he said:

" We have proofs in our possession that during the last few weeks an atomic blast was carried out in the Soviet Union."

Not long after this announcement, a report came from Britain that the authorities had detained Klaus Fuchs, a Jewish atom physicist and Einstein's intimate friend. *The Jews had passed on the secret of the atom bomb to the Soviet Union!*

The formula of the atomic bomb fell into the hands of the Jews in its early stages, soon after research began. At the time of his arrival in America, Einstein was in possession of complete information concerning both Professor Otto Hahn's atomic fission theory and the results achieved up to date by the Kaiser Wilhelm Institute. He advised President Roosevelt to carry on with these experiments with the ultimate aim of producing the atomic bomb for the U.S. From this time on Jews never ceased to swarm around the secret of the atom. Amongst them, Lise Meitner, a female Jewish scientist, is to be specially mentioned, as she it was who passed on the results of Professor Otto Hahn's experiments to America through a Danish atom physicist, also a Jew. Leo Szilárd, another Jew from Budapest, also appeared on the scene, and since then the greatest secret of our present age has been surrounded by a strange and mysterious team of Einstein's protégés. Suddenly the German Jew, Robert Oppenheimer, a graduate of the University of Göttingen, joined this team of Jews. He was a Communist with Communist connections, because *he saw a truer, more ruthless and fanatical fulfilment of Jewish interests in Communism than in the democratic system.* Robert Oppenheimer was above everything else a Jew. He is one of the most characteristic and venerable representatives of Jewish world-conquering chauvinism. While Professor Otto Hahn wavered as to whether he should make or sabotage the atomic bomb for Hitler, or else present it to his own clan and nation, Robert Oppenheimer threw all his knowledge, creative imagination and inspired intelligence into the race to invent the atomic bomb first. He worked day and night without rest or reprieve. He grew lean and haggard; his weight went down to seven stone. He achieved almost fantastic scientific results for the sole purpose of destroying the Germans — the enemies of the Jews.

Naturally he was immediately surrounded by the chairmen and presidents of the various Jewish world banks and finance houses, who saw in the production of the atomic bomb not only a splendid profit but also a national mission. L. Strauss, one of the directors of Kuhn, Loeb and Co., had previously been David Lilienthal's financial advisor. Thus J. Robert Oppenheimer was put in charge of atomic research and of experiments backed with huge financial funds. Einstein let Klaus Fuchs into the experimental and production secrets of the atomic bomb. The works and offices engaged on production soon became choked with Jews from various countries. Unreliable refugees, shady immigrants, German, Ukrainian, Polish and Hungarian Jews took over not only key positions but the small jobs as well. Julius Rosenberg, David Greenglass and their ilk filled all the positions in Los Alamos.

There are doubtless many good reasons for this. There were always good mathematicians among the Jews. Besides, atomic research would appear to rather suit the Jewish mentality. Atomic fission is a typically Jewish science. So far it could destroy only, and as yet create nothing.

Everything else that followed was only the natural consequence of Jewish chauvinism. If one Jew succeeds in occupying any key position he will immediately try to employ as many Jews as possible. This is actually what happens during the judaisation of any institution, section of society or profession. Those Jews who succeed in establishing themselves will help and assist more Jews to settle in too, since in their eyes only their own kind can be trusted in the furtherance of Jewish national aspirations. And so around the person of J. Robert Oppenheimer was formed a fanatical chauvinistic group of Jews. According to American sources, only the labourers in the laboratories of Los Alamos and Honmouth were non-Jews. The names of Julius Rosenberg, Martin Sobell, Harry Gold and David Greenglass became known later during the trials of the most notorious atom spies. Professor Pontecorvo, the Hungarian Professor Jánosi, inventor of the hydrogen bomb, and Edward Teller, all belonged to this atomic sect.

The coil of the symbolic serpent closed tightly round the production of the atomic bomb. The great secret of America, guarded, produced and administered by the Jews, was regarded by Jewry as its own national property. *Thus Jewry regarded it as quite natural to share this secret with the Soviet Union.* The relations between the Eastern and Western Jew were renewed in this field as well. Although the members, or the fathers and grandfathers of members of the atomic sect had emigrated long ago to escape Russian pogroms, *they regarded Bolshevik Russia as much more reliable than America.* The Bolsheviks fought against Hitler fanatically. But in America there were people like Lindbergh, Taft and the isolationists. The atomic bomb, therefore, had to be handed over to the Soviet Union which they believed to be more ruthless and resolute than America.

It was of secondary importance only that there were a number of Communists amongst American atomic scientists. They had their eyes fixed all the time on the more savage, ruthless, fanatical and revengeful Soviet Jews, and they trusted nobody else but them. The Eastern Jews were well aware of this. David Zaszlavszkij and Ilia Ehrenburg referred constantly in *Pravda* to Albert Einstein as one of the six best friends of the Soviet Union in the U.S.A., and as being a personal friend of Stalin. And to make themselves more worthy of the trust of American Jewry they appointed Solomon

Abrahamovich Rebach, one of the leading organisers of the Bolshevik secret police, to the post of High Commissar of Soviet atomic research, and comrade Abrahamovich still holds this post to-day. On the other side of the Atlantic, the representatives of Kuhn, Loeb, the international bankers, played a most important rôle in the production of the atomic bomb. The same big Western capitalists who financed the Bolshevik Revolution in 1917 and who had such splendid connections with Trotsky (Bronstein), this time never bothered to conceal their feelings concerning Eastern Jewry. Albert Einstein himself never denied that, as a staunch democrat, he was enthusiastic about the Soviet. John Rankin, U.S. congressman, *publicly accused Einstein of having connections with the Bolsheviks* Thus we need not be surprised by the testimony of Major George Racey Jordan of the U.S.A.F., in which he said that as early as 1943, *mysterious hands began and maintained a constant delivery to the Soviet of raw materials, equipment and secrets necessary to the production of the War.* During the investigations into the case of radar espionage, *atomic bomb, i.e. in the most critical hours of the Second World* which was closely related to the atom spying, it came to light that twenty-six of the vanished fifty-seven most secret files of the U.S. Signal Corps of Monmouth were recovered in Eastern Germany. All those " scientists " suspended as a result of these investigations belonged without exception to the race of the world conquerors.

Eventually it became evident during the trials in the New York court that *atom espionage was not so much the work of Communists as of Jews.* Those accused admitted that they handed over atomic secrets to the Soviet as early as 1943. They passed on this vital information gratis, i.e. without ever expecting any reward for it, simply driven by the zeal of their Jewish chauvinism. The most remarkable feature in the case of the atom spies was that none of the accused demanded any money from the Soviet Union in return for their services. Julius Rosenberg in one instance only received $500 for defrayal of expenses. Completely obsessed by the most fanatical Jewish chauvinism, they were perfectly convinced that to betray America and thus help the Soviet Union, was the most sacred *duty of Jewry.*

All the accused in the atom espionage trials, without any exceptions, were Jews. And we will see that behind them stood the whole of world Jewry. During the trials the U.S. had to avoid the slightest appearance of " anti-Semitic " tendencies, unless she wanted to be declared bankrupt or have an economic crisis. Thus the case against Julius and Ethel Rosenberg had to be assigned to a Jewish judge— Justice Irving Kaufmann—whom the whole of world Jewry regarded as a destructive, opportunist traitor to the Jewish race. Sypol, the New York district attorney, was a Jew too. Finally, besides the accused, a Jew called Bloch was the defending counsel.

Behind the secret of the atom sits enthroned one of the most mysterious and powerful personalities of world Jewry in the person of Bernard Baruch, " the philanthropist " banker who, in the most obscure circumstances amassed a personal fortune during the two world wars. In the imagination of the American people, perhaps not without reason, Bernard Baruch appears as the " unofficial President of the U.S." and even Churchill has to visit Baruch first, before he calls at Washington to see the official President of the U.S. When Roosevelt became President, Baruch's power and influence was multiplied. Whilst the soldiers of the U.S. were losing their lives at the front during the Second World War, Bernard Baruch, in control of 351 of the most important branches of industry in the United States and of two-thirds of the raw materials of the whole world, used every effort to remove authority over the atomic bomb from the President and the Army of the United States. In this case *Jewry almost completely took off the mask.* If not by word, then by deed and propaganda it declared emphatically that it regarded the atomic bomb as *its own national property* and the means by which it hoped to establish its supranational power. As several American writers and publicists admit, Congress committed high treason when, under the lash of Baruch, it passed the Act which took control over the atomic bomb and its secret of production away from the President and the Army, and established the U.S. Atomic Energy Commission. President Truman, unaware of the consequences, signed this Act.

This commission is more powerful than the President of the U.S. It can act independently of any government on earth, even of the Government of the U.S. According to statements of American official circles, this commission possessed more power than Hitler, Roosevelt and Stalin combined.

When everything had been carefully planned and prepared, the members of the Atomic Energy Commission were appointed. Out of the first five members, three, or perhaps even four, were Jews. They were: David E. Lilienthal (Jew), Lewis L. Strauss (Jew), Robert F. Bacher (Jew), William Wymack (?), and Sumner T. Pike (?). It is noteworthy that although certain changes did take place in America, where the investigations of the McCarthy committee drew the attention of American public opinion to a good many things, the structure of the Atomic Energy Commission could not be changed. As a result of the Oppenheimer case, David E. Lilienthal was removed from the chairmanship of the A.E.C., but Lewis L. Strauss took his place. During this time, Professor Pontecorvo, the Italian Jew, became head of atomic research in the Soviet Union. Under him work the kidnapped German atom scientists, while over all of them Solomon Abrahamovich Rebach, chief atom commissar of the Communist secret police, exercises supreme control.

The atomic bomb fell entirely into the hands of the Jews. The greatest tragedy of history thus took place, and the most threatening menace looms over mankind. The atomic bomb even in the hands of duly elected democratic statesmen is a most dangerous weapon. But the march to Washington of Rabbi Korff and his 600 fellow-rabbis gave the world a reminder of what danger the atomic bomb could become in the hands of a fanatical tribal nationalist group. By the use of the atomic bomb, not only might civilisation be destroyed but the freedom of mankind may be lost for ever. The atomic bomb in the hands of world Jewry is a permanent menace to democracy, to the independence of all nations and to every spiritual or political movement unfavourable to the world conquerors. Those nations disobedient to world Jewry, or who may consider the rate of interest fixed by Kuhn, Loeb is too high, can be easily wiped off the face of the earth. In the hands of Jewry the atomic bomb represents terror and a horrible threat even if it is never dropped. The atomic psychosis, the fear of being destroyed by atomic blast or radiation, can be exploited to the detriment of whole nations. "Surrender your freedom and independence, abandon your Christian faith, for we are holding the atomic bomb over your heads like the sword of Damocles! At the time of the explosion of the first hydrogen bomb, the Jews succeeded in creating the impression that if

America began a war against the eastern half of their world-kingdom, the whole of the universe would probably be blown up as well.

This is not just a political possibility, but the materialisation of the vision in the Revelation of St. John, concerning the power of the beast *" over all kindreds, and tongues, and nations"* (*Revelations xiii.* 7) and foretelling the extermination of two-thirds of mankind. Not even the Learned Elders of Zion, the authors of the *Protocols*, dared to contemplate such a vision fifty to sixty years ago:

" It is from us that the all-engulfing terror proceeds."

The atomic bomb is the horrible agent of this terror engulfing everything, and at the same time it is the most horrifying proof that aspirations for world domination and world conquest actually exist. From 1934 until 1948 Jewish propaganda constantly proclaimed that American democracy together with the freedom of mankind could co-exist in good neighbourly understanding with Soviet tyranny. Since the end of the Second World War their global programme comprised divided world power between the Western and Eastern Jew. It is actually the sharing of the globe between them! It is rule by gold in the West and by tommy-gun in the East. *The supreme aim is the prevention of war and of a showdown with Bolshevism. As we pointed out before, this is the reason why Morgenthau organised the " Society for the Prevention of World War III ".*

Marcel de Briançon, the French author, sees this point clearly when he writes:

" These two apparently opposing, antagonistic and irreconcilable power concepts, which in fact complement each other, say to themselves: ' If the Soviet defeats the U.S.A., world power will be established in the form of a Communist world State by the organisation of a world Soviet. If the opposite happens and the U.S.A. defeats the Soviet Union, a new pluto-democratic world State will inevitably be established following the American victory. After all it matters little whether we Jews hold political world power by our sole possession of concentrated private capital, or whether we exercise the same political world power from key position in state capitalism. To us it does not matter which of these two concepts emerge victorious, for in either case the sole victory at the end will be ours. Under these circumstances is there any need for a showdown?' "

But later on, when world Jewry saw that a clash was possible after all, and when American public opinion had slowly begun to realise that the co-existence side by side of Bolshevism and freedom was not possible, Klaus Fuchs was suddenly arrested for handing over every detail of the atomic secret to the Soviet Union. Two names suddenly emerged from obscurity: those of J. Robert Oppenheimer and Julius Rosenberg. Both of them, as we will see later, can be regarded as symbolic figures of Jewish world-conquering nationalism.

As long as German National Socialism had to be destroyed, J. Robert Oppenheimer worked with the self-sacrifice of an ascetic and the inspiration of a genius to produce the atomic bomb. He was a Western Jew in the full sense of the word, *but even so, he put his trust only in the ruthlessness, bloodthirstiness and fanaticism of his Eastern brethren, and in nothing else!* According to the accusations brought against him, between 1940 and 1942 he supported subversive anti-American Bolshevik activities in the U.S. with large sums of money. He married a Communist. His brother and sister-in-law were also Communists. His Communist wife's first husband was also a hard-boiled Bolshevik and was killed during the Spanish Civil War. Oppenheimer had employed Communists in Los Alamos during the Second World War.

At that time he threw all his knowledge and talent into the problem of solving the production of the atomic bomb. He had no remorse, neither was he in the least conscience-stricken, for he knew that only nazis would be destroyed by the atomic bomb. But when the defeat of nazism was an accomplished fact, and when the H-bomb should have been invented and produced to check the real tyranny of the Soviet system, the great Western brother suddenly became diffident and unwilling to do anything against the Eastern world conquerors. He, of all people, knew very well that these Bolshevik despots and suppressors, though they might be a thousand times worse than Hitler, were nevertheless his brethren. With him they could recite in unison: "We are all the same nation! The same tribe! The same race! We are not Russian, Portuguese or American Jews, but *just Jews and nothing else but Jews!"*

K. D. Nicholson, general manager of the Atomic Energy Commission, wrote:

" Oppenheimer in his official capacity as chairman of the General Advisory Committee to the Atomic Energy Commission, in 1949 strongly opposed the development of the H-bomb and made every effort to persuade the others as well to go slow with this project, even after President Truman gave definite instructions to proceed with the experiments." (*American Hungarian Voice,* April 19th, 1954, page 7.)

The H-bomb should at this time have been dropped on the eastern half of the Jewish world kingdom. And the Western Jew did not want the destruction of the eastern half of his dominion. He, the mathematical master-mind, the wizard of physics with the satanic brain, perceived clearly that *the most favourable conditions for world conquest consisted in the bisection of the globe into two hemispheres, both possessing the atomic bomb, and both in a position to threaten one another constantly.*

The other symbolic figures of this world-conquering nationalism were the Rosenberg couple. They are typically small, unimportant people who perhaps did not help the Soviet Union as much as many observers believed. They handed over the atomic secret out of sheer racial conviction, i.e. doing it as part of their duty towards their own people. They handed over everything to the Soviet Union and, most characteristically, said in their defence that America was her ally.

But the sulphuric flames of supranational " nazism " blazed with a most intense and violent heat when the Rosenberg couple was about to go to the electric chair. According to the law the Rosenbergs were spies; they were traitors to America. Nevertheless, ninety-nine per cent of world Jewry stood up for them in solidarity. The millions of world Jewry, the capitalists and the proletarians, the residents of luxury villas of the Sea Gate and of the slums in the Bronx, the Jews of the West End of London as well as of every capital city in the world, united solidly in demonstrations to force the " nazi-fascist-Hitlerite " Eisenhower to exercise his presidential prerogative of mercy. In the eyes of decent patriotic American citizens, this whole campaign, with its picketing, appeared like a Communist demonstration. " If Ilse Koch, the *murderess of Jews,* could be pardoned "—said placards carried by the demonstrators—" why must the Rosenbergs die?" " Professors Urey and Einstein demand a pardon!" and: "Distinguished leaders in Israel are asking for a reprieve!" was to be seen written on other placards.

In five continents capitalists and Communists, highly cultured intellectuals and simple Talmudists all joined forces to save two Communist spies. The whole nation of totalitarian world conquerors lined up to support the traitors. In London the Rosenbergs' co-racialists knelt down and lay flat in the streets and shouted for pardon in a demonstration which held up the traffic for miles. In Moscow, Budapest and Bukarest, and in other capital cities all over the world, touching stories were written in the national Press about the career of these traitors. On Union Square in New York, the Irish police-men were hardly able to cope with the situation brought about by fainting fanatical Jewesses collapsing when they heard that their adopted country, the United States, had executed the traitors according to the sentence of the Court.

"It was interesting to listen to the New York Radio after the executions took place," wrote the *American Hungarian Voice*. "There were announcers who almost sobbed when giving the news. Other stations after announcing the news began to play funeral music. On Union Square Jewish women threw themselves on the pavement, wailing and lamenting hysterically, and even some of the men started to weep, shouting: 'They killed them . . . killed them!'" (*American Hungarian Voice*, June 29th, 1953, page 8.)

And finally, on Church Avenue, Brooklyn, world-conquering "nazism" held a rally remarkable for its fanaticism. Tens of thousands of people confessed and demonstrated their solidarity with the criminals in the name of their tribal "nazism" since, like the Eastern Jews, they also regarded the executed spies as martyrs to their cause.

At the memorial service, Emanuel Bloch, the defending counsel of the executed Rosenberg couple, said:

"I place the guilt of murdering the Rosenbergs on the doorsteps of President Eisenhower, Attorney General Browell and Edgar Hoover, director of the F.B.I. They gave the orders for the button of the electric chair to be pressed. These two dear, sensitive, tender and cultured persons were the victims of cold-blooded wilful murder. They fought against despotism. America is groaning to-day under

203

the despotism of a military dictatorship, clad in civilian clothes."
(*American Hungarian Voice*, June 19th, 1953.)

From now on, President Eisenhower, the latest successor of Washington and one of the executors of the Morgenthau Plan, could count on the fact that his name too would be on the black-list of " war criminals " and " enemies of the people ". The gallows of Nuremberg were now facing towards the White House and casting their shadows on it. Supranational " nazism " has declared war upon America and upon its faithful servant President Eisenhower. Possibly not only the voice of Emanuel Bloch was to be heard over the coffins of the Rosenbergs, but the echo also of Julius Streicher's words from Nuremberg:

"*. . . you will be hanged by the Bolsheviks!*"

FIFTEEN

THE BETRAYAL OF AMERICA

In finally betraying America world Jewry definitely removed its mask.

Jewry may perhaps feel it has a grievance against every country in the world. The United States, however, gave everything to the Jews a country can offer—money, business, wealth, security, a peaceful life, an unrestricted liberty which was turned into unbridled wantonness and even political influence. America went into battle twice, sacrificing her sons for the sake of the business interests, the profiteering and the political influence of Jewish nationalism; for these were the forces that pushed her into both world wars. America defeated Hitler and also gave eleven billion dollars to the Soviet Union to help liberate the Jewish inmates of the concentration camps. She took her share of the odium resulting from the Nuremberg trials and from dancing attendance on Jewry's desire for revenge.

It took Jewry hardly seventy years to acquire and control the major part of American business and financial life. The destitute little Jew who had fled from Russian pogroms basked in the sunny side of life in the U.S.A., enjoying civic rights and many privileges. During Roosevelt's Presidency, he occupied key positions in political life. He became the owner of an earthly paradise—of much of the riches and wealth of Miami, Florida and California. For him the Promised Land was not Palestine but the United States of America. Palestine, or Israel as it is called to-day, was re-established for the sole purpose of receiving those undesirable types of destitute and cadging Jews who scare New York millionaires, because they carry with them everywhere the germs of " anti-Semitism ".

During Roosevelt's administration America became a land of the Jews. Thus one would expect the world conquerors to remain faithful to America of all countries, and not to turn against the United States when the time came for her to fight against Communism. But the Jews have shown in the case of America also that *they feel themselves safe only as long as they are rulers; and they will be faithful to a country only as long as the interests of that country are identical with their own.*

In the absence of knowledge of the Jewish question, America might indeed have had the right to expect that world Jewry would take her side in the cold war which followed after the Second World War. But exactly the opposite happened. Somewhere behind the veiled privacy of B'nai B'rith lodges the fate of the United States was decided by world Jewry. Surely America's Gentile politicians, though in Jewish hands, did not want to win the Second World War for Jewry alone, to the exclusion of everybody else. Perhaps, with the exception of Roosevelt, they never believed in the possibility of a lasting agreement with the Soviet Union. Senator Truman, who succeeded Roosevelt, said on June 21st, 1941, the day of the outbreak of war between Germany and Soviet Russia: "If we see that Germany is going to win we will help Soviet Russia, but if it is the other way round, we will have to help Germany. *Let's leave them alone so that they will weaken each other as much as possible.*"

Friendship with the Soviet was not in the interests of the U.S., any more than was the cold war after 1945. Both of these things served the interests of world Jewry alone and nobody else. World Jewry's interests played a decisive part in the unleashing of both world wars. But a third world war to defeat and liquidate the Soviet and to liberate the enslaved nations *is not in the interests of the Jews.* On the contrary, at Yalta and Potsdam world power was parcelled out between them.

As the *Protocols* tell us:

"*It is from us that the all-engulfing terror proceeds.*"

According to the well-known catch-phrase America is the "land of freedom", and in the estuary of the River Hudson the Statue of Liberty holds high the symbolic torch. But in reality an "all-engulfing terror" has reigned beyond Ellis Island since the time of Roosevelt's accession to the Presidency. Felix Frankfurter, one of the judges of the Supreme Court of the U.S., said that *"the real rulers in Washington are invisible and exercise power from behind the scenes"*. The American citizen has the right to vote either for the Republican or Democratic Party, but those behind the scenes know very well that real power remains in their hands whichever party wins the election. Anybody daring to rebel, to protest or to utter a single enlightening word concerning this *hidden hand* will be either killed, gagged, driven into suicide or publicly " smeared ".

Gerald K. Smith, the courageous leader of the American Christian Crusade, gives in his book an appalling account of the terror provoked by this *hidden hand* as well as of those patriotic Americans who fell victims to the world conquerors' " all-engulfing terror ". We give here an abridged account taken from his book *Suicide* of how the powers behind the scenes exterminated those Americans who stood in the way of Bolshevism and of a second world war, and consequently opposed the aspirations of the world conquerors.

The reputation of *James Forrestal,* Secretary of War in Truman's administration, was ruined by Drew Pearson and Walter Winchell (Lipsitz), the two radio commentators, exponents of the Jewish " M.V.D." and of the Anti-Defamation League. They made Forrestal's position impossible by stamping him as an " anti-Semite " for opposing U.S. foreign policy in the question of Palestine. Forrestal, after having publicly announced on one occasion that " these Jews will ruin America ", was detained in a hospital, and later mysteriously met his death one morning by " falling " from a sixteenth floor window. Joseph Kennedy, the U.S. Ambassador to Great Britain, had to endure being silenced coupled with a kind of local internment in Florida, because on his return home to America before the outbreak of the Second World War he declared: " Only over my dead body will this country go to war." Kennedy's successor, *John Winant,* after becoming familiar with the circumstances which falsely served to embroil America in the Second World War, was left with the choice of ignominious silence or suicide. This honest American diplomat chose suicide. *Henry Wallace,* who was a member of an odd Oriental sect and believed that with the help of some wildcat serum he would live 150 years, became Roosevelt's Vice-President. But when he turned out to be difficult and not amenable to the powers behind the scenes, he died quite suddenly and quite young. *General Patrick J. Harley* said in 1947 that " there are still several thousand Communists sitting in the State Department ". For this, he was silenced by the mysterious Black Hand of Washington which drove him into exile — disgraced. *The wife of Generalissimo Chiang Kai-Shek,* the daughter of Sun-Yat-Sen, lived in mortal fear whenever she visited America during the Second World War, because she knew that secret agents of the world conquerors' " Gestapo " were planning her assassination. It came to light that the speech delivered by Stettinius, Secretary of State, at the opening of the United Nations, was actually written by a Hollywood Communist film star called Dalton Trumbo. *Morton Kent* killed himself by cutting open a vein. He knew who stole very secret files for the Soviet Union. He knew well that it would make little difference whether he spoke or remained silent; he would be murdered in any case.

Whittaker Chambers Louis Budenz and Tyler Kent still live, but in some danger of their lives. *Budenz,* who previously was one of the leading members of the Communist Party and who exposed several Jewish Communists, sought refuge in the Catholic University of Fordham. Should he step out of the protecting walls of the university buildings he would not live twenty-four hours. The same can be said of the other non-Jewish ex-Communist leader, *Chambers,* who exposed Alger Hiss.

Tyler Kent, who decoded the secret telegrams exchanged between Roosevelt and Churchill — some sent before Churchill was Prime Minister—and thus became one of the most important witnesses of how the world had been driven into war, was jailed for five years in Great Britain, on the Isle of Wight.

That benign and correct old gentleman, *General Vaughan,* had been kept busy removing Jews and Communists from the State Department in considerable numbers. He took a firm stand against David K. Niles, who was the "eminence grise" of the White House during the administrations of Roosevelt and Truman. In his younger days Niles had been convicted and sentenced in Boston to several years' imprisonment for sexual offences. Later he wrote speeches for American Presidents. General Vaughan had strong objections to letting such a Lombroso-type of character live in the entourage of the President of the United States. However, he was silenced, removed from office, and socially ruined under the pretext of "anti-Semitism ".

General Frederick Morgan, U.N.R.R.A. chief in the American Zone of occupied Germany, was an Englishman by birth, who took the liberty to state in writing that the Jews living in Germany were were well provided with both money and food, and thus suffered no need whatever. On the demand of Herbert H. Lehman, Senator for

New York and head of U.N.R.R.A. at that time, General F. Morgan was removed from his post, despite the fact that at first the British Government did not wish to give way to the pressure of American Jewry.

Mr. Earle, U.S. Ambassador to Bulgaria, was similarly silenced. He had been handed a secret memorandum by Von Papen in Sofia, in which Hitler's Government made an offer to keep the United States out of the war. After passing on this memorandum to Roosevelt, Earle was recalled to Washington, then called up for military service and sent out to a Pacific island for the rest of the war. The American people were under no circumstances to be allowed to learn that the hated " nazis " wished for peace with the United States.

The murder of *Huey P. Long,* Senator of Louisiana, was a most mysterious case. Long was one of Roosevelt's rivals with the best possible chances of being elected as President of the U.S. He alleged in the course of a speech to the Senate on August 9th, 1935, that the American " Black Hand ", led by Jews, had ordered his assassination during a meeting in a New Orleans hotel. The Senate laughed off the old fighter at the time. But a month later he was shot dead by a Jew named Karl Weiss.

According to Gerald K. Smith's book, a good many of Roosevelt's opponents perished under similarly mysterious circumstances. Amongst these were *Senator Cutting of New Mexico, Senator Shawl of Minnesota,* and *Mr. John Simpson,* president of the Farmers' Union of Oklahoma.

Keep silent or die! — this was likewise the order to *Admiral Kimmel,* who knew the real story of Pearl Harbour. And the Admiral remained silent, unwilling to risk his life.

Dr. William Wirt, a university professor of Gary, Indiana, apparently as the result of a mistake, received an invitation to a very exclusive social gathering where he heard explained plans and preparations of the Jews and Communists to take over power in the United States. He reported what he had heard to the Press and was consequently summoned to one of the " anti-American activities committees " of the Senate, presided over by Senator O'Connor. The committee stamped Wirt as a liar. Wirt died not long after these hearings in the most suspicious circumstances. But on the first anniversary of Wirt's death, Senator O'Connor visited the grave of this victim and prayed for forgiveness.

Gerald K. Smith, the leader of the American anti-Jewish movement, was once poisoned with arsenic, and the doctors only saved his life with difficulty. This same Gerald K. Smith writes that Gerhard Eisler, a Communist German Jew who emigrated to America and then, having been branded an important Stalin agent, escaped from the American authorities to the Soviet Zone of Germany, ordered the assassination of several thousand American citizens. *Westbrook Pegler*, one of the best known American publicists, lived in permanent fear for his life. Those papers in which Pegler's articles are published exposing the subversive activities of the Communists (Jews) are consistently threatened by Jewry with boycott and terror.

The story of Charles Lindbergh, the valiant pilot who flew the Atlantic, is now well known. Lindbergh opposed the war, and in the course of one of his speeches delivered in Des Moines, Iowa, he pronounced the word " Jew " in a not very flattering tone of voice. Such an intense campaign immediately started for his moral destruction that even to-day in circles of the Anti-Defamation League, the mention of " Lindbergh-treatment " conveys the assassination of a person's character, career and social position. These circles know very well that the elimination of Lindbergh from public life was the work of Jewry. Martin Dies was silenced also by methods similar to the Lindbergh-treatment, because he was the first to try to drag Communists before the Senate and so into the spotlight of publicity. There were attempts to kidnap his son and his wife was constantly threatened. Eleanor Roosevelt and her friends attended the sittings of the Senate Committee to poke fun at its chairman. The Press received confidential instructions to boycott the work of the committee. Yet though Dies was silenced, his committee's work was carried on by Senator *Joseph McCarthy* on whom world Jewry's anathema was declared and who may also be murdered at any time. (*Since the publication of Gerald K. Smith's book, Senator McCarthy has died in the most mysterious and suspicious circumstances. Several American papers hinted openly that he was murdered.*—AUTHOR.)

This was also the fate of the Canadian M.P., Norman Jacques, one of the most popular Members of the Canadian Parliament. Before his death he wrote to several of his acquaintances that: "In my next speech in parliament I am going to open the eyes of my audience and I intend to expose the whole Jewish nationalist conspiracy." But before he could deliver his speech he died from "heart failure".

Gerald K. Smith points out that *the death of Franklin D. Roosevelt* is itself a great mystery. It appears almost certain that *Roosevelt did not die a natural death.* According to some versions he suffered from having a guilty conscience because of Pearl Harbour, or because of that far-fetched Soviet friendship which resulted in a promise to hand over to the Soviet five million people consisting of Germans, Italians, Hungarians, Roumanians and Bulgarians. According to another theory, he wished to be proclaimed President of the World Republic, simultaneously with the establishment of U.N.O., but was forced to realise that the state of his health made him unfit for this office.

Only a single photograph remains to posterity showing the President of the U.S.A. Republic in his coffin. In this photograph a white flower can be seen covering a wound on Roosevelt's head. And when his son Jimmy Roosevelt arrived for the funeral, his mother and family did not dare to open up the coffin so that he might see his father for the last time.

All these facts and events clearly prove that Felix Frankfurter is right. Actual power in America does not rest with the visible Government but is in the possession of individuals behind the scenes. They are the people representing supranational "nazism", whose interests were so well served by the Second World War, *but whose interests would not be served by a third world war in which the sword of America would rip open the Iron Curtain.* What would happen if the Soviet prisons were opened, or if the American soldiers saw the same things in the liberated territories that were seen after 1941 in Soviet Russia by the warriors of Europe? What would happen when the political prisoners were freed together with the slaves of the internment and forced labour camps? Would they not all tell the world who the real jailers, torturers, executioners and usurers of the Soviet régime were? Has not Lenin himself said that "'anti-Semitism' is the means of the counter-revolution"? With the fall of Bolshevism a great awakening of the Gentile nations would

211

follow. The secret archives would be opened. *Woe betide the world conquerors then!*

World Jewry changed its tactics after 1945, because it saw clearly that a showdown between the U.S.A. and the Soviet must be avoided at all costs. The policy now is so to debilitate America that she will have no strength left to defend herself in the end. And so Jewish nationalism, having established unparalleled financial and political power, through armament races, inflation, unemployment, world wars and revolutions, now turns round suddenly and becomes " peace-loving ". It starts the greatest political campaign of its history with the help of U.N.O., U.N.E.S.C.O., the European Council of Strasbourg and various parliaments which are under its influence. With the world Press in its hands, it works with the *sole aim of making America weak and isolated, of leaving her without allies on the day when the clock strikes and she has to face a showdown with the Soviet.* The aim is to make the policy of the United States unpopular with other people, at the time when she should be rallying to her side the Christian nations and other non-Christian people, such as Mohammedans.

Jewry's interests lie in Jewish world government on the concepts of Einstein, and the totalitarian Jewish State. And this nationalism, after having carried out the most bloodthirsty war propaganda campaign against Hitler, now makes a volte-face. Now, the hidden hand, acting quietly behind the scenes, is taking steps to force America on her knees by augmenting as much as possible the strength of the Soviet Union and at the same time *by crippling those forces which consider war against Bolshevism inevitable.*

These tactics have had a certain " merit " in the past. But in Europe they were used only at the end of lost wars. They are known as sabotage and as whispering campaigns that poison the mind. *" Do not fight any longer, you people: The Russians are also humane!"* went the whisper assailing the ears of those ready and willing to defend their country against Soviet barbarism.

Morgenthau's policy plans to crush the might of America by almost identical means.

" After all," say the triumphant Jews to each other — the Jews who beat Hitler — " just read the Book of the Prophet Isaiah and you

212

will see that not only the *Protocols* promised us power over the world, but the Prophet himself too:

"Therefore thy gates shall be open continually; they shall not be shut day nor night; that men may bring unto thee the forces of the Gentiles, and that their kings may be brought." (*Isaiah lx.* 11.)

"For the nation and kingdom that will not serve thee shall perish; yea, those nations shall be utterly wasted." (*Isaiah lx.* 12.)

"Over there, on the other side of the Iron Curtain, 40,000 Soviet tanks, 15,000 aircraft and 175 divisions of the Soviet Army are waiting in readiness to overrun Europe and accomplish the fulfilment of our world power. Churchill said in 1949 that the atomic bomb alone was protecting America and Europe from a Soviet attack. But the atomic bomb, as you know, *is ours!*"

"Those who carry the secret of the atomic bomb to the Soviet Union are all our blood-brothers. It is just as if Einstein had selected them personally and sent them to carry out their great missions. Such are Klaus Fuchs, whose treason speeds up the production of the Soviet atomic bomb by two years, and Bruno Pontecorvo, the Italian Jew, who carried atomic secrets to the Soviet in eleven large trunks. There are also many others such as Harry Gold, David Greenglass, Julius Rosenberg, Emmanuel Bloch, William Perl, Professor of the University of Columbia, Abraham Brothmann, Mirijam Moskovich, Simson the plutonium thief Jew, Jánosi the Hungarian Jew who would protect Lazar Khaganovich's empire with a cosmic ray curtain, John Vág-Weiszfeld, who was Harry Gold's accomplice, David Boehm and Edwin David, all of them members of our race. Why is there not a single Christian among them? Because Gentiles are not reliable! The secret is ours; we do not deny it. Julius Rosenberg admitted frankly to the New York Court that ' Soviet Russia is our ally and I considered her, therefore, entitled to receive such information from us!' . . ."

America possessed hidden weapons which could have made her the leading anti-Bolshevik world power. They were the greatest military secrets of history, with the help of which she could have delivered the world from the menace of servitude. These secrets had to be stolen and sold, so that as a substitute for the powers known as America and Russia, a single power should remain in the world:

213

the world power of Jewish nationalism which keeps at bay both America and the Soviet Union. If it does nothing else, the betrayal of America will prove better than anything that *there is a grandiose Jewish plan in existence to divide the world into eastern and western hemispheres, and consequently to rule both of them, and that this plan has so far been executed with the most ruthless efficiency.*

Radar and the inter-continental rocket were also among the military secrets in the hand of the U.S., and these could have offered her the greatest security, even after the loss of the atomic bomb secret. But to-day it is established by the F.B.I. that Julius Rosenberg was also the head of the radar spying. After investigations, held in the military research institute at Monmouth, it came to light that the culprits who betrayed the radar secrets to the Soviet were almost exclusively all Jews. Professor H. Coleman and Morton Sobell, a spy sentenced to thirty years' imprisonment, Hyman Gerber Yavis, Carl Greenbaum and Miss Glassman can be mentioned amongst others in this connection.

The handing over of China to the Reds is one of the most horrible chapters in the betrayal of America. China was one of America's best markets. She had to be forced into the red hemisphere at any price. Otherwise, in the case of a showdown, the 500 million Chinese, among whom Jewish subversive ambitions were never able to find a favourable soil, could have become a formidable ally on the side of the U.S. It is generally known to-day that Owen Lattimore, an American professor of dubious origin, Roosevelt's chief adviser on Chinese questions, was working against the U.S. in the service of Soviet military espionage. For seven years he was editor of *Pacific Affairs,* a paper issued by the Institute of Pacific Relations, from which the Soviet Union received first-hand information regarding China. The investigating officers of the F.B.I. found 1,700 very confidential files in the offices of Amerasia. The fact that the persons detained in connection with this case were all Jews is important. John Stewart Service, Larsen Mano, Andrew Roth, John Abt, Nathan Witt, Lee Pressmann, Philipp Jaffe, an ex-ambassador, and Maria Bachrach, had all betrayed America, the country which gave them a home, to serve their Jewish world-conquering nationalism.

" The problem was how to bring about the downfall of China so that it would not appear to be caused by the U.S.," wrote Owen

Lattimore. "Due to Amerasia and to the extension of the policy of the fellow-traveller, 665 million souls vanished behind the Iron Curtain!" some American papers stated later. America lost her greatest export market and one of her best trading partners. And the whole position in the Far East was shaken to its foundation. Those who divided the world into eastern and western hemispheres cannot deny the object of their action: *Divide et impera!* Divide your opponents and so rule them. Rule over America as well as over the Soviet Union.

In furthering this aim, the hidden hand had deployed its own men everywhere, upon whom it relied not to serve America but only the interests and power aspirations of Jewry. Before the outbreak of the Korean war a certain Lyman L. Lemnitzer, wearing the uniform of a major-general of the U.S. Army, was the military leader in South Korea, and on him falls the responsibility for neglecting its defences, as was declared in Congress. Later, the half-Jewish general, Mark Clark, son of Rebecca Ezekiel, became commander-in-chief in Korea. This man, while commanding the American occupation forces in Austria, handed over refugees and displaced persons by the thousand to the Soviet. It is no coincidence either that during the Korean war a certain Colonel A. C. Katzin was chief U.N. delegate over General MacArthur, while another Jew called George Movahon directed the Korean section of the U.N. Information Centre. During the time of the Persian oil crisis, a certain Michael J. Lee was head of the Far Eastern Division of the State Department, and it came to light that he emigrated from Soviet Russia into the United States in 1932 and that his original name was Efraim Zinoy Liebermann.

As in the Far East, so in Europe too, the exponents of world Jewry did everything to ruin America's prestige and good name, and to eradicate from the hearts of the people of Europe those ideals which picture her as the land of freedom. We referred already to the fact that the Morgenthau Plan was actually conceived in Moscow. Harry Dexter White, a Russian Jew, was Under-Secretary of the Treasury Department as well as Morgenthau's deputy in Roosevelt's administration. He was one of the most sinister figures of modern times, being at the same time leader of the Communist cells and spy rings carrying on their activities inside the U.S. Treasury Department. He stole and handed over to the Soviet Union the stereo plates, paper material and printing secrets of the so-called "Allied Marks", the banknotes designed for the allied occupation of Germany, and thus caused a financial loss of about 225 million dollars to American taxpayers. But besides the original stereo blocks of the occupation banknotes and printing formulas, there were other most confidential documents received by the Soviet from Harry Dexter White. In the Communist cell under his authority names were found such as Frank Cohen, Harold Glasser, Victor Perle, Irving Kaplan, Solomon Adler, Abraham George, Silverman and Ludwig Ullmann, etc., President Truman appointed White to the chairmanship of the International Monetary Fund, while Harold Glasser became financial director of U.N.R.R.A. It is to be ascribed to the activities of this Jewish spy ring that the gold reserves and foreign exchange bills of the Hungarian National Bank, estimated at 42 million dollars, were also handed over to the Soviet Union.

It is impossible to name here all the hundreds and thousands of Jews who were active in the most important key positions of the occupation zones of Germany, secretly furthering the Soviet cause and doing their best to Bolshevise Germany, as propagandists, C.I.C. or O.S.S. agents, press and theatrical officers, city commandants, financial experts, etc. The files of McCarthy's Investigation Committee tell us more about these things than the best detective thriller and are a most startling historical documentation.

And as if all this was not enough, Jewish nationalism produced from its ranks the chief traitor Alger Hiss, who handed over 110 million Gentiles to the Khaganovich gang at Yalta. And the witness for the defence, who came forward and tried to save him, was nobody else but Felix Frankfurter, Judge of the Supreme Court of the U.S. And the protector of Alger Hiss after his conviction was nobody else but the great senator, the uncrowned king of New York, Herbert H. Lehmann, father-in-law of Buttenweiser, who tried to hide the chief traitor of America in his flat.

But the most characteristic feature of the treason committed against America does not concern the atomic bomb, the radar spy ring or the other spy scandals, but *the active rôle of American Jews in the Communist movements.* Here again the old saying is vindicated that "*perhaps all Jews are not Bolsheviks but without Jews there would be no Bolshevism!*". The majority of America's Jewish population came from countries behind the Iron Curtain. The greatest number of them fled to America to escape pogroms in Russia. America is not ruled by the Czars but by a so-called democratic régime. She gave the Jews everything, including even the privilege of taking part in the administration of the country. Yet despite all this generosity, the Jews were, and are to-day, actively at the head of all anti-American and Communist subversive movements.

The Communist Party has been planted in America and it is led by the same type of people who were leaders of the Russián Bolshevik Revolution. The members of the American Politbureau, popularly referred to as the "Great Eleven" are, not taking negroes into account, almost exclusively Jews: Eugen Dennies, Henry Winston, John Hates, Irving Pothias, Gilbert Green, Carl Winter and Guss Holl.

"If a spy or a Communist leader is detained anywhere," boasts the voice of Old Testament "nazism", "he always comes from our ranks. Judith Coplon, the beautiful Jewish girl from Brooklyn, sold the most confidential files of the State Department to Gubichev, a Soviet agent. And we saw to it that she will not come to any serious harm."

Again we perceive the flashing coil of the symbolic serpent in America, the emblem of Jewish nationalism, the network of which covers and reaches everything. It controls the banks, house property, family life, State, Press, society and the trade unions.

When the Californian Communist conspiracy was detected, the same well-known characters were dragged out of their underground hiding places by the F.B.I. The race of these traitors is stamped on their features, Robert H. Williams' book, *Know Your Enemy,* shows a series of photographs of the Américan traitors. Under characteristic faces appear characteristic names. Alexander Bittelman appears in this picture gallery as one of the founder members of the American Communist Party, and the other leaders with him are: Gerhard Eisler, Jack Stachel, Leon Josephson, Alex Trachtenberg and J. Peters (Goldberger). The participants in the recent Hollywood plot are: "Dr. Sidney Weinbaum, Dr. Jacob Dubnov, Philip Bart, director of the *Daily Worker,* Alex Trachtenberg, V. J. Jerome, leader of the Bolshevik Cultural Committee (whose real name is Isaac Romaine), Simon, Gerson, Elisabeth G. Flynn, Alex Bittelman, Betty Gannet, Isadore Begun, Jacob Minden, Claudia Jones (negress), Israel Amter,

W. Weinstone, George Charney, Fred Fine, Sid Steinberger, Louis Weinstock and Js. Jackson.

The *Reader's Digest* confirms that of the eleven top leaders of the American Communist Party, six are Jews, two are negroes, and only three are American-born citizens. According to the same paper, the most important Bolshevik leaders are: Jacob Stachel, John Gates (alias Israel Regenstreif), editor of the *Daily Worker,* Gill Green (alias Gilbert Greenburg), Gus Hall (alias Arvo Mike Hallberg of Lithuanian Jewish parentage), Irving Potiash, a Soviet Russian Jew, and Carl Winter (alias Philip Carl Weinberg).

Can all this be explained away as accidental? Is it merely a strange coincidence that the names of those directing subversive activities in America are the same as those turning up on the list of leaders of the Soviet Bolsheviks and of Hungarian and Roumanian Communists? Is it another coincidence that the first five men to be removed from the U.S. Army for Communist activities, namely Harry Specor, Phil Weiss, Irving Specor ,Abraham Kotlechuk and Rheabel Mendelsohn, were Jews too? Could it be really just chance that ninety-five per cent of those persons summoned before the McCarthy Investigation Committee for Anti-American activities and found guilty, were Jews as well? And may it not be a sense of guilt that, according to the Congressional Record of May 17th, 1946, *all Jewish members of Congress voted for the discontinuation of the hearings of the Dies committee investigating anti-American activities?* Moreover, did not Senator McCarthy inform Bernard Baruch himself that as all the television networks in the United States were in the hands of the Jews, he would not be given the chance to expose the American traitors by means of the television service.

Another decisive proof of the existence of Jewish " nazism " is the fact that those participating in American Communist movements never come from the " proletariat ", i.e. from the working class or from 'destitute people, but from Jews occupying the highest strata of American society. The publication *Red Stars Over Hollywood* draws attention to the fact that out of those Hollywood film stars whose earnings amount to millions of dollars, one hundred are Bolsheviks and all of these are Jews. To these people America gave glamour, wealth and success. And despite everything they are still Bolsheviks, or to put it more concisely, we think they are Bolsheviks.

These stars, led by Charlie Chaplin (alias Israel Thorstein) are, first and foremost, Jews, who visualise in Bolshevism the perfect accomplishment of Jewish world power, and look upon Bolshevism as a bulwark of that totalitarian Jewish world rule of which they themselves will be the intellectual élite.

The 3,500 American professors who took part in various Communist demonstrations also belonged to the storm-troops of this Old Testament nationalism. The overwhelming majority of them are Jews. The Communist teachers against whom disciplinary action was taken on account of their Bolshevik activities, also belong to the pioneers of this supranational " nazism ". Among them were Abraham Biedermann, Cellis Lewis, Citron, Mark Friedländer, Isadore Rubin, Abraham Feingold, David Friedman, Louis Jaffe and so on. The first saboteurs detained on the outbreak of the Korean war were: Max Schnalzer, Minton Silverman, Samuel Zakkman and Samuel Kerr. At this time Nathan Ostroff sold the Chinese Communists ten million pounds' worth of rubber to ensure that the armies of Red China marched in rubber boots against the soldiers of the U.S. The following were amongst the first batch of the above-mentioned Hollywood Communist film stars and film producers summoned before the Investigation Committee: John Howard Lawson, Dalton Trumbo, Ring Lardner, Albert Malz, Alva Bessie, Herbert Bieberman and Samuel Ornitz, all of them Jews.

World Jewry's greatest act of treason against America is that it undermined the earlier goodwill and trust of other peoples towards America, especially in the Near East and in Mohammedan countries. And it is of little use for the Americans to try to find excuses. This was no mistake of " inexperienced " diplomacy because it was part of *a deliberate Jewish world scheme.*

Corruption became prevalent in the State Department and later grew out of all proportion during Roosevelt's anti-American activities. According to figures quoted by *The Hidden Empire,* eighty-six per cent of the staff employed in the State Department was Jewish. And according to the McCarthy committee, 5,000 homosexuals were then employed in the Civil Service. *Such corruption and degradation proved itself to be the best ally of Bolshevism everywhere.*

Through cracks in the structure of the administration, through faults and weaknesses of dishonest and corruptible civil servants,

Communist spies, agents and gangsters infiltrate into the Government of the country. At the same time Communist propaganda will say to the ignorant masses: "Look at them! Are these men your masters?" But this does not explain the most important point, i.e. that these men or *the majority of them at any rate, are Jews.* When democracy sinks to such a low level that Jews can behave as they wish, then corruption cannot be checked and the rapid progress of Bolshevism is ensured.

World Jewry's programme since 1945 has been to weaken *America as much as possible.* America is to be undermined by Communist conspiracy and corrupt practices. Her armament industry must be disorganised so that Bolshevism — *the higher and safer form of the Communist system and of Jewish world power* — can score an easy victory.

It is true that American Jewish organisations issued a declaration in 1950 against Communism, but this was a deception only! American Jews in fact wish to achieve very different aims from what they say. One of the most influential personalities among American Jews wrote in the leading article of the *B'nai B'rith Messenger* on November 1st, 1948:

"My soul revolts when I hear and have to stomach the fact that Fascism and Communism are concepts of identical composition. Some people talk about Communism. . . . I say: *this is Jewish ideology!"*

And whenever Jewry has taken off its mask for one or two brief moments on various historical occasions, much the same message was delivered.

In celebration of the Bolshevik Revolution, the same idea was expressed in the Parisian newspaper *Peuple Juif,* on February 8th, 1919:

"World revolution, which some of us may live to see, is and must remain our concern, and its preparation must be in our hands. By means of this world revolution *the power of Jewry will be established over all nations of the world."*

Zinovjev-Apfelbaum, the great Eastern Brother, announced the same thing when he received an eleven billion dollars Lend-Lease from the hand of La Guardia:

"We exterminated the capitalists and the landowners in Soviet

Russia, *and we will go to any length to do the same to the intelligentsia of Europe and America."*

And the Jew from Germany, who to-day might be an immigrant in America or a deputy-governor in Germany or perhaps an American press officer, said essentially the same thing in his German newspaper soon after the First World War:

" We must continue our fight not only for our own existence but *to achieve world power for Jewry as a whole; it is for this we have ceaselessly worked during the last 2,000 years."* (*Israelitische Wochenblatt,* January 5th, 1926, Leipzig.)

All nations, including the U.S.A., must vanish. This is after all an old-world programme. That great leader of Jewry, Adolph Crémieux, president of the Alliance Israélite Universelle, said almost a hundred years ago:

" The nations must vanish and religions must be suppressed. Only Israel must not disappear, for this small nation is the chosen people of God."

Why, therefore, do the Americans believe that amongst the various national groups who immigrated to America and settled there, the group composing Jewry is just like any of the others? How could the American people imagine that Jewry will remain loyal to America when they were not loyal to the Roman Empire, to Spain or to Portugal or to any State in the world? There is no doubt that Jewry's most resplendent dream is to become master of the United States and to treat her the same as other nations have been treated.

And why do Americans believe that this is not possible?

The proportion of Communists in those States conquered by Bolshevism was not more than three to five per cent of the population at the beginning of " direct action ". In Russia nobody had ever heard of Bolshevism before 1917 when the Imperial General Staff of the Kaiser permitted Lenin and his gang to pass through Germany on their journey from Switzerland to Russia. Not a single Bolshevik was to be found in Hungary until 1919, i.e. until Béla Kun's short-lived terror régime. The leaders were sent by Lenin and his gang operating from Russia. When in 1945, Mátyás Rákosi-Roth and his confederates returned to Hungary, the total number of underground Communist Party members was only 140. At the end of 1945, during the Hungarian elections, Communists secured seventeen per cent of the total votes. They failed to gather more than three to four per cent of the votes in Austria at that time, though by then the Communists in both Austria and Hungary were supported by the bayonets of the Soviet armies. The position in Roumania, Eastern Germany and Bulgaria was similar. Nevertheles all these States are to-day in the iron grip of Bolshevik dictatorships.

The Bolshevik Party is by nature conspiratorial; it is a fanatical sect. In the beginning Churchill saw this plainly and said so. This fanaticism is able to overcome even the most perfect democracy. Freedom is good because it can be exploited and misused! *The greater the freedom, the greater is the menace of Bolshevism.*

According to American estimates, Communist Party members in the U.S. number about 60 to 100 thousand persons only. Therefore say the Americans, there can be no Bolshevism in America, where the standard of living is the highest in the world. As we can see American democracy works moderately well and such a small Communist majority should stand no chance whatever of subjugating a powerful country of 160 million people.

Edgar Hoover, director of F.B.I., says that to the 100,000 Bolsheviks another 500,000 fellow-travellers can be added.

If this is so, the over-all picture of Bolshevism in America is immediately changed and may be summed up as follows: we have 100,000 conspirators plus 500,000 fellow-travellers (amongst these many holding important posts and key positions), plus five to six million Jews, plus twelve million negroes, plus corruption, plus Soviet espionage, plus the national Press, television and radio network (100 per cent of which are in Jewish hands), and finally, plus the ever-rising crime wave in which juvenile delinquency plays a shocking part.

Amongst the negroes are many God-fearing, civilised and fine citizens. But the negro feels he is a " slighted " person, and the Bolsheviks have always recruited their fifth columns from such people Many Jews are not Bolsheviks at all. But the Jew is always a nationalist and he turns Bolshevik as soon as he recognises the Jewish character of Bolshevism. According to Gerald K. Smith there ar already at least half a million conscientious and fanatical Bolshevik in the ranks of American Jewry. And, according to the highest estimate, the Russian Revolution was started by only 500 Jews

Working along these lines, the American Communist Party, led by American Jews, passed the following resolution on February 5th, 1951:

". . . and our congress accordingly placed on its agenda, as its main concern, the fight for peace, the fight for the working class and for the coloured people, besides calling for the mobilisation of all peace-loving forces in the country."

The Communist wing of Jewry intends, as can be seen from the foregoing, to mobilise the Black population of America. Half a million Jews intend thus to realise a ghastly American-Jewish dream. *They plan to organise and to arm a negro terror-force of one million men, led by American Jewish commissars.*

The Communist wing of Jewry co-operates with those Jews who champion the rights of the Black man. *The Hungarian Daily Journal*, an admittedly Jewish Communist paper, printed a very illuminating article in its issue of April 14th, 1950, under the title: " The Jews fought for the rights of the negroes and workers." The article tells us about E. L. Rose, a Jew born in Poland, who came to America after the defeat of the 1848 Revolution in Vienna, and who made several speeches championing the negroes, and thus became the leader of the movement for the liberation of negroes in St. Louis. The Russian Jew, S. A. Bierfield, is referred to by Jewish Communist propaganda as a martyr of negro-Jewish co-operation, when gangsters murdered him in his shop with his negro servant. The above-mentioned article also points out that when the pamphlet " Labour and Capital ", by Carl Marx, was edited in Yiddish in 1888, enthusiastic Jews of the East Side set out to organise trade unions among the negroes.

Due to the opposition of religious negroes, the great dream of American Communist Jews—the organisation of a large negro terror force—has so far failed, but it will appear less of a dream to us if we read the reports of the American Special Committee on un-American Activities. According to these reports, the American Communist Party had 1,160 organisations among general labourers, farmers and negroes, including political, and even so-called religious, groups and sections.

John T. Flynn, the courageous American publicist, in his book *The Road Ahead*, quotes a rather formidable list of negro Communist organisations. From this we learn that there are eighty-eight large negro organisations working for American Bolshevism. Amongst these are the African Blood Brotherhood and many other movements and sects bearing the most varied titles and operating under the pretext of being religious peace movements.

The Americans are not yet acquainted with the tactics of Jewish nationalism. But the advent of an economic crisis, a third world war, or unstability resulting from a lost war would be quite sufficient for hell to be let loose in America. The devils of Bolshevism were similarly let loose in Russia in 1917, in the Danubian Monarchy in 1918, and in the whole of Eastern Europe in 1945.

And if this happens in America the day of the world kingdom will have dawned. The old promise will be carried out in accordance with the written instructions:

" It is from us that the all-engulfing terror proceeds."

The Black army will march led by the eleven leading members of the American Politbureau, six of whom are Jews. This will be a force of one million fanatics held under iron discipline, to whom American white women will be promised. This will be the world's most gigantic M.V.D., led by 500,000 commissars, officers, agents and secret police of the seed of Abraham, and it will assume power over America. But the ruthless ones will now come out of the ghettos of Brooklyn, of the Jewish quarters of Bronx and the stark masses of East Polish immigrants will be on the move. A Black army will emerge from Harlem too. The hearts of the Black soldiers will be suffused with hatred, and their thirst for blood, now disguised by a veneer of civilisation, will be whetted by Jewish propaganda. These Blacks hate the Whites, but they will not hate Jews whom they believe are their liberators, though in reality they are their lords and masters, and as such will be protected by the brute force of the Blacks.

Private capital amassed by individual Jews and others will be taken over by Jewish state capitalism in order to get complete control over the enormous wealth of the United States of America. Jewry will run the Federal Government as well as the State Governments, and will abolish democracy and voting by ballot.

The Jews no doubt reason somewhat as follows:

" The Americans say: ' This is not possible in our country!' *But so far it has turned out to be possible everywhere.* And if the American people tried to resist us we should erect a gallows on Capitol Hill in front of the White House; and these gallows would be guarded by King David's fierce black bodyguard, by twelve million negroes and six million Jews. This power will be as firm as a rock. Just try to revolt, you people of Washington. . . ! Try to rise against us, you American freedom fighters, and your fate will be that of Wrangel's guards who, once tried to rise against us also! The sword of Damocles is now suspended over your head. *Atomic artillery will exterminate you if you dare to go to war against our great King David.* We should already have erected scaffolds and you must not expect either humanity or philanthropy to be shown once total power falls into our hands. No; it is from us the all-engulfing terror proceeds!

" Just think of what happened to the freedom fighters who defended the various Eastern European cities against our Bolshevik armies. At one end of the street fighting was still going on when we broke out of the ghettos; for we who supposedly never fought, took off our mask at the last moment And when the freedom fighter looked through his sights into the city occupied by our Bolshevik troops, he could see that after half an hour gallows were standing there. We had erected them and we came out of the ghettos to hang our enemies on them — the Christians."

And this vision may become a reality at any time because Jewry has betrayed America. The only question now is: *Will the American people awaken while there is yet time to act?* If they did, another terrible vision might come true, i.e. that of Oscar Strauss, a great American financier and businessman:

" It is my people. I'm telling you my friend, that if my people do not mend their ways and be good citizens and that soon, the time is coming when America is going to see pogroms beside which the pogroms of Europe will have been nothing!"

One thing Oscar Strauss did not point out is that *the way to solve the Jewish problem is not that of the pogrom.* Physical force promotes only disarmed nationalism.

Jewish world conquest must be defeated, but by different methods. For if it is not soon checked, the hours of freedom for Americans and the rest of mankind, are running out fast with the sands **of time**

SIXTEEN

THE FULFILMENT OF THE PROTOCOLS AND THE FAREWELL LETTER OF A HUNGARIAN MARTYR

IN analysing the present-day world position we cannot emphasise enough the importance of a fact that nobody seems to be willing to face, i.e. that Jewry, who suceeded in unleashing two world wars among the Christian nations and who, as we pointed out in previous chapters, was the principal war criminal of the Second World War, *does not consider it to be in its interest to allow a showdown with the Soviet or with Bolshevism generally.* This would not be in the interest of Jewry because once the Bolshevik dictatorship was defeated, the world would learn who were the real murderers, hangmen, commissars and jailers of the enslaved nations and perpetrators of biological class warfare.

Beside their dreams of world power, the horrible alliance of a guilty conscience is the connecting factor between Eastern and Western Jews. People who cannot understand why world Jewry strives to prevent America fighting against Bolshevism and why the Iron Curtain is kept up between East and West, would do well to read the statement of Dr. Goldman, American leader of the World Jewish Congress, according to which "*a third world war would mean the total extermination of Jewry*". Pinkas Lubianker, leader of the Israeli delegation in London, said essentially the same thing. Solem Traitsman, Chief Rabbi of Communist Poland, let the cat out of the bag when he sent out the following circular to world Jewry in 1951, urging them to sign the Soviet peace petitions:

"*For Jewry the end of peace would mean their own end. The third world war is a new weapon in the hands of Jewry's ancient archenemies. The peace petitions, whether they are instituted by the right or the left, must be signed under all circumstances by the majority of mankind, but above all by Jewry. As for Jewry, this is not a question of 'East versus West'. For Jewry this is a question of life or death!"*

The rabbis in France joined the peace movements and made similar statements, and neither is it accidental that in 1950, 160,000 Jews in Israel signed Communist peace petitions. The percentage of those who signed, said the *Daily Worker,* is greater in Israel than in any other country, except the Soviet Union!

Now we can understand better why the Soviets had to be presented with the secrets of the atomic bomb, why the Iron Curtain is kept up as well as the purpose of the false peace slogans and the slogans of co-existence and why the cold war continues. We also see why there is no active European defence community and no European Army. It becomes plainer why nations are enslaved and bisected and why half of mankind tolerates the existence of the Soviet slave camps.

The answer is simple. World power over both hemispheres is in the hands of world Jewry.

It was said that the *Protocols of Zion* were forgeries. But within half a century the Great Vision came true. In this short time world Jewry has passed the first two stages of the struggle for world power and has come close to the third as well, but has not yet definitely removed its mask.

But actual world power is now in the hands of the world conquerors and it is only a question of time until Eastern and Western Jews shake hands openly across the enslaved nations and barbarised masses.

In 1904, Chaim Weissmann commented as follows on Theodor Herzl's *Judenstaat*:

"Four years ago world Jewry was divided into two camps: one on the east and one on the west. And when Herzl arrived and said to us that we must unite Eastern and Western Jewry, and we carried out this order accordingly. *Our unity* to-day is Theodor Herzl's legacy to the Jewish people."

Theodor Herzl's *Judenstaat states*: "Wir sind ein Volk!"—"We are one people!" *And to-day this is the only unity* existing in a world divided into two hemispheres.

"We are one people despite the ostensible rifts, cracks and differences between the American and Soviet democracies. We are one people and *it is not in our interests* that the West should liberate

227

the East, for in doing this and in liberating the enslaved nations, the West would inevitably deprive Jewry of the Eastern half of its world power."

The great programme of the *Protocols* is nearly accomplished and this is the best proof of their authenticity. Fifty years ago the League of Nations and U.N.O. was nothing but a dream, but the authors of the *Protocols* clearly envisaged the rôle and purpose of these organisations.

Thus to replace the unsuccessful and extinct League of Nations U.N.O. was established, with its palace built at Lake Success, where under the blue and white colours of Zion the governments of the world unite. In Korea American soldiers died fighting under Zionist colours. In these circumstances, therefore, *the United Nations can rightly be regarded as the most accomplished and most perfected power organisation of world Jewry.*

The formation of the Jewish world government is not yet announced officially. But Einstein, the prophet, together with the Organisation of World Federalists and the Federalist Organisations of several European countries, are openly proclaiming this. (See the programme of the World Federalists.) In that part of New York State most densely populated by Jews, Senator Herbert H. Lehman and Congressman Jacob Javits are elected under this programme.

The most important section of the United Nations is U.N.E.S.C.O. (United Nations Educational, Scientific and Cultural Organisation). It is almost exclusively in the control of Jewry. U.N.E.S.C.O. wishes to direct and control the education of the entire youth of the world. This is, in fact, also one of the instructions of the *Protocols*:

" We must so direct the education of the Goyim communities that whenever they come upon a matter requiring initiative they may drop their hands in despairing impotence." (*Protocol* V.)

U.N.E.S.C.O. is, therefore, the leading organisation envisaged by the authors of the *Protocols,* which was established at a given moment to produce and train a world youth consisting exclusively of atheistic world proletarians, who would have no loyalty to their own country and national traditions and who would regard everything unfavourable to Jewish world conquest as despicable " anti-Semitism ".

" In place of the rulers of to-day we shall set up a bogey which will be called the Super Government Administration," is prophesied in

Protocol V. " Its hands will reach out in all directions like nippers and its organisation will be of such colossal dimensions that it cannot fail to subdue all the nations of the world."

In U.N.O. the Western democrat, the Eastern Soviet Jew, the New York rabbi and the Soviet commissar, sit to-day side by side in full co-operation. While Gentile soldiers are busy shedding each other's blood, a war is carried on even inside U.N.O. itself, where the famous dictum of Theodor Herzl influences every peace declaration of the United Nations:

" We are one people. We are all the same people!" *And everything besides this is a farce, just a put-on show.* In the Atomic Energy Commission of U.N.O., Jews talk to Jews masked as either democrats or Bolsheviks, and discuss among themselves the most formidable problem of the world. Though the author of the United Nations Charter, Leon Pavlovsky, is an American Jew, he copied out the Soviet constitution word for word into the Charter of U.N.O. Information considered suitable for the Gentile nations must be passed down by the Information Centre run by a Jew, Jacob Sappiro. In the Atomic Energy Commission, Bernard Baruch represents the United States and in the Political Committee, D. J. Manuilsky, a Soviet Jew, represents Soviet Russia. The International Labour Organisation of U.N.O. is directed by David A. Morse, whose real name is Maskovich a Russia Jew. Though the Secretary-General of this powerful world organisation is not a Jew, nevertheless, Benjamin Cohen, Assistant Secretary-General is one. It is also most remarkable that *during the Korean war, Constantin Zinkovich, a Russian Jew, was chief of the Security Service of U.N.O. And this meant, in fact that he was the boss of General MacArthur during the Korean operations.*

From now on it will not be the American Congress that decides the fate of America but an unknown organisation, controlled by Jews. Thus Turkish soldiers must die at the behest of Jews in the United Nations, and these very same Jews may sabotage those who are struggling against Bolshevism. And again, U.N.O. will dictate and tell France, Greece or Western Germany whom these countries may accept as citizens, whether they can receive loans, and what kind of labour regulations are to be adopted. We will deal with this in the next chapter.

Let us see to what extent the instructions laid down in the *Protocols* have been carried out in both East and West. We will first deal with Bolshevism. From a comparison it is clear that it would be more accurate to regard the *Protocols,* rather than Lenin's works, as the Bible of Bolshevism.

" The people under our guidance have annihilated the aristocracy . . ." (says *Protocol* III, written in 1897) " who were their one and only defence and foster-mother for the sake of their own advantage which is inseparably bound up with the well-being of the people. Nowadays, with the destruction of the aristocracy, the people have fallen into the grips of merciless money-grinding scoundrels who have laid a pitiless and cruel yoke upon the necks of the workers."

But, in fact, much more than this was achieved by world Jewry in half a century. It succeeded in destroying not only the aristocracy based on birth but that also based on ability, as well as the intellectual *élite,* regardless of whether it belonged to the working class, landed peasantry or to the " aristocracy " of the middle classes. The intellectual decapitation of Russia was completed after 1917, and instead of Dostoievsky and his class, people like Ilia Ehrenburg represent to-day the " intellectual *élite* " in Soviet Russia. Half of the European *élite* was executed, some under the pretext of liberation, and others because they were found guilty of war crimes. The people fell indeed into the " grips of scoundrels ".

To-day, while this chapter is being written, one can take a look at what is happening in Russia and behind the Iron Curtain. Firstly, the kings were dethroned and their sceptres and crowns taken from them, next the aristocracy was destroyed, then the middle classes of the various countries were shot and buried in common graves on the pattern of the Katyn Wood murders or deported to slave labour or extermination camps, and now it is the turn of the workers' leaders to suffer the same fate.

" What we have to get at is that there should be in all the States of the world, besides ourselves, only the masses of the proletariat, a few millionaires devoted to our interests, police and soldiers." (*Protocol* VII.)

This aim has been completely achieved in the Soviet Union, and its achievement in the other countries behind the Iron Curtain is well on the way. The Jewish world kingdom has taken material shape in the form of Bolshevism, in which there is nothing to be found but enslaved masses and Jewish commissars.

" In this way . . . we shall destroy among the goyim the importance of the family and its educational value and remove the possibility of individual minds splitting off . . ." says *Protocol X.*

Jewish teachers in the schools of countries behind the Iron Curtain teach artificial insemination to thirteen-year-old children. In the people's colleges, thirteen- to fifteen-year-old boys and girls sleep together. In Soviet Russia family life is scattered, but not by deportation only. The railway workers or postman born in the Ukraine is sent for duty to Vladivostok and vice versa. The Soviet youth movements ruthlessly detach the children from the family circle.

The following quotation from authentic American reports proves that part of the programme of the *Protocols* has been accomplished in America as well:

" Juvenile delinquency is growing at an alarming rate in America to-day. The police cannot name a section of the criminal code with which American youth, girls and boys alike, would not be familiar. The murder of parents and of brothers and sisters as well as all sorts of sexual murders, robberies, hold-ups, bank robberies, common kidnappings and dope smuggling are not uncommon amongst juveniles. The picture reflected by the statistics is simply appalling." (*The Hidveroek,* December, 1955, page 939.)

In *Der Weg,* Vol. VI, No. 8, we read that in an interview, Herbert Hoover, head of the F.B.I., gave even more shocking figures. There was a total of 1,790,030 cases of crime during 1951. The daily average of persons murdered or attacked was 301; of houses broken into, 1,129; of persons robbed, 146; and of motor cars stolen, 468. Thus, in every five minutes, one murder, robbery or kidnapping took place. The most disturbing feature of the crime wave is that juveniles are so often involved. Almost daily one reads cases of fifteen-year-old boys, armed with revolvers, committing hold-ups and armed robberies. According to statistics, hundreds of thousands of young people carry guns. To-day in America a criminal atmosphere appears to have been *intentionally produced* which is inhaled with every breath. This begins with children regularly reading lurid stories in the so-called picture comics. More than a hundred of these gutter-publications produce over forty million copies. Ninety per cent of the children in the six to eleven year age group read these horror-stories. Detective and crime stories flood the bookstalls in lots of 100,000 or more. Six hundred "authors" are working full time writing and producing them. Perhaps it is right to add that more than ninety per cent of these "authors" are Jews.

The artificially created criminal atmosphere is even more intensified by television, explains the article in *Der Weg*. Last year, according to the scripts, 16,932 violent deaths were to be seen on the luminous screens of television receivers — 9,652 persons were shot dead by revolvers and 762 more were mown by machine guns. Various investigations held in the high schools brought to light the fact that about half of the students under eighteen are habitual dope addicts; marihuana, heroin and morphia were mentioned among the narcotics they take.

Since we know that the films, television, radio and Press in America are almost exclusively in the hands of Jewry, this crime wave can scarcely be regarded as accidental. The authors of the *Protocols* knew well that the stability of their rule dependend upon the masses being rendered corrupt and characterless. The programme of the *Protocols* was accomplished:

"... the Goyim are bemused with alcoholic liquors; their youth has grown stupid." (*Protocol* I.)

"In our programme one-third of our subjects will keep the rest under observation from a sense of duty, on the principle of volunteer service to the State. It will then be no disgrace to be a spy or informer, but a merit. ..." (*Protocol* XVII.) To-day in the offices, factories and workshops of the bolshevised countries, several hundreds of thousands of informers and agents of the régime compete in observing and reporting even the most unimportant matters. *Protocol* XI tells us:

"The Goyim are a flock of sheep and we are their wolves. And you know what happens when the wolves get hold of the flock. ..." The lethargy of the masses and the terror induced in them proved to be important safeguards for the survival of the Bolshevik régime.

"Not a single announcement will reach the public without our control," states *Protocol* XII, and to-day all censorship in countries behind the Iron Curtain and especialy in Soviet Russia is one hundred per cent in Jewish hands.

232

" When we are in the period of the new régime transitional to that of our assumption of full sovereignty we must not admit any revelations by the Press of any form of public dishonesty; it is necessary that the new régime should be thought to have so perfectly contented everybody that even criminality has disappeared . . . cases of the manifestation of criminality should remain known only to their victims and to chance witnesses — no more." *(Protocol* XII.) To-day behind the Iron Curtain, police news and crime reports are missing from the Press. The secret Jewish command in the *Protocols* was faithfully carried out by the " new régime " fifty years later.

" When we come into our kingdom it will be undesirable for us that there should exist any other religion than ours . . ." the Learned Elders of Zion state in *Protocol* XIV. And it is said that in the Soviet Union to-day the Jewish faith alone enjoys religious freedom.

". . . we shall make it our task to see that against us such things as plots shall no longer exist . . . we shall slay without mercy all who take arms (in hand) to oppose our coming into our kingdom. Every kind of new institution of anything like a secret society will also be punished with death. . . ." *(Protocol* XV.) This Jewish order was carried out with almost classical severity by the M.V.D., led by the Jews. The purges and massacres in Soviet Russia and in the countries behind the Iron Curtain prove that the Jews in power are carrying out the instructions of the *Protocols* ruthlessly.

" Every kind of new institution of anything like a secret society will also be punished with death; those of them which are now in existence, are known to us, serve us and have served us, we shall disband and send into exile to continents far removed from Europe. In this way we shall proceed with those Goy masons who know too much." *(Protocol* XV.) This explains why freemasonry was liquidated in Eastern Europe after the establishment of Communism, despite the fact that it had paved the way for Bolshevism. Freemasons behind the Iron Curtain to-day live in a rather remote land — in Siberia in fact! *Protocols* VIII and X tell us:

" For a time, until there will no longer be any risk in entrusting responsible posts in our States to our brother-Jews, we shall put them in the hands of persons . . . who in case of disobedience . . . must face criminal charges." ". . . we shall arrange elections in favour of such presidents as have in their past some dark, undiscovered stain, some ' Panama ' or other — then they will be trustworthy agents . . . out of fear of revelations. . . ." (*Protocol* X.)

This system was employed with ghastly thoroughness by the Bolsheviks in the countries behind the Iron Curtain until their power was firmly established. It can be best illustrated by examples in Hungary. Since 1945 the real holder of power in Hungary was a Muscovite Jew called Mátyás Rákosi-Roth. The first President of the Republic was Zoltán Tildy, an alcoholic Calvinist priest whose wife, Elizabeth Gyenis-Gruenfeld, is a Jewess. The second President was Árpád Szakasits, an informer for the Gestapo whose wife was sent to prison for shoplifting. The third President was a gipsy called Alexander Rónai-Roma who had a Jewish wife. But real power is always in the hands of the Hungarian secret police (A.V.H.) led by Jews.

". . . it cannot be allowed that out of fear of a possible mistake an opportunity should be given of escape to persons suspected of a political lapse. . . ." says *Protocol* XVIII, which goes on: ". . . in these matters we shall be literally merciless . . . there is no possibility of excuse for persons occupying themselves with questions in which nobody except the government can understand anything. . . ."

And indeed, in Central Europe most political prisoners are rotting in Soviet prisons, in the internment camps of the enslaved countries or in deportation colonies. Political " criminals " were punished by the enforcement of retroactive laws. According to the statistics of the American Federation of Labour (A.F.L.), fourteen to twenty million slaves are building the structure of the Jewish world kingdom in the forced labour camps of the Soviet. The *Protocols* even give a prescription as to how political prisoners must be treated in order to prevent people feeling sympathy for them :

" In order to destroy the prestige of heroism for political crime we shall send it for trial in the category of thieving, murder, and every kind of abominable and filthy crime. Public opinion will then confuse in its conception this category of crime with the disgrace attaching to every other and will brand it with the same contempt." (*Protocol* XIX.)

Anybody closely watching political trials behind the Iron Curtain would realise that here too the leaders of the Soviet Union are following the fifty-year-old instructions of the *Protocols*. Thus, under duress, Cardinal Mindszenty was made to confess that he had dealt in currency smuggling; Bishop Lajos Ordass was forced to admit smuggling dollars, and László Rajk, an ex-Communist minister for home affairs, had to plead guilty to larceny. All those who do not like Jewish rule coated with Bolshevism are enemies of the people. They "commit crimes" against one race, i.e. against Jewry.

The authors of the *Protocols* are thinking not only of the present but of the future also. They want to secure world power for ever, and the only possible way to achieve this is to blot out the historical past from the minds of the youth of all nations. Then these young people will grow up to swell the ranks of the servile masses, bereft of any tradition. "Classicism, as also any form of study of ancient history, in which there are more bad than good examples, we shall replace with the study of the programme of the future," we read in *Protocol* XVI. Marxism and Leninism also teaches that: "We will obliterate from the memory of Man all the historical facts of past centuries which could be unfavourable to us. We will abolish all private schools and private education."

All this programme has been carried out behind the Iron Curtain with extreme precision, the above quoted instructions being followed word for word. The classics are no longer being taught in Soviet schools. The youngsters have to learn the doctrines of Marx and Lenin, together with details of the various five-year plans and of programmes relating to the future. All private teaching is abolished. The Latin language is banned and replaced by Russian. The besmirching of the past and the falsification of history is being carried out systematically. Jewish world rule, pulverising and rotting everything, can here be seen in its absolute form — in Bolshevism.

Jewish propaganda has recently suggested that "anti-Semitism" exists behind the Iron Curtain. The show trials of a few Communist Jews would appear to corroborate this argument, e..g. the cases of Slansky-Salzman, Anna Pauker-Rabinovich, Gábor Péter-Auspitz and the execution of Beria

". . . we have sacrificed many of our own but for that we have now already given them such a position on the earth as they could not even have dreamed of. The comparatively small numbers of the victims from the number of ours have preserved our nationality from destruction." (*Protocol* XV.)

This explains away the so-called " anti-Semitism " of Soviet Russia. The bodies of Pauker, Beria and Slansky appear to be rungs in the ladder leading upwards to world power.

What hopes have you got for the future, you men of the West, living in " free " lands, bombarded as you are by empty phrases proceeding from the lips of Jew-run statesmen and leaders? Can you not see that *your much extolled democracy is really no democracy, but Judeocracy?* In the East it is the tommy-gun, in the West it is gold coupled with political influence. Have you any hope, you men of the West, of escaping the fate of your Christian brothers and sisters in the East, whom you have deserted? Perhaps those who are promising you better things are really referring to you amongst themselves in the words of the *Protocols*:

" The Goyims are a flock of sheep, and we are their wolves."

How much of the programme of the *Protocols* has been carried out in America up to the present time?

When Roosevelt broke off diplomatic relations with Germany on account of " the persecution of the Jews ", it became clear that the United States of America were by this time in the hands of the secret Jewish government. The Quebec conference as well as the adoption of the Morgenthau Plan proved that power over America had passed almost completely into the hands of Jewry. The aerial bombings of the Second World War, the revenge campaign of Nuremberg and the Soviet alliance, all reflected an America *which retained few of the traditions of the past.*

" The administrators, whom we shall choose from among the public, with strict regard for their capacities for servile obedience, will not be persons trained in the arts of government, and will therefore easily become pawns in our game in the hands of men of learning and genius who will be their advisers, specialists bred and reared from early childhood to rule the affairs of the whole world." (*Protocol* II.)

F. D. Roosevelt was such a pawn. As we pointed out before, the number of Jews amongst Roosevelt's seventy-two presidential advisers was fifty-two.

" The formula of gradual subversion and the scientifically planned destructive disintegration which has been applied in the case of the U.S. is prescribed by the Protocols:

" This evil is the one and only means to attain the end, the good. Therefore we must not stop at bribery, deceit and treachery when they should serve towards the attainment of our end. In politics one must know how to seize the property of others without hesitation if by it we secure submission and sovereignty." (*Protocol* I.)

In this connection, in order not to offend America, it is enough to quote an article entitled " Return to Paganism ", which appeared in the American Catholic paper *The Wanderer,* on July 23rd, 1950:

" The citizens of this country had to witness throughout the past years a shameful theatrical play in which the leading members of our Government, both in foreign and home affairs, were exposed as Communists and traitors. Others were found guilty of perjury, and some of larceny, blackmail and forgery. *Reliable observers think, that according to the most modest estimate, there are at least 5,000 homosexuals employed in the State administration in Washington, and that amongst the heads of departments of the administration not a single person is to be found willing to try to put things right and clean up this mess in our public life."*

The *Protocols* describe this state of affairs fairly accurately:

" If already now we have contrived to possess ourselves of the minds of the Goy communities . . . if already now there is not a single State where there exists for us any barriers to admittance into what Goy stupidity calls State secrets: what will our position be, then, when we shall be acknowledged supreme lords of the world in the person of our king of all the world?" (*Protocol* XII.)

The American spy scandals, the giving away of the secret of the atomic bomb, the passing on of confidential matter from the State Department and the stealing of military secrets, all show that Jewry was following out instructions from the *Protocols* since, as we have already pointed out, these crimes were committed almost exclusively by Jews.

Simultaneously, with the corruption of the American upper classes and State administration, the demoralisation of the masses began through their entertainments. The ignorance of the American masses concerning public affairs is not natural to the American character. This result has been artificially achieved and corresponds with the commandments of the *Protocols*:

" In order that the masses themselves may not guess what they are about we further distract them with amusements, games, pastimes, passions, people's palaces. . . . Soon we shall begin through the Press to propose competitions in art, in sport of all kinds. . . ." (*Protocol* XIII.)

American films are produced to-day by Louis B. Mayer, Jack Warner, Harry Warner, Nick Schenk, Joe Schenk, Goldwyn, Zukor and other film kings of similar names. Amongst the leading film stars there are more than one hundred Reds and Communists. Eighty-five per cent of the Press is controlled by Jews. These same elements also cater for the masses on radio and television. And so refrigerators are more important to-day than the manufacture of weapons to defend the " free " world.

" Growing more and more disaccustomed to reflect and form any opinions of their own, people will begin to talk in the same tone as we, because we alone shall be offering them new directions for thought . . . of course through such persons as will not be suspected of solidarity with us." (*Protocol* XIII.)

All this has happened. To-day, the Press, the radio, the films and television divert public attention from vital national and international problems. The gigantic network of the entertainment industry represents not only the " sunny side of life ", but remains at the same time the most formidable weapon for the destructive ambitions of a certain race.

Not a word is uttered by the Press against this state of affairs. The very emphasis of the word " freedom " is often nothing else but hypocrisy, or perhaps an excuse for Jewry to do as it pleases. It is enough to read Dorothy Thompson's article, in which she admits that she was unable to find an editor willing to give space in his paper to her serial condemning the hatred artificially created in order to wage war. The freedom of the Press is either dead or is turned into a monopoly, and only things favourable to Jewish interests are published. This state of affairs was also prescribed by the authors of the *Protocols*:

" And if there should be any found who are desirous of writing against us, they will not find any person eager to print their productions." (*Protocol* XII.)

Those American papers which understand the Jewish questions are kept going only by private donations. Their circulation is small and their influence is negligible. The truth that they champion and preach cannot reach the great reading public.

"We have got our heads into the administration of the law, into the conduct of elections, into the Press, into liberty of the person, but principally into education and training as being the cornerstones of a free existence." (*Protocol* IX.)

The notorious Felix Frankfurter is to-day one of the judges of the American Supreme Court. In his book, *The International Jew,* Henry Ford raised objections many years ago to the Judaisation of the administration of justice. To-day in New York courts of justice, Jews make up the majority of the judges. Justice is no longer blind-folded; she looks out carefully so as to recognise and favour the world-conquering race. As at Nuremberg, Jewish nationalism administers the kind of justice that favours Jewish nationalists.

It is well known that public education is in the hands of Jewry. Various " educational " organisations, leagues and associations supply young people with obscure and misleading socialistic ideas. The American Liberty League, under the direction of Robert Filene, the well-known Jewish multi-millionaire of Boston, is the largest of these organisations. As Flynn writes in his book, *The Road Ahead,* it came to light that between sixty and seventy professors of Chicago and Harvard Universities were active members of the Communist Party. One of these professors belonged to fourteen Bolshevik-front organisa-tions. In several colleges the teachers and professors were all Jews. The result is that the next generation is being brought up on Bolshe-vistic ideas leading to moral depravity.

"We have fooled, bemused and corrupted the youth of the Goyim by rearing them in principles and theories which are known to us to be false. . . ." (*Protocol* IX.)

And the lurid game which consumed and plunged into poverty and servitude the people of Eastern Europe is being played out in America also.

"We shall raise the rate of wages which, however, will not bring any advantage to the workers for, at the same time, we shall produce a rise in prices of the first necessaries of life. . . ." (*Protocol* VI.)

Although the great wealth of the soil raised the living standards of American workers to fabulous heights, the end of this economic game is always the same. During the heyday of armament production

239

wages rose, but the price of everything else went up too. The dollar lost half of its purchasing power during the armament boom.

" What we have to get at is that there should be in all the States of the world, besides ourselves, only the masses of the proletariat, a few millionaires devoted to our interests, police and soldiers." (*Protocol* VII.)

To-day the American worker still possesses his own house, his motor car and refrigerator, and yet by means of the sham fight between capital and labour, the Jews are leading him inexorably towards Bolshevism.

The Christian sects have also become embroiled in a war of nerves. The principle of " Free State Religion " weakens the Christian Churches. The Jewish rabbis protest against having Christian songs in the schools at Christmas time.

" When we come into our kingdom it will be undesirable for us that there should exist any other religion than ours. . . . We must therefore sweep away all other forms of belief." (*Protocol* XIV.)

The theory of " The Kingdom of God ", which we dealt with in the earlier part of this book, is a very effective way of inducing a sham Christianity with a Jewish and Bolshevik twist. Moreover, in the background of the various sects the same mysterious power is found which is referred to by the *Protocols* and known as Freemasonry.

" Meanwhile, however, until we come into our kingdom . . . we shall create and multiply freemasonic lodges in all the countries of the world, absorb into them all who may become or who are prominent in public activity, for in these lodges we shall find our principal intelligence office and means of influence. All these lodges we shall bring under one central administration, known to us alone and to all others absolutely unknown, which will be composed of our learned elders." (*Protocol* XV.)

B'nai B'rith, the largest Jewish freemasonic organisation, has to-day 267 lodges under a central direction. This alone secures more influence for Jewry than all other similar organisations put together.

Protocol XV, amongst many other things, tells us:

" In these lodges we shall tie together the knot which binds together all revolutionary and liberal elements. Their composition will be made up of all strata of society. The most secret political plots will be known to us and will fall under our guiding hands on the very day of their conception. . . . It is natural that we and no other should lead masonic activities, for we know whither we are leading, we know the final goal of every form of activity whereas the Goyim have knowledge of nothing, not even of the immediate effect of action."

In America all this has been happening for a long while. Freemasonry is the real governor of American democracy and constitutes a most powerful and obedient auxiliary in the cause of Jewish "nazism". It is an invisible S.S., recruited from leaders of all nations and from members of all social classes. It played a leading rôle in the French Revolution, in the first Hungarian Bolshevik dictatorship of Bela Kun, in starting the anti-clerical and anti-religious movements and in the elaboration of the Versailles treaties after the First World War. As a consequence of all these things, both freemasonry and its subsidiaries, the Rotary Clubs, were condemned by the Pope.

One thing is certain. Freemasonry is the very negation of democracy. When leadership is exerted by a secret organisation and when laws are conceived and elaborated in the lodges before being submitted to parliament, there can be no talk of the expression of the will of the people. Under these circumstances democracy becomes a shadow. When a State is guided by freemasonry, which is controlled by Jews, its democracy represents nothing else but a stage in a rapid descent towards Bolshevism.

The great Hungarian patriot László Endre, a high authority on the Jewish question in Europe, shortly before the outbreak of the Second World War wrote a most interesting book about the *Protocols of the Learned Elders of Zion,* whose authenticity he establishes by diligent study and research. Is it any wonder, then, that in 1946 he was among the first to be dragged to the gallows in bolshevised Budapest? This man who endured martyrdom for his ideals, wrote a farewell letter during the night before his execution. In this letter, dated March 21st 1946, he states:

"The *Protocols of the Learned Elders of Zion* are true . . . the means to establish a world kingdom are in their hands and they will destroy everything that might constitute an obstacle to their formation of the new World State. Everything happening here is for the sake of prevention as well as revenge, and of course has nothing to do with the administration of justice. For Jewish policy is *to exterminate not only those who did something but even those who might yet do something or could have done something. . . ."*

The *Protocols of the Learned Elders of Zion* are true. The reason for accepting their authenticity is not because a Hungarian martyr thought them to be true, but because *everything written in them has so far come true.* Can a better test of veracity be found?

SEVENTEEN

THE KEY-POSITIONS OF JEWISH
WORLD-POWER

MODERN civilisation is governed politically and controlled economic-
ally by men in key positions. Influence exercised through men in
key positions is often more decisive than rulings of heads of State
or resolutions of parliament. The Jews have always understood how
to occupy and keep these key positions for themselves, and also
how to utilise them either for grabbing political power or for the
purpose of governing behind the scenes.

The news services of the world are practically all in the hands of
a few big Jewish news agencies. Therefore some 2,000 million people
hear news that is generally favourable to the Jews and to the aspirations of Jewish nationalism. The Jews control the *cinema and the
film industry,* not only in America but in almost all countries of the
world, including the Soviet Union. The *textile industry and the
cotton trade* is also nearly everywhere in the hands of Jewry. *The
gold trade and gold production* is associated all over the world with
the following names: Rothschild, Bleichroeder, Mendelsohn, Japhet,
Seligman, Lazard, Strauss, Morgenthau and Schiff. The Oppen-
heimers control almost the whole *diamond production* of South
Africa and nearly all world trade in diamonds. The hostile political
influence of one member of the Oppenheimer family is well known
to ministers of the South African Government. Through the Diamond
Trading Company Sir Ernest Oppenheimer built up one of the greatest
monopolies in the world, which had even its own secret police. This
monopoly consists almost exclusively of Jews and it keeps Western
Germany under a boycott even to-day. Consequently Germany's needs
in industrial diamonds can only be covered through the black market
or with the help of smugglers. (*Der Spiegel,* Vol. XI, No. 35.) To
the Oppenheimres belong 100 of the world's greatest diamond, gold,
copper and uranium mines. His private fortune is about a billion

dollars. Though Sir Ernest has died recently, the position of the Oppenheimer monopoly remains unchanged.

Lord Melchett (Alfred Mond) controls the *nickel,* while the *wheat trade* is in the hands of Louis Dreyfus.

The *Jewish Encyclopædia* gives a very interesting survey of how the Jews gained influence in the various countries by loan transactions. The Sterns and Goldschmidts in Portugal, Baron Hirsch in Turkey, the Rothschilds in France, the Strassbergs in Roumania, Poljakov, Speyer and Co. in Russia, and Kuhn, Loeb and Co. financed the building of the railways in the United States. The *Jewish Encyclopædia* also confirms that the *mercury trade* is in the hands of the Rothschilds; Barnato Brothers and Wernek, Bett and Co. control an important part of the *diamond trade;* Levinson and Guggenheim the *copper trade;* and Graustein and Dreyfus the *paper industry.*

But even more interesting than the *Jewish Encyclopædia* is an issue of the *Edmondson Economic Service Bulletin,* dated 1939, from which it can be seen that the 440 wealthiest American families, meaning here old established Gentile millionaires, possess altogether twenty-five billion dollars, whilst a handful of American Jews possess wealth computed at 500 billion dollars. Even such a small and relatively little-known Jewish concern as the Insull Brothers exercises control over five billion dollars.

Syria is a typical example of the malign influence of the world conquerors. *Hatikva,* the Zionist paper written in Hungarian, boasts that the whole economic life of Syria is under the control of a 60,000 Syrian Jewish minority. Almost 100 per cent of the professors in the University of Damascus are Jews. According to Zionist sources, the 60,000 Syrian Jewish minority holds key positions in the economic life, and plays a major rôle in the cultural, industrial and commercial life of Syria.

As a result of this, Syria, while living in a realm of fantasy, is drifting dangerously nearer to becoming a Soviet satellite.

The Suez Canal itself, the nationalisation of which almost embroiled mankind in a third world war, was controlled for almost 100 years by the financial interests of the world conquerors. Originally, Disraeli, the Jewish Prime Minister of Great Britain, acquired a large holding of the canal shares for the British Government. The Rothschild banking house of London made a profit of more than 100,000 pounds sterling on the first credit transaction alone. When the Egyptian President Nasser wanted to terminate one of the greatest business interests of the world conquerors, Israel, Great Britain and France vainly attempted to protect them with fleets, tanks and rockets.

In previous chapters we have quoted the *Protocols*, and pointed out paragraphs giving directions how to establish a government over all other governments. It is stated in *Protocol* V that: " In place of the rulers of to-day we shall set up a bogey which will be called the Super Government Administration." With this is closely connected some of the most important instructions of the *Protocols*, which tell us that *as long as it is not advisable to put Jews into the highest positions the important posts will be filled by persons of doubtful character.*

It must be noted that Jewry, as a most disciplined nationalism, obeyed this order without fail. Be it Soviet dictatorship or American democracy, Jews everywhere fill positions behind a Gentile front. A Gentile puppet is in the forefront as head of the State, Prime Minister, etc., but at his elbow stands a Jew. Eisenhower comes first but next comes Baruch who is much more influential. Similarly, Stalin was followed by Khaganovich. It is noteworthy that this plan was carried out not only in cases affecting the most important key positions but often in those concerning posts of lesser importance also. The head of the office is a Gentile, his deputy is a Jew. The commander-in-chief of the occupation forces is an American or Soviet general, but his deputy is a Jew. At Nuremberg, Gentile judges sat on the bench, but Robert M. Kempner, helped by 2,400 other Jews, toiled in the background.

The first president of the old League of Nations was a Jew called Hymans. But he was quickly replaced by a Gentile. The time had not yet come to put Jews into the leading positions. Yet according to reports in the *New York Times* of August 22nd, 1922, Nahum Sokolow emphasised in a speech delivered to the Zionist Congress at Carlsbad, that the establishment of the League of Nations was " a Jewish idea ".

Dr. Dillon, referring in his book to the Versailles peace conference, tells us that the most influential exponents of the whole gathering and those with the most characteristic interests were Jews who came from Palestine, Russia, the Ukraine, Greece, Great Britain and the Netherlands. But the Jewish delegates sent from the United States were the most important of all. It may surprise the reader to know that most of the delegates were convinced that the real influence behind the Anglo-Saxon people was Jewish.

The Jews stood behind a Gentile front here too. The delegates receiving the publicity and those who signed the treaties were Gentiles. But those who acted as advisers and represented the real power were Jews.

To-day Jewish world power is based on the system of a Gentile front. This is a kind of mimicry. "Secrecy is the character of our power." If a map of Jewish world power could be drawn up it would actually represent a pattern of the key positions held. We might add that this map can never be perfect and it is very incomplete even to-day. It would show those key positions so far occupied by Jewry, or a small fraction of them, from which it dictates world policy to the Gentile front.

The United Nations (U.N.O.) became the most powerful organisation of world Jewry. The U.N. is the chief organisation of Eastern and Western Jewry. It is the beginning, and a sample, of supranational world government, and on its staff both Eastern and Western Jews, capitalists, and Bolshevik Old Testament "nazis" meet. On top of the glass palace of the United Nations in Manhattan the flag of U.N.O. is displayed, the pale blue and white colours of which are strikingly identical with those of the Israeli flag. But it is not only the colours of the flags that are similar. The people represented by the flags are alike too. The most important key positions in the world are occupied by men of the same race. Taking 1951 as the basis for our survey, we give a list of names. It is almost as sinister as the list of the Russian Bolshevik leaders in 1917.

THE SECRETARIAT OF THE UNITED NATIONS

Dr. H. S. Bloc, head of the Armament Dept.
Antoine Goldet, Principal Director, Dept. Economic Affairs.
Ansgar Rosenberg ,special advisor Dept. Economic Affairs.
David Weintraub, director Economic Stability and Development.
Karl Lachman. head of the Fiscal Dept.
Dr. Leon Steinig, director of Narcotics Division.

Henry Langier, deputy-chief of the Department of Social Welfare.

Dr. E. Schwelb, deputy-chief of the Dept. of Human Rights.

H. A. Wieschoff, in Administrative Dept. of the Non-Autonomous territories.

Benjamin Cohen, Assistant Secretary-General Public Information Dept.

Dr. Ivan Kerno, Deputy Secretary-General Legal Dept.

Abraham H. Feller, head and chief advisor of the Legal Dept.

J. Benoit-Levy, director Films and Visual Information Bureau Division.

Marc Schreiber, legal advisor.

G. Sandberg, legal advisor to the Dept. of Codification of International Law.

David Zablodowsky, head of the Printing Dept.

George Rabinovich, head of the Dept. of Interpreters.

Max Abramovitz, deputy-chief of the Planning Office.

P. C. J. Kien, head of the Accountancy Dept.

Mercedes Bergmann, official of the Personnel Dept.

Dr. A. Signer, head of the Health Clinic.

Paul Rodzianko, secretary of Appeals Board.

U.N. INFORMATION BUREAU

Jerzy Shapiro, head of U.N. Central Information Bureau in Geneva.

B. Leitgeber, head of U.N. Central Information Bureau in New Delhi.

Henri Fast, head of U.N. Central Information Bureau in Shanghai

Dr. Julius Stawinski, head of U.N. Central Information Bureau in Warsaw.

INTERNATIONAL LABOUR OFFICE

David A. Morse (Mocovitch), head of the Dept. of I.L.O., Geneva.

Three of the four chiefs of I.L.O. are Jews. They are:

Altman (Poland), David Zellerbach (U.S.A.), Finet (Belgium).

V. Gabriel-Garces, Ecuadorian correspondent and delegate.

Jan Rosner, Polish correspondent and delegate.

FOOD AND AGRICULTURAL ORGANISATION

André Mayer, first Vice-Chairman.

A. J. Jacobsen, Danish delegate.

M. M. Libman, head of the Dept. of Chemical Fertilisers.

E. de Vries, Dutch delegate.

Gerda Kardos, head of the Fibres Dept.

M. Ezekiel, head of the Economic Analysis Branch.

B. Kardos, head of the Dept. of Miscellaneous Commodity Section

M. A. Hubermann, head of the Technical Forestry Dept.

J. P. Kagan, technical officer Logging and Equipment Section

J. Mayer, head of the Food Office.

F. Weisel, head of the Administrative Dept.

EDUCATIONAL, SCIENTIFIC AND CULTURAL ORGANISATION (U.N.E.S.C.O.)

Out of the four members of the Executive Committee Alfred Sommerfelt and Paul Carneiro are Jews.

J. Eisenhardt, president of the Re-educational Committee.

Miss Lauffman, head of Dept. of International Understanding and Education.

Dr. O. Klineberg, departmental head.

H. Kaplan, head of the Public Information Bureau.

C. H. Weitz, head of the Administrative Dept.

B. Abramski, head of the Dept. of Housing and Travel

S. Samuel Selsky, head of Personnel Bureau.

B. Wermiel, head of the Administrative Employment.

Dr. A. Welsky, head of the Office of Scientific Co-operation.

INTERNATIONAL BANK OF RECONSTRUCTION AND DEVELOPMENT

M. M. Mendels, secretary.

Leonhard B. Rist, economic director.

Leopold Chmela, president and chairman of the Board

E. Polask, member of the Czechoslovakian Board of Governors. Governors (Czechoslovakia).

P. Mendès France, member of the French Board of Governors

A. M. de Jong, of the Board of Governors of Holland.

D. Abramovich, of the Board of Governors of Yugoslavia.

INTERNATIONAL MONETARY FUND

Josef Goldmann, of the Board of Governors (Czechoslovakia).

Louis Rasminsky, Canadian managing director.

W. Kaster, Dutch deputy-director.

Louis Altman, deputy managing director.

E. M. Bernstein, head of the Department of Enquiries.

Joseph Gold, leading counsel.

Leo Levanthal, leading counsel.

INTERNATIONAL REFUGEE ORGANISATION

Mayer Cohen, head of the Health and Welfare Dept. of I.R.O.

Pierre Jacobsen, director of the Repatriation Dept.

R. J. Youdin, director Repatriation Division

WORLD HEALTH ORGANISATION

Z. Deutschmann, head of the Technical Dept.

G. Mayer, head of the Dept. of Translations.

M. Siegel, head of the Financial Dept.

Dr. N. Goodman, managing director Co-operation Dept.

A. Zarb, director Legal Section.

INTERNATIONAL TRADE ORGANISATION

Max Suetens, president of the organisation

INTERNATIONAL TELECOMMUNICATION UNION

F. C. de Wolfe, U.S. delegate in the Administrative Council.

Gerry Gross, deputy managing director of I.T.O

H. B. Rantzen, president of the International Telecommunication Committee.

ORGANISATION OF CIVIL AVIATION

A. G. Berg, head of the organisation

MISCELLANEOUS PROJECTS

Col. A. C. Katzin, representative of U.N. in Korea.

George Novshon, U.N. information officer in Korea.

Ernest A. Gross, second delegate of the U.S.A. to U.N.O.

Isador Lubin, head of the Economic and Employment Committee

Julius Katz-Sochy, permanent delegate of Poland.

Dr. Ales Bebler, permanent delegate of Yugoslavia.

The lists already quoted show that *the vital key positions are held everywhere by Jews.*

Let us now make a detailed examination of the highest political government of the United States. Between 1945 and 1951, the non-Jewish Harry Truman stood in the forefront, but according to a statement in the *Chicago Tribune,* the second line, the secret government of the U.S.A., consisted of the following members: Morgenthau, Herbert H. Lehman and Felix Frankfurter. At the same time as Marshall was Secretary of War, Mrs. Anna Rosenberg, a Jewess from Budapest, acted as Deputy-Secretary of War. During the Truman administration, although Dean Acheson was Secretary of State, foreign affairs were, in fact, directed by Felix Frankfurter. At the same time it was said that Bernard Baruch was the real President of the U.S.A.

Since, according to the *Hidden Empire,* eighty-two per cent of the employees of the State Department were Jews, we cannot be surprised at this state of affairs. The sad picture is completed by the key positions in the American immigration office, together with those in big capital, the Press, the film industry, radio and television being in the hands of Jewry. Here we may add that, according to the same authority, Jews controlled at least sixty per cent of the national income of the U.S.A.

In any case it must be put to the credit of the "little" Harry Truman that during his administration the investigations of the McCarthy Committee were able to progress undisturbed. After Roosevelt's death, the White House, which Harry S. Truman took over, resembled a synagogue. When Truman left there were hardly any members of the world conquerors in the White House. David K. Niles was evicted from it, and so was Samuel Roseman.

During the Eisenhower administration the position has not improved but has become rather worse. The McCarthy investigations ceased and the world conquerors evicted by Truman were replaced by other Jews. The pamphlet, *The Coming Red Dictatorship,* edited as a special issue by the American paper *Common Sense,* gives an appalling picture of the real set-up of the Eisenhower administration. Eisenhower's chief economic adviser, for instance, is a young Jew called Arthur F. Burns, one of Bernard Baruch's men planted in the White House. The chairman of the Atomic Energy Commission is L. Strauss; the military expert on Far Eastern questions is General Lyman Lemnitzer; the head of the secret world government is James

P. Warburg, the banker; and one of the chief U.S. delegates to ττ Ν. is Jacob Blaustein. Isidore Lubin directs German reparations. It would take too long to enumerate all the key positions occupied by the world conquerors in the Eisenhower régime. But it is certain that the position is, if anything, worse to-day than it was during the time of Roosevelt.

In conjunction with the U.S.A. we now turn to the Soviet Union. Rumour would have us believe that the overwhelming majority of the Jewish participants of the 1917 Revolution was driven underground, and that subsequently a great Russian or Pan-Slav movement got the upper hand. This was said to be evident at least in the Politbureau and in the most important governmental positions.

It would be an absolute misconception of Soviet affairs to think that so-called " Muscovitism " constituted the Jewish form of Bolshevism, or that Titoism and National Communism was in the slightest degree " anti-Semitic ". *Muscovitism represents no doubt the most perfected form of the Jewish system of world domination.* The essential character of this system is that the civilised, cultured and intelligent workers in all countries behind the Iron Curtain must be ruled by Russian methods, regardless of the fact that these methods were originally prescribed for Soviet citizens only. Lazar Khaganovich, no doubt, was the most determined exponent of this plan. It is, on the other hand, perfectly possible that there were certain Communist leaders in the various States behind the Iron Curtain who refused to submit to Muscovitism. Slansky-Salzman and Anna Pauker were themselves Jews and Communists. It was not, therefore, the Jewish character of Khaganovich's Muscovitism that called forth their objections. They reasoned, however, that the schedule prescribed for home use was not suitable for the Czechoslovak, Roumanian or Bulgarian worker. *They wished to adopt those methods to which Roumanian, Czechoslovak, Bulgarian and Hungarian Jews had long been accustomed.*

All this is far from meaning that the Soviet Union has turned " anti-Semitic ". Louis Levine's conclusion in 1945 that the Soviet Union was governed by one million Jews in key positions still holds good to-day. The Soviet Jews firmly believe that the *Muscovite type of Communism represents the most perfected form of Jewish world domination,* and they will, therefore, ruthlessly exterminate even

251

other Jews who are unwilling to share their views on this point.

In the Soviet Union, Lazar Khaganovich was as predominant an exponent of how the world conquerors rule behind the Gentile front as is Bernard Baruch in the " democratic " United States of America. The real dictator is here, whether it be behind Stalin, Malenkov or Kruschev that he acts. His younger sister Rosa Khaganovich was Stalin's third wife, while his son Mikhail Khaganovich married Stalin's daughter Svetlana.

The recent removal of Khaganovich does not mean much. He retired for the time being but the one million world conquerors in key positions remain the real masters of Soviet Russia.

Molotov's relations are interesting to record. He is not a Jew, but his wife Karpovszkaja, the younger sister of Samuel Karp, the American multi-millionaire oil magnate, is a Jewess.

Out of the nine members of the former Politbureau, Khaganovich and Mikoyan were Jews, Saburov most probably also belonged to the world conquerors, and Swernik was a substitute member.

Like the democracies, a characteristic feature of the Soviet system is that the visible leaders are not usually the real rulers. *Thus Vladimir Ashberg, a Jewish banker, plays a most important rôle in the Soviet Union.* His position resembles that of Morgenthau during the Roosevelt era. He is in various degrees of relationship with all the important Jewish banking families, and he is also a member of the Jewish World Congress. He is the chief financier of the Soviet Union.

If we examine the holders of key positions in the *Soviet Union,* we will see that this country also *is under the control of the Jews.* The year in question is 1951.

Professor Mark Mitin, president of the Science Academy of the Soviet Union, the highest authority on Marxist-Leninist ideology, and editor of the Kominform paper *For Lasting Peace and People's Democracy*—is a Jew.

Also a Jew is Pavel E. Yudin, one of the most important people in the Soviet Union, head of the History Department of the Soviet Union's Science Academy, deputy-chairman of the publishing house of popular scientific works, editor of the Kominform paper which publishes official Soviet propaganda, one of the chief leaders of the " purges " behind the Iron Curtain, political adviser of the Red Army in the East German Occupation Zone and the present dictator of Eastern Germany.

M. Z. Saburov, president of the State Planning Office and Planning Committee, is a Jew.

A. I. Lavrentiev (real name Lippmann), deputy foreign minister, former ambassador to Czechoslovakia, bosom friend of Alger Hiss, director of Soviet diplomatic espionage all over the world and head of the network of foreign espionage which organised the Persian disturbances, is a Jew.

Eugene Varga-Weiszfeld, head of the World Economic and Political Institute of the Soviet Union, one of the most important leading officials of the Soviet's economic life, is a Jew too.

Ilia Ehrenburg, propaganda chief, writer of *Pravda* leading articles, leading publicist of Soviet ideology, and the director of the Kominform " Peace Movement ", is a Jew.

Leonid Menikov, Soviet ambassador to Roumania, is a Jew.

I. Nosenko, minister of heavy industry and transport, is a Jew.

Anatole Yakovlev, Soviet ambassador to the U.S. during the hearings of the Rosenberg treason case, and now one of the heads of Soviet espionage, is a Jew.

M. N. Svernik, former President of the Soviet Union, and now leader of the Russian trade unions, is a Jew.

A. F. Gorkin, Secretary-General of the Presidium of the Supreme Soviet, is a Jew.

David Zaslawsky, editor of *Pravda,* is a Jew.

S. A. Losowsky, former head of the Soviet Foreign Office, and now director of the Soviet Information and News Service, is a Jew.

Prof. I. P. Trailin, attorney-general of the Soviet Union, former Muscovite member of the " Committee for the Prosecution of War Criminals ", and director of the Law School of Moscow, is a Jew.

Boris Stein, director of the Diplomatic Service School of the Soviet Foreign Office, one of the Soviet delegates to U.N.O., is a Jew. The Soviet Foreign Office is so full of Jews that Russians humorously refer to it as the " Synagogue ".

Franktine Schul, one of the leading exponents of world Communism, who speaks sixteen languages, is also a Jew. In 1950 he was leader of the Red terrorists in Indo-China, and at present he is head of N. 3 Group; as such he directs the extermination of anti-Communists behind the Iron Curtain.

S. V. Kraftenov, Minister of University and High School Education in the Soviet Union, is a Jew.

General K. Gorshenin, Minister of Justice, is a Jew.

Jacob Malik, previously chief Soviet delegate to U.N.O., and at present Soviet ambassador in London, is a Jew.

Major-General Boris Rasin, military attaché in Great Britain, is a Jew.

Solomon Abrahamovich Reback, deputy-director of the Soviet Atomic Energy Committee and also security chief of the special department of M.V.D. which controls the atom scientists, is a Jew.

Colonel I. Vigdor, counter-espionage officer commissioned to the security service of Soviet Atomic Research, is a Jew.

Major Kahan, secret police official, detailed to the Atomic Energy Committee, is a Jew.

A. Mikoyan, member of the Politbureau and Minister of Commerce, is an Armenian Jew.

M. M. Brodin, Press chief, is a Jew.

Peter Levitsky, vice-president of the Council of the Soviet States, is a Jew.

D. Manuilsky, dictator of the Ukraine, is a Jew.

A. Kornejchuk, author and nominal President of the Ukrainian Republik, is a Jew.

A. N. Jacobson, dictator of Estonia and delegate representing Estonia, is a Jew.

N. Jakovliev, head of Soviet public education, is a Jew.

Yu Masenko, special expert on Indian affairs and director of the Communist movement in India, is a Jew.

G. I. Levinson, expert of the Oriental Section of the Soviet Science Academy on Chinese affairs, and one of the Chinese Communist leaders, is a Jew.

A. D. Danyalov, member of the Presidium of the Supreme Soviet, is a Jew.

F. T. Gusev, Deputy Foreign Minister, is a Jew.

S. Y. Romin, Minister of Building and Road Construction, is a Jew.

D. I. Fumin, Minister of Food and Raw Materials, is a Jew.

Jacob Suritz, Soviet ambassador to Brazil, is a Jew.

Colonel Rudenko, chief public prosecutor delegated by the Soviet to the Nuremberg trials, is probably a Jew.

Isaac Zaltman, director of tractor production, is a Jew.

I. G. Bosakov, director of the cinema industry, and possessing ministerial rank, is a Jew.

Prof. Pontecorvo, director of Soviet hydrogen bomb production, is a Jew.

S. Z. Ginsburg, president of the State Bank, is a Jew.

K. R. Herzberg, chairman of the Torg Bank, is a Jew.

A. G. Samuelenko, chairman of the Vnieshtorg Bank, is a Jew.

X. Yacob Simenov, chairman of the Prombank, is a Jew.

We should also bear in mind that the members and leaders of the Soviet Science Academy are almost exclusively Jews.

In 1957 the most shocking disclosures were published regarding the extent of the world conquerors' influence on Russia. Joseph Stalin, the most powerful and ruthless dictator, built up Soviet power to what it is to-day, and this he achieved with the help of the Jews. His wife was Rosa Khaganovich, and the Khaganovich family exerted a terrible influence in the Soviet Union. We know from authentic Jewish witnesses that only for Jews is the Soviet Union a Garden of Eden, since here they enjoy key positions in the Government, in the Army, in the academies, in planning offices and factory managements. According to reliable British and American reports, Yiddish was often spoken in Stalin's house in general conversation.

But Stalin, originally a great friend of the Jews and the second spiritual father of Bolshevism, was shaken in his convictions by events. This is affirmed by Emmanel Birnbaum, a Jewish writer, and also by an article in *Aufbau*. Stalin's faith in the Jews was shaken when Hitler's armies reached the circular railway lines on the outskirts of Moscow, enabling Stalin to see what degree of panic spread among the 500,000 Muscovite Jews, who fled leaving to its own devices " the great and glorious Bolshevik Revolution " which had done so much for them.

In the light of this, the exposure published in *France Soir* of June 7th, 1957, carries the mark of authenticity. In the article referred to, the French paper throws sharp light on the circumstances of

Stalin's death, which were described to members of the Polish Press by Ponomarenko, Soviet ambassador to Poland.

According to the ambassador's account, in February, 1953, Stalin submitted to the Presidential Council of the Soviet a decree to the effect that all Jews in the Soviet Union were to be deported to the Soviet Republic of Birobidjhan. Many Poles, Russians, Georgians, Estonians, Latvians, Lithuanians, Hungarians and others — more than the total number of Jews in the Soviet Union — had previously been deported on Stalin's orders, but against these deportations not one of the Soviet leaders ever raised a word of protest.

But when, as we learn, Stalin wanted to touch Jewry, all the Soviet leaders immediately turned against him. Khaganovich and Molotov, whose wife is Jewish, immediately stepped in, and Voroshilov, whose wife is also Jewish, said that he would quit the Communist Party at once if Stalin dared to touch Soviet Jews.

According to the account of Ponomarenko, Stalin flew into a livid rage, as a result of which he suffered a heart attack from which he collapsed and died on the spot.

The account of the Soviet ambassador at Warsaw is perfectly credible. But Stalin's death was said to be in March and not in February, 1953. If that is so, perhaps his death was not instantaneous, due to a heart attack, but caused by something else . . . *perhaps a dagger thrust, a revolver bullet, or poison killed him. The avenging arm of Jewry can reach far.*

But this story becomes even more sinister if we examine what happened after Stalin's death.

The well-informed Hungarian weekly *Way and Purpose* (Vol. IX, No. 8, page 10) published a most interesting article portraying Kruschev.

This paper states that Kruschev's biography was recently published in America. It was written by a Jew and from it we learn that Stalin's successor, the most powerful person in the Communist Party, comes from the Ukraine and is the son of a Cossack blacksmith. While a young man he lived in the Ukrainian town of Mariupol (Zhdanov), a port on the Sea of Azov, and as a turner earned good wages. He lodged with Jews and enjoyed their company so much that he learned to speak Yiddish. This orthodox Jewish family became rather fond of the young man, who was readily at their service on Saturdays, when he usually lit the kitchen fire as well as the fires in other rooms of the house, and who ate with an excellent appetite the stuffed fish and other especially tasty dishes of Jewish culinary art, to which his kind-hearted landlady was pleased to treat him. At that time life was not too good for Jews living in the Czar's empire. In those days the Beilis case was being heard before the Kiev courts. Beilis was charged with ritual murder, i.e. with having killed a young Christian boy and taken his blood. This case engendered great hatred against the Jews and an "anti-Semitic" organisation known as the Black Hundreds terrorised Russian Jewry. The excited population carried out pogroms in various parts of the country. The situation was rather dangerous in Mariupol too. The local leader of the Black Hundreds, a master butcher, was instigating the population in the market-place to start a pogrom, and it seemed quite likely that the Jews of Mariupol would not escape a dreadful fate. To prevent the pogrom, a Jewish teacher hastily organised a body of men to disperse the crowd that had gathered for the massacre of the Jews. Kruschev volunteered, and when it came to action he took part bravely in the fights. Bleeding from head wounds he returned to the Jewish family, who in the meanwhile had begun to suspect him of belonging to the Black Hundreds. But this incident dispelled all suspicion, and the Jews washed and cleaned the wounds of the limping Kruschev, while the cobbler, his landlord, announced with satisfaction : "This is a decent chap and I am sure he will never harm us!"

This he certainly never did and the Jews were not ungrateful to him. The cobbler's son, who was no other than Lazar Khaganovich himself, helped Kruschev throughout his life, supporting him in every difficulty. He brought Kruschev into the Bolshevik movement and exerted his influence in his favour whenever possible. Khaganovich brought him to Moscow from the Ukraine and introduced him to Stalin. There is no doubt, therefore, that Kruschev's relations with the Jews are excellent and that he has proved to be a faithful servant of those aspirations to world power laid down in the *Protocols of the Learned Elders of Zion.*

Certain Western intellectuals have tried to produce all kinds of evidence to establish the so-called "anti-Semitic" attitude of the Soviet. They quote evidence such as the liquidation of Beria, the trials of the Jewish doctors, the recent removal of Khaganovich, the Slansky case and the peaceful despatch of Anna Pauker-Rabinovich.

But to believe that Bolshevism could be capable of such a basic change would be to misunderstand the essence of the Soviet system.

In the usually well-informed Jewish newspaper *Aufbau* of New York, the organ representing Jews who fled to America from Hitler, a very interesting article was published on May 4th, 1951, from the pen of Jehojachim Alkalai, a Jew of Tel Aviv. At a time when Stalin was already suspected of " anti-Semitism " it informs us that during the German invasion of Russia, those Jews who had to flee from Hitler's invading troops were sent by the Soviet Government to Central Asia for resettlement. This ensured that more than 400,000 Jews were not only safe from further German persecution but that at the same time they were found excellent posts in the Republics of Kazakhstan, Uzbegistan and other Central Asian member-states of the Soviet Union. These posts were in those territories where the Soviet Union's great new centres of armament production and atomic research were to be built.

The article points out that with the resettlement of the Jews the Soviet Government achieved several important objects. In the first place, *the Jews were removed from those parts of the Soviet empire where the majority of the population is made up of Russians who, according to past experience, are prone to " anti-Semitism ".* The Jews were also preserved from any further suspicion on the part of a certain fraction of the Bolshevik Party possessing " cosmopolitan " features in their ideology, since among the inhabitants of Kazakhstan and Uzbegistan they had no chance whatever of expressing any of the so-called Western sympathies they were alleged to hold. But the most important aim of this resettlement was to ensure that the Soviet heavy armament industry to be established in these districts should be in reliable hands.

" For the time being it seems certain," writes Jehojachim Alkalai, " that due to their more than average intelligence, as well as to their long-standing experience, the Jewish scientists, technicians and administrative experts are almost indispensable to the Soviet Union."

It is also pointed out in this article that there are three Jewish ministers in the Government of Uzbegistan and two Jewish deputy-ministers in the Government of Khazakhstan. *" In the ministries of*

these States a long list of important key positions are filled by Jews."
The Jews are very strongly represented in the State planning office
known as " Gosplan " which *controls the entire economy of the State.*
Among the party executives, this same paper informs us, are many
Jews and they abound especially in " Agitrop " (the Ministry of
Propaganda). In commercial, trade and industrial organisations Jews
are also employed as directors and leading scientists. Finally, this
well-informed *Aufbau* article concludes by stating that the economic
and social position of the Jews is much better in the Central Asian
Soviet Republics than in any other part of the Soviet Union.

What in fact happened was that Soviet Russia successfully transferred the basis of her power. The best and most indispensable
elements of Jewry were transferred to the new and vitally important
industrial regions. The armament industry and the uranium production
of the Soviet Union is in Jewish hands and under Jewish administration. *Thus a second and a third* Iron Curtain was built hiding the
world conquerors behind the Ural Mountains. As a result of this,
European Russia, which is thoroughly infected with " anti-Semitism ",
is almost devoid of the Jewish scientists, works managers and State
planning designers who constitute the indispensable basis of Soviet
power. They are far away in the new vital production centres of the
Soviet Union which are hardly accessible even to long-range
American inter-continental ballistic missiles.

It is also worth noting that according to the report in *Aufbau* in
1951, Lazar Khaganovich was still controlling this new strategic
Soviet power centre. He was elected into the Soviet Politbureau by
the Tashkent district of the Republic of Uzbegistan. It is also certain,
according to *Aufbau,* that these high Jewish officials, leaders of the
Soviet's political, economic and cultural life, were sent to these regions
with a definite mission.

A gigantic ring of key positions has been erected behind the second
and third Iron Curtains, which governs the entire Soviet Union. On
this is based the whole future of the Soviet system. And yet by the
detention, trial and acquittal of a few Jewish doctors it could conveniently be advertised to the outside world that " we are ' anti-
Semites ' . . ." or " anti-Zionists ". Although Lazar Khaganovich was
removed from the visible post he previously held in European Russia
where he was well known, he was nevertheless neither hanged nor

259

imprisoned. The political observer of to-day might rightly wonder what Khaganovich was doing in the new power centre of the Soviet, where the hydrogen bomb, the inter-continental ballistic missiles and the sputniks of the Soviet are being produced.

In 1956 a delegation of the French Socialist Party, led by its secretary-general, Pierre Comin, visited the Soviet Union. Upon his return home, Pierre Lochak, the Russian-French interpreter, published the shorthand account of the whole material of the conversations which took place during this visit between Kruschev and Khaganovich on one side and the French delegation on the other side. During the course of these rather frank exchanges, Lazar Khaganovich replied to French remarks about Western humanitarianism:

"There is no place left for humanitarianism until we have secured the final victory of the Soviet Revolution. The sole duty of the proletarian dictatorship is to secure and complete the total victory of the Revolution. . . ."

According to Khaganovich, the victory of the Revolution cannot be anything else but absolute world domination. And Kruschev, also, promptly added that the Soviet Government is based to-day on Jewish leadership and that it was due to certain considerations only that Jewry was masked by a Gentile front.

"*If Jews to-day occupied everywhere the first positions in our Republic,*" said Stalin's successor, "*they would most probably not be very popular with the native Russian population.* If, for instance, we appointed a Jew to a high administrative position in the Ukraine and he then proceeded to surround himself with Jewish personnel, this would certainly arouse the jealousy and animosity of the local population towards the Jews. *But we are not ' anti-Semites '. If you look at Mr. Khaganovich you can see he is a Jew. And Mr. Mitin here is also a Jew. And dear Lydia Faktor, our interpreter, is Jewish as well. I, myself, have a half-Jewish grandchild. We all fight against ' anti-Semitism '.*" (*Sueddeutsche Zeitung,* July 5th, 1957.)

It is a corollary of the Soviet system that in order to mislead the Western world, and especially the anti-Israel Arab nations, it needs to create occasionally a false appearance of "anti-Semitism". But the real power of the Soviet Union — the heavy industry and war production based on Jewish leadership still exists to-day behind the second and third Iron Curtains. Neither has the Soviet Union forgotten the pronouncement of the venerable rabbis in 1951 which we have already quoted, namely, that " a third world war would result in the total extermination of the Jewish population of the world ". And if world Jewry perished, Bolshevism would perish with it. Kruschev, Molotov, and the entire new Soviet intelligentsia could, of course, end by becoming farm labourers. But this is exactly the thing which even the Gentile section of the Bolshevik movement would not like to see happen.

The Western Press likes to spread various tales about the " anti-Semitism " of Kruschev and of the Soviet in general. The *Rheinischer Merkur*, the West German Christian Democrat paper, reputedly close to Chancellor Adenauer, published recently a lengthy article written by Stephen Pollak, a Jewish publicist in London. This well-informed and honest Jewish journalist complains in his article that the Soviet system strangles Jewish culture. In the Soviet Union the Yiddish theatres are closed and several Jewish actors have been executed. He lists as a grave complaint the fact that there is no chief rabbi in the Soviet Union and that facilities in the rabbinical training colleges are insufficient. He bitterly complains that the development of cultural life among three and a half million Soviet Jews is made impossible *But this holds good for all other nations of the U.S.S.R.* Bolshevism succeeded in smothering Russian culture itself.

" During the Jewish World Congress in London," writes Pollak, " Dr. Levenberg, representative of the Jewish Agency in Britain, said most interesting things about the social and economic position of Jews living to-day in the Soviet Union. Whilst in 1933 there were 270,000 Jews in agriculture, *to-day the entire Jewish population of the Soviet Union works in the cities as civil servants, doctors, scientists, etc. They even fancy themselves as the holders of a few key positions from which the Russians have not yet been able to evict them. According to official statistics there are still 25,000 Jewish scientists working in the Soviet Union."* (*Rheinischer Merkur* No. 50, of December 13th, 1957.)

A most important fact is admitted here, though it is wrapped up in the guise of a complaint. The facts and figures recorded by Louis Levine fully agree ·with Dr. Levenberg's statistics: Soviet Russia is governed by about three million Jews in key and administrative positions, 25,000 *of them working in the top scientific appointments of the Soviet responsible for the atomic bombs and space rockets.*

This question of so-called "anti-Semitism" in the Soviet can be answered without bias by quoting Kruschev himself. As we know, Eleanor Roosevelt paid a visit to Kruschev in 1957, and the first thing she did was to question Kruschev on the position of the Soviet Jews. And this is what Kruschev said to her:

"*The Communist cannot be 'anti-Semitic' for Communism is against every form of racial discrimination.* And if any member of the Communist Party was known to be an 'anti-Semite', none of us would shake his hand. *How could a Communist become an 'anti-Semite' when Karl Marx was himself a Jew?* My own son who was killed in the war, married a Jewish woman. Soviet Jews have every chance of securing both the best education and the highest positions." (*Bridge Builders,* Vol. X, No. 23.)

In this respect Poland's position is most enlightening. The policy of the Gentile front is demonstrated here most conspicuously. Jewry has carefully avoided appointing a Jew Prime Minister of Poland. But Poland's archbishop, during his visit to America in 1946, emphatically stated that the majority of the Polish Communist Party consisted of Jews who ruthlessly terrorised Poland. The Polish Premier was never a Jew. The Gentile front to-day consists of the Pole, Gomoulka, but behind him are the real holders of power: Roman Zabrovszky (Jew), secretary-general of the Communist Party; Hilary Minc (Jew), Minister of Economy; and Jacob Berman (Jew), Under-Secretary of the Ministry of Economy. Jews occupy the key positions in the Polish Government from which they dictate to the unfortunate Polish people.

The fate of Hungary, especially after the attempted rising to secure independence in 1956, is another striking example of the Gentile front. In 1951 the President of Hungary was Sándor Rónai, a half-gipsy by birth, though his wife was a Jewess. The President of the Hungarian Politbureau is also a non-Jew called Istvan Dobi—a hard-drinking railway worker, always at the beck and call of Moscow in return for a few drinks.

Until the spring of 1956 Mátyas Rákosi-Roth was the real Jewish dictator *behind the scenes.* He was secretary of the Communist

Party. Another important Muscovite Jew called Ernoe Geroe-Singer took over this rôle from Rákosi later.

Allowing for a few changes and replacements here and there the Jews were the masters of Hungary.

Josph Révai, alias Moses Kahana, Minister of Education, the notorious instigator of the Mindszenty trials, is a Jew.

Mihály Farkas, Minister of Defence (real name Israel Wolff), another Muscovite Jew, was formerly a printer in Kassa.

Ernoe Geroe, alias Singer, played an important rôle in the Spanish Civil War on the Communist side. Later in the Second World War he helped to organise the treacherous organisation known as Freies Deutschland—Free Germany—under General Paulus, and was for a long time afterwards Stalin's personal representative in the Far East. Ernoe Geroe Singer's radio speech on October 23rd, 1956, did much to provoke the Hungarian rising, because in the course of it he asked the Soviet to maintain their occupation of Hungary. The enraged young Hungarian workers and university students replied to this by a spontaneous revolt.

Zoltán Vass, alias Weinberger, Minister of Economy and director of the Komlo mining trust, was also a Jew. His wife, who was one of the doctors in the Jewish hospital and who handed over the wounded and sick patients under her care to the Soviet executioners, was a Jewess.

Gábor Péter, alias Benjamin Auspitz, the notorious chief of the Hungarian M.V.D. (secret police) was, naturally, a Jew also. From being a small town tailor's assistant he became head of the Hungarian Communist secret police and is responsible for the murder and torture of 30,000 persons. Later he fell into disgrace and, according to what meagre news there is concerning his fate, was sentenced to nine and a half years' imprisonment.

The Minister of Foreign Affairs, Erik Molnar, was, of course, a Jew too. He had written a long " scientific " treatise concluding that the Hungarians as an " Asiatic " people, should be resettled on the steppe of Golodnia.

Ivan Boldizsar, alias Bettelheim, propaganda chief of the Hungarian Communist régime, was also a Jew.

Jews grabbed the key positions of the entire network of the Communist secret police in Hungary. They became the commissars, the leaders of local government and the directors of the people's factories.

The shifts and changes that took place in Hungary between the Gentile front and those forming its background are not difficult to follow. In 1956 Rákosi was replaced. His successor in the post of secretary to the Hungarian Communist Party, i.e. in the dictatorship, was another Jew, Ernoe Geroe-Singer, who represented the very same Muscovite and pro-Zionist line as did his predecessor. When the Hungarian uprising began on October 23rd, 1956, the young Hungarians who during the previous twelve years had been educated in Communist ideology and consequently had no knowledge whatever of the Jewish aspirations for world power, wanted Imre Nagy to become Prime Minister.

Very few people know that Imre Nagy was a half-Jewish smallholder from Western Hungary and that his real name was Grosz. His mother was Hungarian but his father was Jewish. His wife is a Jewess. He lived for a long time in Moscow and was a student under the Stalinist régime. His rôle as a leader in the Hungarian rebellion appears to have been *ineffective and his behaviour suspicious.*

However great the crime he may have committed against the Soviet Union *he was not placed on trial until very recently.*

Both the Hungarian fight for freedom, as well as its suppression, proved that *although many things may change in Communism, its Jewish and Zionist world-dominating features are permanent and unchangeable.* After the Soviet attacks on November 4th, 1956, Hungarian key positions were once again occupied by the Jews who act now as ruthless dictators over the unfortunate suppressed Hungarian people. They dictate in the factories, in the party centres and from all leading positions of the reorganised secret police.

The position of Roumania is also interesting and worth a closer study. This courageous young nation of Central Europe has for centuries been familiar with the aspirations of Jewish world power and might have been one of Hungary's best allies. Just before the Second World War a new movement won support from all sections of the Roumanian people; it was known as *the Iron Guard.* The old concepts of Socialism were adopted by this fanatically Chauvinistic group which, unfortunately, often clashed with both the Hungarians and other neighbours. But behind Carol, the Roumanian king, his mistress, Mrs. Lupescu, alias Maggie Wolf the Jewish red-head, carried on her intrigues and persuaded the king to uproot the movement, which he actually did. It is appalling to think that even Hitler's Germany, in the pursuit of its own "great political concept", misunderstood and helped to liquidate this Roumanian movement, whose leaders sat with Jews in the concentration camps until 1944. It took the treason of King Michael to awaken the German leadership to the importance of the Iron Guard, which was thereupon organised into an anti-Bolshevik legion. Their training was completed and their equipment issued during the last few months of the war, and on May 8th, 1945, the legion of the Roumanian Iron Guard constituted the last armed resistance to the Bolshevik units.

After the war a Gentile front was organised with great efficiency in Roumania. George Groza became the Prime Minister but behind him stood the Jewess Anna Pauker-Rabinovich, a most faithful disciple of Stalin. Kisinevszky, first secretary of the Roumanian Communist Party, was, of course, a Jew. Theohary Georgescu-Lebovich, Minister of Internal Affairs; Maurice Roller, head of public education; Maurice Bercovici, head of foreign trade; Max Salamon, head of propaganda; and Mondy Kerkovici, who with Rebecca Nathason were leaders of Soviet-Roumanian cultural affairs, were all Jews.

With Georghiu Dej's assumption of power and with the removal of Anna Pauker-Rabinovich, the position may seem changed, but that is only a superficial view. The unfortunate Roumanian people are still subjected to the same terror previously exercised by Anna Pauker-Rabinovich.

Czechoslovakia presents yet another example of the Gentile front. Here the Prime Minister, comrade Gottwald, was a half-Jew. But behind him Slansky-Salzman was first secretary of the Czech Communist Party, leader of biological class warfare and a characteristic Jew. Slansky-Salzman, like the non-Jewish Hungarian László Rajk, was executed, although a Communist, because he was not willing to accept the Muscovite type of Jewish world domination. He wanted to secure power for the Western Jew only. At the present time a Jew called Dr. Kosta is head of the foreign Press service of this hybrid State. Dr. Eugen Loebl, assistant secretary of foreign trade, is a Jew. Ludwig Frejka, economic adviser to President Gottwald, is also a Jew. Vasely, head of the Czechoslovak secret police, the Czech replica of Gábor Péter (Benjamin Auspitz); Bruno Kohler, commandant of the militia, together with Lomsky, Bubona, Fuchs and Taussigov, important district secretaries; Bistricky and Goldstecker, Czech ambassadors; Truda Jakaninova Cakutrova, head of the Czechoslovak delegation to U.N.O.; Jiu Hironek, departmental head of the Ministry of Information, as well as Augenthaler and Gottlieb, the two senior officials of the Ministry of Foreign Affairs, are all Jews.

The half-Communist Hungarian paper, *Világ* (*World*), wrote on March 15th, 1953: "With the help of the Soviet M.V.D. many Jews succeeded in occupying leading positions in the Communist Party."

With the execution of Slansky-Salzman, the Jewish background appeared to have been liquidated. The anti-Jewish Czech workers had to be shown that Bolshevism was not Jewish. Nevertheless the Jewish background is still retained holding, in its grasp the real power.

Yugoslavia is another example of the foregoing. Marshal Tito—real name Joseph Broz—is a non-Jew. But until his recent death, a Jew, Mojse Pijade, wielded actual power here. The name of Mojse Pijade is connected with the murder and starvation of 200,000 members of the German community and also with other macabre cases of genocide in Yugoslavia. Thirty thousand Hungarians fell victim to the systematic extermination of racial and national groups in Yugoslavia.

Wilhelm Grothewohl, Premier of Eastern Germany, is a non-Jew. But Gerhard Eisler, the Jew behind him, is the sole possessor of real power. He acts as with the authority of both Eastern and Western Jewry. He is the faithful follower and protégé of Eleanor Roosevelt. Paval E. Yudin, Soviet commissar, wielder of Soviet power in Germany, is, naturally, a Jew. The terrorist organisation is in the hands of the bloodthirsty Jewess, Hilda Benjamin.

The above list, of course, is far from being complete. But it gives some information about the organisation of the Gentile front, i.e. about the real face of the masked Jewish power. We also know that the number of Jews in key positions and leading posts is actually much higher in the enslaved countries behind the Iron Curtain than our lists show. This is due to the fact that Bolshevik Jews live everywhere under different cover-names, and most of them have even changed their first name in order not to be recognised by their previous Old Testament names. Of all the countries behind the Iron

Curtain, Poland appears to be the most dominated by Jewish power. Cardinal Hlond's statement made in America on July 6th, 1946, draws attention to this. He said:

" Jewish leadership in the Government created a form of rule disliked by the majority of the people. The important question is not how many Jews sit in the Government but, rather, what *kind of positions do they occupy?"*

Usually the first secretary of the Communist Party is the real dictator in the countries behind the Iron Curtain. He has at his command the complete machinery of the political police, the Communist Party and the Soviet administration. For this reason it is a most dangerous sign that in 1951, Bulgaria excepted, the position of first secretary of the Communist Parties of all the countries behind the Iron Curtain *was held by Jews.* This is true even in Tito's Yugoslavia. Jews are also the chiefs of the political (secret) police, or alternatively, they hold the post of Minister of Internal Affairs. Moreover, it would seem that the ministerial posts of education, propaganda and defence are also gradually being taken over by Jews. It is also revealing that at the same time Jews are desirous of obtaining the post of Minister of Defence in the Western world. At this moment Jules Moch is Minister of Defence in France, Emmanuel Shinwell in Great Britain, whilst in the U.S.A. Anna Rosenberg is Assistant Secretary of War. Mr. Eisenhower has lately appointed a Jew as Assistant Secretary of War to Mr. McElroy.

Mr. Bernard Baruch, America's " Elder Statesman ", who controlled the 351 most important industries of the U.S. during the Second World War, said proudly:

" It is undoubtedly true that I probably had more power than any other man in the war! "

I had more power than anybody else! — says Baruch, and this power itself is part of the Jewish world power.

It is a clearly discernible political fact in the Western world that the more Jews there are sitting in the key positions of a democratic State, the quicker will this State drift towards Bolshevism. For instance, the whole political position and outlook of France to-day can be explained by the immeasurable Judaisation of French political life. As we write these lines the French Premier is Pierre Isaac Isidore Mendés-France, son of David Mendele Cerf-Hirsch and Sarah

Farburger Cohen. Akin to the power-pattern of the States behind the Iron Curtain, Robert Hirsch, as chief of the Sûreté, wields supreme police power in France. Jacques Duclos, the second most important Communist of France, is a Jew too. Jules Moch, one of the most influential personalities of the French Social-Democratic Party, who was Minister of Defence for a long time in post-war French Governments — and was thus one of those sabotaging the integration of German divisions in the European Army—comes also from the ranks of the world conquerors to take over the glorious traditions of a napoleonic inheritance.

Paris remains the centre of Diaspora, the *Monde Juif* tells us with pride. And France meanwhile hurtles dizzily down the slope of corruption following the example of the perished Roman and Spanish Empires.

Since the American occupation, German heavy industry has been infiltrated by so-called " American " capital, the pressure of which dominates Western Germany to-day. In West Berlin, the late Ernst Reuter, only, was acceptable as burgomaster—he who had been before first secretary of the German Communist Party and who was, of course, a Jew. Meanwhile, a Jew called Lipschitz is Minister of Internal Affairs in West Berlin.

We have already pointed out that in 1951 all the first secretaries of the Communist Parties in countries east of the Iron Curtain were Jews. With the removal of Slansky-Salzman in Prague; Gábor Péter, alias Benjamin Auspitz, terror chief, in Hungary; Anna Pauker-Rabinovich in Roumania, and Beria in the Soviet Union, certain shifts seemed to have taken place in the key positions. Western radio propaganda, also firmly in the grip of the world conquerors, likes to ascribe this to " anti-Semitism " in the Soviet Union and in the enslaved countries. But " anti-Semitism " is simply non-existent. With the detailed data given relating to the Soviet Union and to the countries forced behind the Iron Curtain, *we proved that there also power is firmly in the hands of the Jews.* The fact that political figures are shifted in these countries, and that at times certain unpleasant tasks are assigned to non-Jewish Communists, means absolutely nothing. Neither does the occasional liquidation of one or two Jews bear any significance, since the *Protocols* say that one or two of their own ilk will be sacrificed. This is the explanation of the liquidation of Beria, Slansky,

Peter-Auspitz and Pauker, in view of the fact that the population of these countries suffering under their tyranny slowly became aware of the predominantly Jewish character of Bolshevik power, and in their rage turned against the bosses of the terror. Thus Beria and a few others had to be sacrificed to *create the illusion* that the State was against the Jews. All those who carried through these measures were themselves Jews. Nobody knew the real reasons and motives for their actions better than they did and Western Jewry understood them perfectly too. When here and there in the Western world signs of anti-Bolshevik tendencies become noticeable it is expedient to distract public attention from the Jewish character of Bolshevik power.

"We are one people," wrote Theodor Herzl.

Until the truth of this is recognised by the non-Jewish world, all talk about differences between the Western and Eastern world is sheer lies and stupidity. There are no differences whatever! Jews are sitting in the key positions of the Eastern Hemisphere as well as the Western Hemisphere, and they will never attack or harm one another for they know that they would only destroy themselves. They would thus destroy Jewish world power. *These considerations gave rise to the idea of co-existence, the sabotaging of European re-armament and the patriotic popular movements, the sale of the atomic bomb and all those discoveries and inventions offering to the Eastern and Western Hemispheres the possibility of living side by side.*

A long as this is the position, all talk on the radio of Western nations about " anti-Bolshevism " is a lie. And as long as it cannot be frankly stated in the West that Bolshevism is nothing else than the most perfected form of the Jewish world power, it is useless to talk about the free Western world and Western democracy. And similarly, until it can be pointed out freely in the East that the Western world is not governed by " imperialist capitalism " but by the silent terror of political influence and by ruthless exploitation on the part of the Jewish money power and Press, it is dishonest to talk about the prevailing system of the suppressed States behind the Iron Curtain as " Socialism ".

The Jews are trading to-day with our wheat, diamonds, clothing, religion and prayers. They control the Communist Parties in China and India, as well as the Republican Parties of the free Western world, as was seen when they planned the destruction of Senator McCarthy. They command the U.N. armies against the North Koreans, and they stand behind the North Koreans facing the forces of the U.N. In Viet-Nam they oppose the Communists, and while many thousands of non-Jewish " legionnaires " died heroically at Dien-Bien-Phu, they kept the Bolsheviks advised of French moves from the French National Defence Council itself. While championing the re-unification and integration of Europe they render it simultaneously impossible. They speak of the possibility of securing co-existence, although they know very well that co-existence is, in fact, perfectly possible. The Western and Eastern Jew have always understood each other. In 1917, during the war of intervention, the Western Jew helped the Eastern Jew by the material building up of the Soviet, and during the Second World War he helped by the eleven billion dollar loan, by the Lend and Lease Act and by the support given at Yalta, Teheran and Nuremberg. It comes to this: the Western and Eastern Jew, by selling each other the secret of the atomic bomb, displayed the black flag of a possible atomic death above the heads of the non-Jewish nations, in order to establish their rule over the world.

The Western world does not lack its daydreams. " Moderate " Bolsheviks, pink intellectuals and so-called anti-Bolsheviks have to learn that mankind cannot be classified correctly into groups of Bolsheviks, " moderate " Bolsheviks, and " anti-Bolsheviks ". The correct classification is into the two groups of those who see and recognise the danger of Jewish nationalism, and of the others who deny it. *Anyone who is " pro-Jewish " or denies that the main features of Bolshevism are Jewish cannot be at the same time a true anti-Bolshevik!*

" We are one people! We are the same people!" said Theodor Herzl.

The Gentile front is for the " man in the street ", for " our creature and slave "; for the masses. It is an illusion, like the sovereignty of the White House, or democracy or equal rights. But in the second line, behind the scenes in key positions, are Bernard Baruch, Frankfurter, David Lilienthal, Strauss, Oppenheimer and the iron fist of Jehovah wielding the power which will smash kingdoms and democracies to pieces. For the masses of the Eastern Hemiphere, the non-Jewish Kruschev is god; but the second line is held by the Khaganovich dynasty, by Yudin, and the tommy-guns of the M.V.D. and the steel-helmeted Maccabees.

"We are one people!" But a people who will desert their host-nation whenever their interests dictate it. On one occasion they abandoned even the Soviet Union itself. This happened when the European armies stood athwart the circular railway system on the outskirts of Moscow. The Jews, having expropriated for their sole use the last motor cars and vehicles and loaded them with all the treasures of the Soviet people, ran away, leaving behind the angry Russians.

But now, as a result of their great victory in the war, they can say: "We have conquered the world. We control mankind from key positions behind the scenes."

EIGHTEEN

SECRET POWERS

THE world conquerors would not be able to maintain their power for a moment without their auxiliary troops which they command from key positions. It is an appalling feature of our present-day world that the democracies and a certain section of the Christian Churches are controlled just as much by these auxiliary troops as are Bolshevik dictatorships and masonic lodges. Parliaments and rulers, as well as the media of public entertainment such as the stage, radio and television, which are engaged in the systematic drugging of public opinion, are organised to act the part of auxiliary troops just as much as is the party congress of the Bolshevik dictatorships. But behind the governments, commissars and puppets of the opposition stands the Satanic Director — the Golden Calf — the "money power", washing gold from the blood and sweat of the 2,500 million inhabitants of the earth.

How did this come about? Is the world really governed by a dark and evil power?

On the Russian front during the Second World War an officer of the Spanish Blue Division found a file containing records of unique interest near the body of a Bolshevik police officer named Guzmin. These records, drawn up in 1939 by Guzmin, contained a statement by Rakovszky, then Soviet Ambassador in Paris, who was incriminated in the great conspiracy against General Tuhachevsky. In the records, the authenticity of which seems to be beyond question, the veil obscuring Bolshevism is lifted and one of the greatest secrets of the world is exposed. They were dictated by an authentic witness, one of the closest collaborators of Lenin. Needless to say, Rakovszky was a Jew.

Rakovszky frankly admits in the records that at the end of the First World War the position of Bolshevism became extremely critical due to the spread and progress of the Russian counter-revolution. At the end of 1917 the Bolsheviks had been driven back as far as the territory of the principality of Moscow. But *at this moment a higher power appeared, which, according to Rakovszky, governs the world.* This higher power acted from the West and stopped the flow of military and economic supplies for the counter-revolution which up to then had been steady and reliable.

In a series of confidential confessions Rakovszky also states in the records that the great financial crash on Wall Street in 1929 was the work of a mysterious group consisting of a few persons directed by a higher power. This same world power put to work Roosevelt's famous New Deal, but on the other hand it also supported Hitler's movement in its initial financial difficulties *through the help of Schacht, who was a freemason.*

"This world power is greater and more omnipotent than the Komintern itself," said Rakovszky.

To Guzmin's repeated question as to who were the holders of this world power, Rakovszky gave various evasive answers, such as: "Them"; "Those people", etc. Apparently he did not want to pronounce the word Jew!

He said he did not know exactly who these people were. But he knew that they were omnipotent and within call anywhere. They had no visible form and appeard mostly in the guise of international financial interests. They are sometimes referred to as the "money power". But one thing was certain: this world power would be sure to intervene should any overwhelming force arise to destroy Communism. Trotsky, more closely acquainted with these circles, on one occasion said to Rakovszky: "The man who has succeeded in breaking the blockade closing round the Soviet is Walter Rathenau, the millionnaire member of the Weimar government."

These records also hint that this unknown world power is embodied in some kind of freemasonic organisation. But it is even more interesting to learn from Rakovszky that Karl Marx was not the real founder of Communist world revolution. Its true father was Adam Weishaupt, founder of the freemasonic order of the Illuminati. This Weishaupt, who came from Germany, was a pupil of Moses Mendelssohn, the Jewish philosopher.

Kuhn, Loeb and Co., according to 1935 statistics, controlled a fortune of four billion dollars, and to-day no doubt control much more.

The world policy of this secret power is most interesting. Jewry's hatred of the Czarist Russia was so great that this same bank, Kuhn, Loeb and Co., made a loan of 130 million dollars to the Japanese in order to finance the Russo-Japanese War. In later years, when it appeared that the Bolsheviks would be defeated, at the end of the First World War, it saved Bolshevism too. It knew very well that the victory of the counter-revolution leading to the revenge of the tortured and cheated Russian people would end in the destruction of Russian Jewry.

But the most horrible chapter of this satanic policy is when, according not only to Rakovszky but to other reliable German sources, this same world power gives still larger sums to Hitler and National Socialism, in order to help Hitler and his movement over initial difficulties. They knew that if Hitler suceeded in taking over power Germany could be forced into a new war. *The real aim was not only the destruction of German National Socialism, but something even greater: the realisation of the final great and glorious aspiration, which is the biological destruction and enslavement of all non-Jewish nations.*

Certain parts of Rakovszky's statements attain impressive heights. He must have been familiar with the nature of this secret world power to have prophesied from a prison cell as early as 1938: " Hitler will shake hands with Stalin in order to be able to liquidate Poland, and Stalin will accept Hitler's offer. Though both of them will thus have attacked a Catholic country important to the West, nevertheless the West will declare one of them only to be the aggressor, and that will be Hitler's Germany."

Grand Orient records relating to the Great Council's meeting on May 29th, 1939, fell into the hands of the German counter-espionage service before the outbreak of the last war. From these it becomes evident that Groussier, the Grand Master, at this time had important consultations with Roosevelt's ambassador at Paris, Mr. Bullit, who was informed of the viewpoint of the Grand Orient, according to which *all possible steps were to be taken to prevent any understanding on the Polish question being reached either between Hitler and the Poles, or between Hitler and the European powers.* Chamberlain was told as early as March, 1939, that if he continued his conciliatory

274

policy, the U.S.A. would withdraw all moral and financial support from Great Britain.

The records of the Jewish Congress, which was held in Paris well before the Second World War, were published in the *Catholic Gazette* of February, 1936. At this congress, we are told, the secret world power demonstrated the full magnitude of its arrogance. The speakers referred proudly to the fact that the most important leaders of all nations were freemasons and were thus mobilised for the promotion of Israel's aspirations.

" We are masters of war and of peace! " sounds the confident challenge of the world conquerors. " France fell into our hands; Great Britain depends upon our money and is our slave. Many other States and nations, including the U.S.A., bow before our power and organisation."

That this world power not only exists but is in fact master of the world, is strongly emphasised, firstly by Rakovszky's statements, secondly by ex-King Alphonso XIII, thirdly in secret reports found by the Germans after the occupation of Paris, fourthly by Forrestal's diary, and lastly by the confidential papers of a Polish diplomat.

Count Jean Szembek, one of the leading officials of the Polish Foreign Office, published his diary in France under the title *Journal 1933-1939*. Here he records his talk with the King of Spain, Alphonso XIII, on February 19th, 1939. " The Spanish king has formed a very pessimistic opinion of the world situation," says the diary. " World Jewry and freemasonry play a very important rôle in the attempt to unleash war.

On July 6th, 1939, Jerzy Potoczky, Polish ambassador to the U.S.A., returned to Warsaw from Washington to report to his government. In the course of his account he says: " There are all sorts of people in the West driving us to war: the Jews, the big capitalists and the armament firms. They feel they are entering an era of prosperity. They regard and handle us like negroes, whose only duty is to work and sweat in the interest of multiplying their capital."

The Jews and freemasons found allies in unexpected circles. On March 19th, 1939, Count Szembek visited Count Ledochowszky, the General of the Jesuit Order, and recorded the following: " I happened by chance to be present during Count Ledochowszky's consultation with Cardinal Marmaggi about the arrival of a deputation from the

Spanish Falange. During their talk both of them sharply condemned Fascism and Hitlerism and arrived at the conclusion that the Falange was a similar movement. Ledochowszky referred to all of these systems as the 'opera del diavolo', i.e. 'works of the devil'. . . ." On April 21st, 1939, Monsignore Montini, the papal legate to Poland at that time, told Count Szembek that *according to the official viewpoint of the Vatican, should Poland decide on war, it would be a just and rightful war.*

Szembek also records in his memoirs that on August 11th, 1939, the Polish ambassador to the Vatican said to him that "an unbending attitude is to be maintained towards Germany and that this policy is openly encouraged by the Vatican"!

And so we find even the Vatican itself ranged among the satellites of the world conquerors, without apparently pausing to consider the inherent danger of Bolshevism.

We have dealt already with the key positions held by the world conquerors. But the political advance was only a rather modest consequence of that economic world power which world Jewry captured as early as the beginning of this century in order to dominate the nations.

The appearance of this mysterious world power was referred to by Marxists, Leninists, and other dreamy-headed Socialists, as "dollar imperialism". Though the flags of the "dollar imperialists" were carried by Americans who died defending them, nevertheless behind these flags of a politically ignorant and inexperienced new and powerful nation stood the world conquerors, who, in fact, are marching to-day towards the subjection of all free and independent peoples.

We will give a few examples to illustrate this. Speyer and Co., the great Jewish banking house, in 1903 gave Mexico her first twelve and a half million dollar loan. They acquired by this transaction all oil concessions in Mexico. Rockefeller, Morgan, Jacob Schiff and the other great Jewish financiers followed suit and thus almost all the natural resources of Mexico fell into Jewish hands. Bernard Mannes Baruch, the National City Bank under Jewish management, and Guggenheim, the Jewish copper magnate, became the real masters of Mexico.

In 1906 the same world conquerors obtained monopolies over

Nicaragua's national income from customs and excise and also over her railways and shipping lines.

The banking houe of Kuhn, Loeb and Co. was one of the founders as well as chief financier of the Panama Canal Co.

The major part of Cuba's industry is controlled by the Guggenheims.

Bolivia was turned into a colony of " dollar imperialism " by Speyer and Guggenheim, who exploited the zinc mines.

Since 1935, thirty-five per cent of the potassium nitrate and ninety per cent of the copper industry of Chile is in the hands of the Guggenheim and Morgan Trusts.

In Peru the copper mines are in the hands of the Seligmans and Goldschmidts.

Lord Melchett, under his original name of Mond, controls the nickel industry of Canada. Out of a total of thirty billion dollars which constitute the national assets of Canada, a total of three billions is in the hands of the Jews.

Foreign trade with China was organised by the Morgans and also by the National City Bank and, of course, by Kuhn, Loeb. Later, the International Banking Corporation, led by Edward Harriman the railway king, and Isaac Guggenheimer, began the economic " exploitation " of China. Schiff, Morgan, Kuhn, Loeb, and Harriman made fortunes out of railway construction in that country.

According to Rakovszky, similar forces rescued Bolshevism, and with the ultimate aim of destroying Germany, supported Hitler's movement in its early days. They were also behind the Stalin pact and total aerial warfare, the expulsion of eighteen million Germans from their homelands leading to the enslavement of Europe, and the suppression of those Asiatic nations struggling for independence. This world power identifies itself with the Nuremberg trials, with the sordid bargaining at Yalta, whilst the death of the democrat Forrestal as well as that of the Communist Zhdanov was due to the fact that these men wished to bring about a showdown between the Bolshevik and capitalist world. It exterminated many of the leaders of the European Christian peoples under the pretext of " war crimes ", and from this has been hatched the latest theory of co-existence to save the Soviet Union. Rakovszky informs us that this " higher " power disclosed its real identity during the trial of the atom spies.

Why did Julius Rosenberg refuse to tell the court the names of those who gave him his orders, though he could have saved his own and his wife's life by doing so?

The answer is simple! This small and unimportant Jew was, together with his accomplices, the agent of this "higher" power. It was not on his own initiative that he passed on atomic secrets to Khaganovich and his friends. Certain persons ordered him to do so; certain persons succeeded in convincing him that it was a sacred, patriotic and religious duty for him—a small but loyal Jew—to pass on to the Kremlin the secret of the atomic bomb, and by so doing to prevent a third world war which would lead to the total extermination of Jewry.

What is certain, however, is that these comparatively unimportant Jews, Rosenberg and his wife Ethel, died like martyrs, taking with them to the grave one of the greatest secrets of the twentieth century. Those Jews who followed their coffins to the cemetery in a funeral procession enlivened by dramatic and fanatical incidents, knew very well that this couple had sacrificed their own lives for the survival of world Jewry. And thus the names of the real culprits were never disclosed.

In its issue of June 15th, 1955, *La Voix de la Paix,* a French paper, published an interesting article from the pen of a leftist writer, throwing, though surely quite unintentionally, a very sharp light on the basic nature of " democracies " governed from key positions.

"The French Parliament itself," he writes, "is a type of closed society in which the representatives of the great banking groups meet. These consist of: (1) L'Union des Banques Américaines which is represented in the French political field by René Pleven, who began his career as Jean Monnet's secretary; (2) L'Union Européenne, to which the banking houses of the Rothschilds belong. This group is represented politically by René Mayer, a former director of the Rothschild concerns."

In this short article a startling picture is presented, showing that the France of St. Louis is to-day under the dictatorship of various Jewish financial groups aided by rotten democratic parliamentarians, and that at the same time she serves as one of the main bases of the international conspiracy which is strangling the world.

Among the many exposures of this secret world power to appear after the Second World War, perhaps Francis Quisney's article is the most remarkable. It was published in the periodical *Der Weg,* edited in Argentina, and dealt with the world policy of the Rocke-fellers. To put it shortly, the present head of the " Christian " banking house of Rockefellers, Nelson Aldrich Rockefeller, has been working for a long time in close touch with the Jewish banking house of Kuhn, Loeb & Co. of New York. During the Second World War Roosevelt appointed Nelson Aldrich Rockefeller to the post of Co-ordinator of Hemisphere Defence, the purpose of which was " to keep in hand " the South American States and to control the South American markets.

It would fill a volume to attempt to describe in detail the fatal rôle played by the head of the Rockefeller banking house in the Bolshevisation of the world while under the influence of Kuhn, Loeb and Co., who financed the Bolshevik Revolution and the atomic bomb. In the *Wall Street Journal* of May 13th, 1948, Ray Cromley, an American journalist, confirmed that not only at Yalta but well before that conference, a secret agreement had been concluded between Nelson A. Rockefelle on the one hand and Gromyko, the Jewish representative of the Kremlin, on the other, to divide the globe into two hemispheres. The demarcation line bisecting the globe runs by the Eastern frontiers of Finland, and continuing along the shores of Sweden, cuts through divided Germany to run along the Eastern frontiers of Austria, from where it follows the Northern limits of Turkey and ends at the Persian Gulf. This secret agreement between the Eastern and Western conspirators took into consideration the fact that the rich oilfields of Saudi Arabia must remain under the control of the Rockefellers and of the Jewish oil magnates behind them. Another alarming part of this exposure is the statement, duly supported by evidence, that the oil delivered by the Saudi Arabian plants of Rockefeller and of Kuhn, Loeb and Co. for the Communist war machine, made it possible for the Korean Reds to carry out their attack on South Korea.

Upon several occasions Bolshevism was saved from destruction by a secret Western conspiracy. The same secret power originally saved it through exerting pressure through the British trade unions and American bankers to put a stop to the anti-Bolshevik war of intervention; later on it helped Stalin in the industrialisation of the

Soviet Union. It saved the Soviet Union again when at the time of the Ribbentrop-Stalin pact Hitler only was singled out as the enemy. It saved the Soviet once more when La Guardia handed over the eleven and a half billion dollar cheque to Litvinov, and yet another time when the second front was prematurely established by the invasion of Europe without waiting for the armies of the German and Russian dictatorships " to bleed one another to death ".

This was done, although Truman, whom we can regard as the only " anti-Semite " President of the U.S. since Jefferson, had said at the time of the outbreak of the Soviet-German War in 1941:

" Let them kill one another. We will later have to support the weaker party."

Truman was still only a Vice-President and Roosevelt nearing the end of his days when the suggestion settling the Soviet question for good was being seriously considered by the Western world. Truman even conceived the possibility of destroying Bolshevism and Hitler together in one opportune swoop. *This was the very last chance for the democracies and for the free world to secure real victory.*

Consultations were begun with the military leaders of the defeated German Army. It was proposed that after a formal capitulation the Germans would join forces with the Western allies and fall on the exhausted Soviet armies. All those who lived in Europe during those feverish times sensed that the world was on the threshold of a new clash which would decide the fate of mankind. It appeared that although German nazism might be destroyed, nevertheless, the victorious Wehrmacht would march again in alliance with the even more victorious British and American forces.

In March, 1945, the operators of the German and Hungarian radio stations, and the General Staffs, knew that the Soviet Union was at the point of collapse. In Hungary and in the East German territories the coded messages sent to Moscow by the various Soviet commands were intercepted and decoded. They all consisted of desperate calls for the " victorious " Soviet generals for help — for weapons, ammunition and reinforcements.

But at this time, when the democracies had the opportunity of wiping out Bolshevism with the help of German National Socialism, the mysterious power mentioned in Rakovszky's records once more intervened through the person of a typical puppet — General Dwight Eisenhower, who later became President of the United States.

The news of the negotiations between the German Wehrmacht and the British were no idle tales. Rokossovsky, the " red " Field-Marshal and recent Commander-in-Chief of the Polish Communist armies, brought to light some remarkable details about this matter. He said that Marshal Zhukov possessed proofs of the fact that in April, 1945, the British intended to conclude an agreement with the German Wehrmacht to swoop down on the Soviet armies which had advanced far into Western Europe. Meanwhile the Soviet High Command intercepted and decoded the telecommunications between British and German headquarters. The sole condition was that the German Army should offer its capitulation by April 22nd, 1945. A combined attack would immediately follow in order to force back the Soviet armies, at least as far as the Oder.

A British Army colonel was believed to have given this plan away to Eisenhower, who in turn promptly told the British that if they helped the Germans against the Bolsheviks, he would cut off all vital war materials from Great Britain who would be obliged to go it alone.

And to-day Marshal Zhukov refers to the moment constituting perhaps the last chance for the freedom of manking by saying: " The intervention of *my good friend* Eisenhower foiled this treacherous plan." (*Das Neue Zeitalter,* of September 28th, 1957.)

And so Roosevelt's tame general, the influential master of American freemasonry, of whom General MacArthur remarked tartly: " Eisenhower was not my staff officer but my clerk " — destroyed the last hope of mankind. The Soviet Union was not only saved but became one of the strongest powers in the world. After this, it was only natural that the favourite of Baruch and Morgenthau and the executor of the Morgenthau Plan, should become President of the United States, while the powers behind the scenes prevented the nominations of Taft and MacArthur for the presidential elections. Once Eisenhower was elected to the presidential post the investigations of the McCarthy Committee were stopped. The world conquerors returned to the White House, and in view of subsequent events even a child can understand the indifferent attitude towards the historical Hungarian rebellion on November 4th, 1956, as well as this omission to give it any effective help.

Thanks to Mr. Eisenhower the Eastern half of Jewish world power was saved again. Through the irresponsibility of this careerist puppet-soldier the secrets of the rockets fell into Soviet hands also. On learning of the approach of the Bolsheviks the German scientists evacuated Penemuende in 1945. The V-1 and V-2 types of rocket had been made here, and the V-9, the equivalent of the Soviet sputnik of 1958, was also ready. The German scientists brought with them fifty-four waggons of blue-prints and scientific material which they intended to hand over to the Americans. The American C.I.C., which at this time consisted almost exclusively of world conquerors, ordered the German scientists to leave the fifty-four waggons of scientific material in the hands of the Soviet. The scientists themselves would be allowed access to the territory occupied by the American forces, but bringing only 100 pounds of personal luggage per head. It may be asked whether these things were known to Eisenhower—Morgenthau's C.-in-C. This may be open to question. But the fact remains that the secrets of the rockets, like the secrets of the atomic bomb, fell into the hands of the Soviet.

So to the question, " Is there a supranational conspiracy covering all nations?" we cannot give any other answer but a definite " Yes!" This conspiracy has taken form and intervened in every great crisis affecting mankind. It had its hand in the French Revolution, in the Socialist-Communist movements of the 19th century and in the peace treaties after the First World War. Its features became visible for an instant in 1917 when Czarist Russia was destroyed, and according to the above quoted records of Rakovszky it was owing to this conspiracy that Bolshevism was saved during the time when the Russian counter-revolution was on the point of achieving success. This mysterious power started the Second World War, destroyed Christian Europe and exterminated the European intellectual *élite*. This mysterious conspiratorial power passed on the secret of the atomic bomb to the Soviet, and it betrayed America.

Who, then, are the members of this conspiratorial group? There is no doubt that in the first place are to be found the leaders of world Jewry, the obsessed fanatics of Old Testament world-conquering " nazism ", directed by the bankers of the great international

282

finance groups and interests and also by the chief commissars of Bolshevism, i.e. the masters of the Kremlin. Perhaps all of these cannot be included, but there are many amongst them fighting under the leadership of Khaganovich for the establishment of the Jewish world kingdom.

Almost more dangerous than these conspiratorial leaders are the "auxiliary" troops they succeeded in rallying to their cause nearly half a century ago. According to the latest statistics there are more than six million freemasons in the world, and four million of them are in the United States. The majority of these freemasons are probably not Communists, but none the less they are unintentionally promoting Communist aims. Furthermore, motivated by financial or material interests or convictions, they are consciously serving the Jewish aspirations, the final target of which is Communism, and through Communism the establishment of totalitarian Jewish dictatorship and the complete abolition of human freedom.

To understand the colossal dimensions and consequences of this conspiracy we must realise that mankind lives to-day in what we might term a "threshold age", and has perhaps already passed from the iron age into the atomic age. It does not need much imagination to see that the world is over-populated and that the future of the whole globe — the life and bread of the population — depends upon greatly increasing production through the most efficient use of atomic energy. This energy, which might be a source of evil or, on the other hand, a heavenly blessing, is controlled by a closed group of the prophets of supranational "nazism". The majority of mankind is already helpless against this group which by means of atomic blast experiments served its own profit-making interests only, regardless of the fact that is has by now possibly poisoned our water and our bread and even affected the genes of our unborn children by atomic radiation. What will happen if this group takes over exclusive control of this fatal energy under the title of "atomic energy for peaceful purposes"? It is neither an Utopian concept nor a nightmarish dream but, on the contrary, highly probable that this energy may prove to be the medium for the establishment of world dictatorship. Only that continent which submits unconditionally will receive fuel and electric energy. Those not prepared to serve this Jewish group and thus to ensure retaining their position near the top of the social pyramid enjoying the sunny side of life, but who would dare to resist the general exploitation, will perish miserably. For this Old Testament " nazism " knows neither mercy nor humanity.

If its power is not soon eradicated, and if it continues to enjoy political, economic and intellectual monopolies, then in one or two decades the totalitarian world terror will come, bringing the destruction of human freedom, together with that of the free spirit of mankind and of all human ideals, including the concept of one's own native land and of national pride. There will remain in the end, on one side, the helot-masses amounting to four billion enslaved people without national, racial or religious ties, and on the other, fifteen million chosen people who fulfilled the prophecy in Torah and *became indeed the masters of all nations.*

NINETEEN

THE HUNGARIAN FREEDOM REVOLT

In October, 1956, fighting broke out in Hungary for national freedom. An entire nation rose up—not only against the East, but simultaneously against the West as well. The Hungarian freedom fighters who with undaunted gallantry turned against the secret police of the A.V.H., run by the Jews, with equal heroism refused to accept the corrupt cheque-book régime of Western capitalism.

Though a free Hungary could not be born yet, a new world was envisaged in the hearts of men. The several-thousand-year-old concept of Socialism took shape and materialised once more in the heart and imagination of the masses—a concept which could also be regarded as being part of a new exemplary world containing the most modern social order. The exploited slave of the mines and factories of Soviet state capitalism, the pupil of the Marxist-Leninist institute, the officer of working class origin in the People's Army and the small peasant, all rose unanimously against Bolshevism, the most developed form of Jewish world domination.

The freedom fighters appear to have avoided raising the problem of Jewish dominion. The leaders and terrorists of the secret police (A.V.H.) were exterminated, not as Jews but as common murderers and as anti-social elements guilty of crimes against the people and humanity. Nevertheless, in its essential features, this freedom-fighting constituted the first real revolution against the world conquerors, for the leaders of the Bolshevik terror régime in Hungary, occupying key positions in the terror organisations of the police and of the army, were almost exclusively Jews. *The character of the terror itself was predominantly Jewish* and only Slav-Bolshevistic to a small degree.

" It is from us that the all-engulfing terror proceeds," say the *Protocols*. And everything prophesied and envisaged in the *Protocols*

285

concerning the Jewish secret police was here materialised and highly developed. The State Security Department, which was solely controlled by Jews, had everybody in Hungary registered in its police files on the card index system. These so-called "cadre cards" gave details about each member of the population. In them each person's character, peculiarities, etc., were recorded with meticulous care, including even occasional expressions of his or her views or ideas. It was known that the worst possible entry on anybody's card was to be recorded as an "anti-Semite". We know of the case of a young clerk who was stamped "anti-Semite" just because she was not keen on seeking the friendship of her colleagues, who thus "sensed" that she was perhaps not fond of Jews.

The State Security Authorities (A.V.H.) employed a staff of 40,000 to keep these secret records, compiled by 400,000 spies out of items passed on from factories, works, offices and every walk of life. Everyone summoned to the State Security Department was treated with the utmost cruelty and ruthlessnss.

In 1945-46 the Fraternal Society of Jewish Labour Companies organised the Communist terror police in Budapest. This organisation was headed by Dr. Zoltan Klar, the former notorious Jewish millionaire doctor in Budapest, who is now active in America as an "editor". The various groups of this society regularly visited the prisons and other places of detention where they raped the women prisoners several times daily. They invented such bestial methods for torturing people that their equal cannot be found even among the methods of Chinese torturers. Prisoners with long-term sentences were obliged to stage quarrels ending in bloody fights during their daily walk in the prison yard. It is of interest to note that the present Premier, Janos Kadar, was also tortured when for a short time he dared to defy the Muscovite system. All his fingernails were plucked out and, according to reports that appeared in several Swiss newspapers, he was castrated.

Thousands of similar cases were reported by the freedom fighters and by those released from the Communist prisons who came to the West. When the freedom fighters succeeded in occupying the buildings of the secret police, they found further proofs of a terror almost incredible to the Western world. Huge halls and large rooms were stuffed with the most unimportant telephone conversations recorded on tape and filed. Unimportant letters from abroad had been photo-graphed on microfilms and filed away in a gigantic card index system. On Tisza Kálmán Square in Budapest, a secret prison with 3,000 cells had been built and equipped on the site of a half-finished under-ground railway station, the existence of which was unknown until the freedom fights started. Similar underground prisons were also detected in provincial centres together with subterranean passages to enable Communist " leaders " to escape in an emergency.

And so, if we take into consideration that in Hungary the leaders were Jews, it can truthfully be said that *here the most extreme dream of Jewry's world kingdom materialised.*

This Jewish world kingdom had other means at its disposal besides terror. As well as biological class warfare which physically destroyed the most gifted personalities in Hungarian social life, there was also political class warfare. Anybody whose grandfather had been a smallholder, the owner of twenty to twenty-five acres of land, or whose father had been a minor civil servant before 1945, was declared to be *"class-alien".* Such a man might possess the highest qualifications as a doctor, university professor, lawyer or scientist, nevertheless all these were useless once he was declared " class-alien ", upon which the only employment open to him was in the capacity of an un-skilled labourer. Positions thus rendered vacant were partly filled by ignorant and uneducated Communists and also, in greater part, by those Jews who occupied key positions in the régime. At the same time 50,000 Intellectuals were deported to the provinces, where they existed in most miserable conditions. In 1953 there were about 95,000 political prisoners put to slave labour in the internment camps, while about 25,000 were in the various prisons. Furthermore, *accord-ing to the records of the Communist régime,* 15,000 *" official " executions took place between 1945 and 1956.* This latter figure came to light when the freedom fighters liberated the Central Prison on November 1st, 1956.

These are startling figures. In the whole of Czarist Russia there were only 40,000 exiles, and in Hungary between 1867 and 1939 the total number of persons killed during strikes, riots and disturbances, in consequence of the lawful use of force by the armed services, only amounted to seventeen.

Clearly the object of these atrocities was to reduce the Hungarian people to an intimidated mass of slaves in accordance with the formula of the *Protocols,* and so to establish Jewry's dominion over them. Against the dominion of this Jewish world kingdom the Hungarian nation rose on October 23rd, 1956, because in spite of everything it had not proved possible to break and reduce this people into an anthropomorphous, unthinking mass.

On the blood-soaked pavements of the capital city of Budapest both aspects of the world conquerors were attacked at the same time. The Hungarian proletariat together with university students, arms in hand, desperately fought against the third stage of Jewish conquest —against the terror campaign with its organisation of suppression. But the Hungarian people were equally opposed to the second stage, which consisted in the re-introduction of liberal capitalism.

Their unwritten programme was: Socialism without terror! National freedom without economic subordination!

It is quite evident that this programme could not be tolerated by the East any more than by the West. The Hungarian fight for freedom was of a nationalistic character. It was consequently as much opposed to Moscow as it was to the alternative terror and the slave system of U.N.O.

The reality of the world's division into two hemispheres was well demonstrated when the Hungarian people tried to break out of the Eastern Hemisphere, and when the Arab world, led by the Egyptian nationalists, tried to break out of the Western Hemisphere. It appeared quite natural that Khaganovich, once more in the limelight, should start rolling Zhukov's armoured divisions into Hungary. But on the other hand it did not appear to be quite as natural for Israel, in alliance with Britain and France, to attack Egypt so suddenly.

Almost on the same day events proved that *the existence of the two hemispheres was a sober fact.* And of course the Yalta and Potsdam agreements were also in force, together with the Gomberg Plan. The demarcation lines laid down in these agreements cannot be transgressed either by Hungary or by Egypt. Otherwise, the armoured divisions of Ben Gurion and of Khaganovich will come and obliterate every form of nationalism with its longing for freedom and independence.

The Hungarian freedom uprising started on October 23rd and the Israeli forces crossed the frontiers of Egypt on October 29th. It was reported on this same day by the radios of the Hungarian freedom fighters that strong Soviet units had begun to invade Hungary from the East.

The Western world grossly betrayed Hungary and Egypt. New York Jewry held a special gathering in the early days of the Hungarian rebellion and promptly stamped the Hungarian war of independence as an "anti-Semitic" movement, so U.N.O. quickly decided not to help the freedom fighters but to give a free hand to the armoured divisions of the Soviet. Meanwhile Britain and France, in alliance with Ben Gurion, made haste to bomb the "anti-Semites" of Port Said.

But the treason of the Western world was more insidious and fatal than the open brutality of the Soviets. The Western world betrayed its own interests as well as its own much advertised principles, not to mention democracy and humanity, when it became more and more certain that behind the bombastic phrases uttered during the Suez crisis there lurked an alien interest, namely, the interest of Jewish world nationalism. Needless to say, nobody dragged Ben Gurion before the Court of Nuremberg "for planning an aggressive war", for which Generals Jodl and Keitl were executed. Meanwhile the United Nations, with its 1,200 Jews out of a total of 1,800 personnel, looked on without a murmur while the Soviet committed acts of the most horrible genocide under their very eyes.

But all this was natural and according to plan, since the complete and perfect Jewish world kingdom was restored in Hungary, even without Mátyás Rákosi-Roth.

It pleases a certain section of the Press in the Western world to spread the rumour that the Hungarian Communist "government" formed after the suppression of the uprising is actually "anti-Semitic". Let us examine what lies behind the headlines. Here can be seen an excellent example of the working of the "Gentile front". Here, the puppet, János Kádár, whose real name is Csernák, is in fact of Slav rather than of Jewish origin.

But the two deputy Prime Ministers, Antal Apró-Apfelbaum and Ferenc Muennich — are both Jews. The Minister of Foreign Affairs, Imre Horváth, together with his two deputy Foreign Ministers, Endre Silk and István Sebes are Jews. Moreover, Géza Révész, Minister of Defence; István Antos, Minister of Finance; Ferenc Nezvál,

Minister of Justice; Sebestyén Bakonyi, First Deputy-Minister of Foreign Trade; János Tausz, Minister of Home Trade; Gyula Kállai (Campescu), Minister of Education, and his deputy-minister, György Aczél, chief organiser of the Anti-Religious Campaign and of the persecution of the Churches, are all Jews.

The world conquerors swarm in the Central Committee of the Hungarian Communist Party, an authority which is more important than the Government itself. The Jewish members of the Central Committee are at present (1958): Antal Apró-Apfelbaum, György Aczél, Janő Fock, László Földes, István Friss, Imre Horváth, Gyula Kállai (Campescu), Károly Kis, Ferenc Műnich, Dezső Nemes, chairman of the Editorial Committee of the Hungarian Communist daily of *Népszabadság,* Ferenc Nezvál, Sándor Nógrádi, Lászlo Orbán and Kálmán Révai.

The ill-famed secret police (A.V.H.), with its organisation of terror, torture and murder, was set up again, and as before, its leaders almost exclusively consisted of members of the Jewish fraternity.

We do not feel guilty of prejudice in stating that the Hungarian fight for freedom in 1956 was of considerable historical importance. It proved that *every form of Marxism* had completely failed to win over the workers and genuine Socialists, despite the fact that in the promotion of the Jewish world kingdom values had been levelled downwards for more than a century. World power exercised from key positions also failed, since both workers and proletariat joined forces instinctively with the intellectual sections and their first action was to liquidate these key positions. It became evident in Hungary that the workers as well as the rest of the nation no longer desired the so-called Western capitalist system. They refused to accept either the Eastern or Western form of exploitation. *The Hungarian nation desires the means of production to remain in its own hands, and this not in the form of national Communism but on the basis of a new national and socialist system free of totalitarianism.* This concept ought to give food for thought to the Western capitalist world and to the Western workers as well. Humanity can be saved from the horrors of atomic warfare and atomic death only by the Western world showing to the workers of the East that same form of socialism which was born during the Hungarian freedom fighting of 1956, the charter of which has yet to be written. Such socialism could take the tommy-gun away from the terror groups, smash the Golden Calf and liquidate the power of Jewish International Finance.

Only a socialistic society that has been purged of its hatreds can save mankind. Until the world is free of the hatred with which it has been infected by Jewish mentality for the last 2,000 years, the danger of atomic death or endless servitude will be ever with us.

The first step to take should be the abolition of all childish forms of " anti-Semitism ". It must be made plain that we are not " anti-Semites ". We condemn " anti-Semitism " first of all on a racial basis, for the real Semites, the Arab nations, are our brothers and natural allies of all nationalist forces in the global struggle.

Neither are we " anti-Semites " in the Hitlerian meaning of the word, i.e. on racial grounds, because we neither teach nor accept the superiority of any race.

We are not " anti-Semites " in the religious sense of the word either, for we are liberal-minded enough to respect one religion as much as the other.

And finally we are not " anti-Semitic " at all in the sense of hating any Jewish personal characteristic. We do not mind either the shape of his nose or his social mannerisms.

What we hate is *Jewish world power with its* 2,000 *years of " nazi " scheming and plotting to drive the whole of mankind into servitude, atomic death and exploitation.* Therefore we must not attack the personal, racial or national characteristics of the Jews, but on the other hand, whether as democrats, socialists or national socialists, *we should carry out our duty as human beings in resisting by all lawful means — and even, if necessary, by revolution — the survival of any form of Jewish world domination. We have every right to stand up against an illegal power to remove those in key positions behind the Gentile front.*

Wherever this domination is exerted its identity must be mercilessly exposed. For this and other reasons an international—or better still — a supranational anti-Jewish world organisation should be established.

This organisation would define the tactics to be employed according to the characteristics of the various countries. It should not attempt to prescribe to the various nations the form of government to be adopted, or to advise them on policy. Perhaps the best weapons in

America would prove to be the democratic ones of the vote, backed by a policy of general enlightenment together with social and financial boycott if necessary. In the so-called fascist countries it would be necessary to win over the central power and in the socialist countries to convince the honest and sincere socialists. Behind the Iron Curtain it would entail fighting guerilla and partisan campaigns against the Jewish leaders of the régime. Here the tommy-gun is a lawful weapon in the struggle which those heroes of the Hungarian freedom fighters waged with such exemplary resolution. Terror is the reply to terrorism, *but it must be used against terrorists only.*

Law and order does not mean the suppression of freedom. The only " freedom " to be abolished is that spurious kind of toleration which enables the exponents of tribal " nazism " to do anything they please. When all the " liberties ", so far restricted to the " chosen people ", permitting them to spread terror, exploitation and unlimited profiteering, are abolished, then Jewry, bereft of its privileges and monopolies, will be faced with the great question of its own fate.

How long can the present trend of events continue? For how much longer must the nations be dragged from one deception to another? How long can Bolshevism be maintained, and when will America at last awake? Are the nations to continue in servitude—suppressed and cheated—and from time to time subjected to wage bloody wars which are planned by an alien nationalism?

Although this world conquest has been continuing with growing impetus during the last 2,000 years, it has always relied on the bayonets of other nations. " The Western Jew will equip an army of twenty million in the East . . ." presaged the Hungarian prophet. But the greatest and mightiest forces of world Jewry, the Soviet Red Armies, were shaken by the sacrifices of the Hungarian proletariats. In the northern provincial city of Miskolc in Hungary, the officers of the Russian armoured divisions ordered to advance against the university students, committed suicide in the street by putting bullets into their own heads rather than carry out their murderous tasks. The Russian soldiers frequently gave themselves up, saying they would not shoot at their Hungarian brothers. During the most critical moments of the uprising at Budapest it often happened that entire Russian armoured units went over to the side of the freedom fighters and together with them fired on the terrorists. It is reliably reported that a great Russian armoured division unit with 400 tanks sent envoys to the Hungarian freedom fighters saying that it was prepared to turn its T-54 guns against their oppressors provided the Hungarians refused to negotiate with the Western capitalists. (An agreement was concluded but it was too late. On November 4th, 1956, the Russian divisions were ordered to attack, and for the time being military discipline proved stronger than the individual sentiments of the soldiers.)

The confidence and faith of world Jewry's greatest army was shaken. So also was the confidence of the soldiers of other suppressed nations who openly took the part of the Hungarian people. The Roumanian Army could not be sent to Hungary because the Roumanian Jewish leaders warned Moscow that its units would go over to the side of the Hungarians.

"When the hour strikes," said a high-ranking Russian officer to the leaders of the Hungarian freedom fighters, "we also will turn our weapons against our Jewish oppressors, as you did. Your mistake was only that you acted prematurely!"

The powers behind the scenes cannot rely on the Russian soldier any longer.

But can they rely on the *American* soldier? Despite the fact that American political life is to a great extent still geared to the Morgenthau outlook, nevertheless, the U.S. Army has learned a great deal since 1945. It saw the crushed body of General Patton, the sufferings of the German people, it was profusely bled in Korea and it witnessed how world Jewry removed General MacArthur, the victorious American military leader.

The Hungarian rising of 1956 was not the end but the beginning. And for the world conquerors this beginning posed the great question — how long can we go on?

Is it possible to continue being conquerors for ever? Is it possible for ever to go about in armoured cars like Rabinovich, Rákosi-Roth and their sort, guarded for the time being by Mongolian, Hungarian or Roumanian body-guards? Can we be certain that the Mongolians will not rebel one day? Can we sail in luxury yachts off Florida and sit on top of civilisation without being a prey to unceasing fears that at any moment our power may collapse? How much longer can the world be mesmerised into believing that everybody who sees through our designs is just a hate-mongering "anti-Semite"? And how much longer must fires of burning hatred be kept alive between the nations in order to repeat the horrors of another Auswitz in America?

For how much longer can we send the *élite* of the nations to the gallows and yet cry "anti-Semitism" when they rise up against our nationalism? How long can internationalism be preached by us to the nations while we ourselves practise the most extreme racial and tribal nationalism? How long can we maintain the fiction that if any harm comes to us that is "anti-Semitism", but when *we* kill anybody or slaughter entire nations, that is the act of either American democracy or Soviet liberation? When we destroy, that is construction; when we murder, that is freedom; when we terrorise the whole world, that is democracy; but when one member of the holy seed of Abraham is lost then it is the duty of the whole world to mourn with us! If we exploit other peoples as befits our selfish principles, that is not nationalism, but if other people want to live their own independent life — that is barbarism!

How long will all this continue? When is the world going to wake up? How long will a state of double morality be tolerated, according to which a Jew is free to commit almost any crime against other people? When will the world hit upon the truth that behind the wars, revolutions and slumps it is our plans that prosper? The coil of the symbolic serpent has encircled the entire globe and also the life, mentality and morale of the nations. It has levelled the masses downwards and destroyed individuality in order to enslave the people. When, then, will our creature and slave — the barbarous masses — rise? When will the world find out that there is no such thing as a chosen people, but oppressors only? Might it not be better if we ourselves could wake up and find a country we could really call our own? In this country we should be oppressors no longer, but free citizens; not hated foreigners but natives of the land. Would it not be worthwhile to sacrifice the Golden Calf and the tommy-gun and found a country of our own by toil and sweat? Would it not be better to have secure homes in our own country rather than live a dangerous life as oppressors, bankers, dictators or as a ruling class, always haunted by the eternal trepidations and uncertainty of our position?

The Learned Elders of Zion must have thought all this before, but no compromise is possible on the slopes of such Chauvinistic lunacy. Still less is it possible when dealing with a nationalism of several thousand years' standing, which has no other choice to-day but victory or death — *world domination or destruction!*

But the Christian people declare that there is yet another better way. For the enslaved world throttled by the grip of the symbolic serpent's coils, there is the example of Christ with his scourge — Christ, the greatest " anti-Semite " of all. Behind the crucifix of Sadducean hatred he raises high the scourge among the money-grabbers of the temple. This is the Christian counter-revolution which will replace all those values Judaism took away from mankind: respect for personal authority, the restoration of independence to the nations and of justice to the poor. It will favour the lot of the proletarian masses and will turn men's eyes away from the material world towards the stars.

This is the Christian Resistance, this is the spirit of Maundy Thursday rising up against the world kingdom of the Jews. This is the New Testament, the truth of which will perhaps be victoriously vindicated in the last hour.

For St. Peter stands once more before the deceived masses of the people and, inspired by the Holy Ghost, cries aloud to those Judaised Gentiles who are " under the law " of the Jews:

" Save yourselves from this untoward generation! " (Acts *ii.* 40.)

Against the fulfilment of the commands in the *Protocols the message of the New Age* sounds clearly with its promise of freedom. During the last century another slogan said: " Workers of the world unite! " But to-day, in this suffering, half-ruined civilisation, the new slogan for an awakening people must be:

" Anti-Jewish people of the world unite before it is too late."

EPILOGUE

The fight for freedom waged by Hungarian workers, peasants and middle classes puts all men of goodwill under an obligation. It affects not only the Hungarians but all the nations of the earth. We must join forces to break the power of the world conquerors, otherwise there will be a third world war and the survivors will either be the wretched slaves of Jewry or human wrecks and idiots degenerated by atomic radiation and strontium effects.

It was this belief, and not hatred, which prompted me to write this book. We are not anti-American, because we like and admire the American farmers, workers and brave pioneers. It is only the America of Morgenthau and Baruch that we in Europe detest. Similarly we are not the enemies of the Russian people, but we are the mortal enemies of Kaganovich's Soviet Union and of Jewish Bolshevism.

In the future, if there is to be peace in this world, there must be no " chosen people " but free nations with equal rights only. This is the truth! In the end truth must surely prevail.